# FAMILY FUTURES

## Childhood and poverty in urban neighbourhoods

Anne Power, Helen Willmot and Rosemary Davidson

First published in Great Britain in 2011 by

The Policy Press
University of Bristol
Fourth Floor
Beacon House
Queen's Road
Bristol BS8 1QU
UK

Tel +44 (0)117 331 4054
Fax +44 (0)117 331 4093
e-mail tpp-info@bristol.ac.uk
www.policypress.co.uk

North American office:
The Policy Press
c/o International Specialized Books Services (ISBS)
920 NE 58th Avenue, Suite 300
Portland, OR 97213-3786, USA
Tel +1  503 287 3093
Fax +1 503 280 8832
e-mail info@isbs.com

British Library Cataloguing in Publication Data
A catalogue record for this book is available from the British Library.

Library of Congress Cataloging-in-Publication Data
A catalog record for this book has been requested.

ISBN 978 1 84742 970 4  paperback
ISBN 978 1 84742 972 8  hardcover

Cover design by The Policy Press.
Front cover: image kindly supplied by www.thirdavenue.co.uk
Printed and bound in Great Britain by Hobbs, Southampton
The Policy Press uses environmentally responsible print partners

# Contents

# List of tables and figures

## Tables

## Figures

# Acknowledgements

This study was funded over eight years, between 1998 and 2006, by the Economic and Social Research Council (ESRC) and the Nuffield Foundation. Additional funding was provided by the Esmée Fairbairn Foundation, Sport England and the Department for Environment, Food and Rural Affairs (Defra). We thank all of them. The 200-plus families that helped us over this long study offered us the greatest support, and we cannot thank them enough for sharing their understanding of family lives in low-income areas. The local authorities, community organisations and government bodies that helped and advised us were also invaluable.

Many researchers played roles in this study, but in particular, the interviewers of the families: Katharine Mumford, Helen Bowman, Bani Makkar, Astrid Winkler, Lalita McLeggan, Rosemary Davidson and Helen Willmot. A particular debt of thanks is owed to Katharine Mumford, who set up the study, devised the methods and the questionnaires and worked out how to identify the families. Other people gave us advice along the way, including Jane Waldfogel, Ruth Lupton and John Hills. Nicola Serle of LSE (London School of Economics) Housing and Communities masterminded, systematised, stored and tracked the information. Her work in identifying quotations, tabulating information, storing interview schedules and researching sources was invaluable. Other people played a very important role, including in particular Olga Gora, Laura Lane, Libby Parrott, Abenaa Owusu-Bempah and Anna Tamas. We are deeply indebted to this large body of helpers, and to the research team of the Centre for Analysis of Social Exclusion at LSE, without whom the book would never have been written. The Policy Press has been an outstanding publisher throughout, with constant advice, encouragement and support. Naturally, we accept responsibility for any mistakes or misrepresentations.

# ONE

# Introduction

*I'm torn between staying loyal to the neighbourhood, and trying to better ourselves and get away from where life's a struggle.* (Phoebe, The Valley)

*Family futures* is about family life in areas of concentrated poverty and social problems, areas where it is difficult to bring up children and where surrounding conditions make family life more fraught and more limited. Neighbourhoods for families aren't just the houses they live in and the routes they take to school, the shops they buy from and the facilities they use. They are communities of people and clusters of connecting activities. These places form a web around people's lives, both anchoring them, and providing the basic services they need – or in disadvantaged neighbourhoods, depriving local families of what they need for their children to progress. Home and neighbourhood carry special meaning for families, because where they live, how they fit in with their neighbours and how their children grow up all intertwine, to build a sense of community. Schools, health centres, local police, shops, parks, play areas, the streets themselves and bus routes all build up local connections, yet too often they fall short of families' needs and ambitions.

Families are at the forefront of change and progress as children are our common future, and what we do to them today will shape all our tomorrows. Poorer communities combine many strands of disadvantage because one problem compounds another, making these areas unpopular with families and other households with choice.[1] Poor neighbourhoods become home to low-income families because they are dominated by subsidised homes for rent and therefore cheaper to live in, more attractive to people on low incomes and less desirable to people in better-paid work. Poorer families with children need affordable housing above all, so they are concentrated in areas of social housing.

Families also need social support, local contacts, local services, familiar faces and community activity, in order to build their family lives within the local area. This makes them value highly a sense of community and a sense of belonging. Many studies support the popular notion that community matters,[2] that where you live is a major determinant of your family's progress, that community capacity and solidarity can combat crime and other social ills,[3] that over-rapid change and loss of family connections can undermine community identity.[4] A sense of belonging or community is more important in low-income areas because most families do not have cars, and with limited incomes they are highly dependent on local services and connections for most of their needs and for most of their children's activities.[5]

*Family futures* is based on the idea that parents with little choice about where they live have a stronger than average concern about their neighbourhoods. They worry about schools, play spaces, the need for children 'to let off steam', crime prevention and safety, health, housing, the local environment, regeneration plans that affect their daily lives and their whole futures. They have little control over most key decisions and for almost all services, programmes, interventions and conditions they rely on the wider society, the city and government. They try to control and shape their immediate surroundings but for this they are highly dependent, not just on who their neighbours are and what family members they live near, but on a range of local and wider structures and services that they cannot shape on their own. This need to influence and shape their futures and the relative powerlessness they feel drives low-income families' need for community and their ambition to be involved in area activities.

In *Family futures* we explore how multiple disadvantages in poor urban areas affect families bringing up children, and what actions help or hinder their progress. There are three important questions:

- What are the main challenges facing families in poor areas?
- How have the areas changed and the challenges been met over time?
- What role have government efforts over the past decade played?

*Family futures* draws on the lives of 200 families in four urban neighbourhoods that suffer multiple problems of deprivation: two in East London (Hackney and Newham), and two in the North of England (Leeds and Sheffield). This study, carried out over 10 years from 1998 to 2008, collected families' views on area and community problems and on how the areas had changed during that time. Since 1998, many public and private initiatives have targeted area conditions and low-income families, but it is rare to hear what families say about what they need, give their views on what works and doesn't work, explain what helps and what hinders their children's progress, what more needs to be done and what new approaches may help.

New Labour promised in 1998 that no one would be seriously disadvantaged by where they live.[6] Programmes directed towards low-income areas and their schools, parks, jobs, training, housing, health, local environments, security and crime would open up opportunities for all, help 'abolish child poverty' and make 'every child matter'.[7] Neighbourhoods would be 'cleaner, safer, greener',[8] and parks and play areas would help all young people to access space to explore, grow and become better citizens.[9] This book examines the record of progress towards delivering these commitments and uses 200 families as a barometer of progress.

## Poor areas, poor families

The four areas are dominated by council estates and other social rented housing, but around one in five of the families have become owner-occupiers, usually through the Right to Buy a council home in which they were sitting tenants. Although an ownership stake helps create more stability and commitment to the area, the fact of owning a home does not in itself protect families from area problems and the families, whether they rent or own their own home, share similar local conditions and services.[10]

These neighbourhoods have long been poor, working-class areas; their large estates were a product of earlier slum clearance and rebuilding before and shortly after the Second World War. The proportion of newcomers, usually migrants from abroad, in all the areas has grown rapidly since the 1980s, following the loss of traditional local jobs and better housing options elsewhere for local families with more choice. This has compounded the pressures on already highly disadvantaged areas. Three of the areas have become highly diverse as many families from a minority ethnic background now live there. Only one area, a large council estate, is almost entirely white (97 per cent), while it shares similar social problems with the other three areas: low income, high worklessness, high crime, concentrated lone parenthood and poor school performance. All the areas have many local facilities and services, added incrementally over years of effort to improve social conditions and to reduce neighbourhood problems, but the overall condition of all the areas is poor.

*West City* is the neighbourhood closest to central London, on the edge of the City, a densely built-up, low-income area bordering on the world's biggest financial centre. The large council estates, old industrial buildings, traditional market area and occasional pockets of gentrified street properties, salvaged from earlier demolition, give it a lively and diverse East London flavour that incomers and locals value.

*East Docks*, bordering the old Port of London on its eastern side, is a confusing mixture of busy dual carriageways, postwar estates, recent affordable housing developments and an imposing new conference centre alongside one of the reclaimed docks. This area feels as if it 'lost its heart' when the docks closed in the 1960s and the old industries vanished. It has the fastest growing minority ethnic population in London, now a large majority locally.

*The Valley* in a Northern inner city comprises dense, old streets and small modern estates in a neighbourhood that rises steeply from the city centre. There are many street-front shops and small businesses catering for its diverse communities. Its multi-racial population suffers extremely high joblessness at the heart of a former industrial area that lost most of its major employers in the 1980s. The Valley is the most mixed of the four neighbourhoods – some stone terraces lining old streets are gentrifying and some unpopular council blocks are decaying while awaiting demolition. There are several different social and private landlords in the area, which is home to a significant refugee population.

*Kirkside East* is on the outskirts of another large Northern city. It is different from the other areas because it comprises one large inter-war, cottage estate, exclusively council-built, and prior to the Right to Buy, 100 per cent council-owned and rented. It has a settled white population with many family connections on the estate, giving it both a strong sense of community and a traditional character, unlike the other three much more diverse areas.

Table 1.1 summarises the main features of the four areas and Annexes 1 and 2 (available online at www.policypress.co.uk) provide information about the areas' conditions and a more detailed summary of their main characteristics.

This book explores the intrinsic assets, particularly the human assets, of disadvantaged areas that make interventions worthwhile. It examines the multiple approaches developed since 1998 to tackle area problems and the effect of these interventions on families' confidence in the areas. Efforts to help the poorest neighbourhoods are often challenged, because they are too narrowly focused and ignore the more dispersed and hidden poverty in the wider society. Compensatory programmes, targeting disadvantaged areas, are expensive, short term, and often fail to fulfil all their promises. Yet targeting help at the worst problems is often far cheaper than allowing problems to accumulate to the point where wholesale area demolition becomes the easier option. All four areas have been subject to elaborate demolition proposals at different times since 1998 because of the intensity of their problems, but over the 10 years of our work, they all largely survived.

**Table 1.1: Main features of the four neighbourhoods**

| **West City** (London inner) | **The Valley** (Northern inner city) |
|---|---|
| - Several large council estates – mainly flats – mixed in with Victorian street properties, very near City | - Close to the city centre, up a steep hill lined with stone terraces |
| - Near local markets | - Many different styles of housing – some large Victorian houses, some unpopular modern flats |
| - Right To Buy is now very expensive | - Very low demand at outset but increased demand over course of visits |
| - Some people on a higher income buying into the estates | - Decayed properties and shops but a major facelift of older properties happening on main road and some estates; some gentrification near the park |
| - Gentrification nearer the City – main road divides the south (gentrifying) and north council estates | - Some recent housing association development |
| - Trendy bars, boutiques, tattoo parlours and specialist shops opening | - Some blighted council blocks – demolition planned |
| - Rapid ethnic change, with new minorities dominating many areas and white population declining, leaving mainly the elderly | - Some visible drugs problems, leading to strong police intervention |
| - Fractured social networks but many activities for families | - Growing diversity of minority ethnic populations including refugees |
| - Major investment through New Deal for Communities but slow to take off and upgrading is piecemeal | - Visibly very poor, with high crime and drugs area |
| - Tenant management organisation has taken over biggest estate | - Beautifully restored local park |

| **East Docks** (London outer) | **Kirkside East** (Northern outer estate) |
|---|---|
| - Now well connected to city centre with new tube line and Docklands Light Railway extension | - Large low-income outer council estate, built before and just after the Second World War |
| - Docks form focus for regeneration | - 'Cottage'-style semis, some prefab concrete 1970s houses |
| - Big new conference centre – attracts many outsiders | - Several rows of shops, a big new Tesco and a new adult education college |
| - New 'urban village', attracting people on higher incomes but socially and geographically isolated from existing 'core' community | - Lots of open space, park, stream, woods – all poorly supervised and maintained |
| - Dome is visible across the river | - On main bus route to centre with several local schools, including an all-girls secondary school, very popular with Asian families from inner city |
| - Much of area dominated by a very busy main road | - Some community facilities but few sports facilities |
| - Noise and dirt of dual carriageway dominates local environment | - Few minorities, some mixed-race children |
| - An ugly underpass provides a crucial link | - Strong family networks – three quarters have relatives nearby |
| - Lots of unused and unattractive spaces | - Many complaints about repairs until estate was taken over by an arm's-length management organisation |
| - New secondary school and adult education college in the docks | - North and south of the estate have very distinct reputations and family networks, eg 'hot spot' for teenage car crime in the south |
| - Some council housing is being demolished | - Minimum spending programme with unfunded proposals to 'regenerate' the estate |
| - Some new housing authority building | |
| - Strongly growing minority ethnic population – particularly African – leading to rapid change | |
| - Declining white working-class population hostile to changes | |
| - Run-down appearance of local shops, some of the blocks and many of the streets | |

There are two cross-cutting distinctions between the four areas which shape the parents' experiences. The two London areas experience the stark divisions and tensions, the pressurised environments, lack of space and pace of community change that reflect London's global city status. Yet East London, like the North, is also shaped by its industrial past, and shows long-lasting, entrenched patterns of poverty as a result. It has retained its cumulative disadvantages in spite of London's general prosperity. East London offers a harsh environment for children. The two Northern areas are also extremely disadvantaged and, like East London, experience divisions and tensions, but they are less pressured by lack of space and have lower concentrations of newcomers from abroad. Many other differences emerge between the Northern and London areas, in work experience and jobs, in the significance of open space and public transport, in training and education, in scale and density. As we go through, we highlight these differences wherever they are significant.

The other cross-cutting distinction is between inner-city and outer areas; there is one of each, in the North and in East London, and here the distinction is not North versus South but inner versus outer. The two inner-city areas are denser, busier, more diverse in their activities and services, much closer to city centres, more threatened by gentrification, more attractive to young in-work families than the outer areas. Large-scale demolition is less of a threat, although both inner areas, but particularly in the North, have seen some demolition in the last decade as a way out of extreme decay. The two outer areas are less dense, less well connected, less mixed, harder to diversify; at the same time, they have more rooted traditional working-class communities and are under less development pressure, although the East London outer area is being subjected to radical clearance.

## Two hundred families

*Family futures* is part of a long-run study of neighbourhood conditions as they affect parents bringing up children. We visited 200 families with children every year over a period of seven years between 1999 and 2006. Over 60 per cent of the families we recruited in 1999 and 2000 were still involved at our last visit in 2006. Wherever possible, when families moved out, we followed them, but in most cases this proved impossible. When families were lost from the study, we found closely matching families within the areas, so there were still around 200 families giving us their views at the end of our visits. Annex 3 (available online at www.policypress.co.uk) explains in detail the methods we used in our research.

The 200 families in *Family futures* lived in the four areas described in Table 1.1. We found 50 families in each area, chosen to reflect as closely as possible the population composition of the areas in 1998 when we began our visits. We found some sharp contrasts between East London and Northern families, between inner and outer areas, but the families shared many similar characteristics, particularly low incomes and generally low skills. Most obviously they all had school-age children in 1998.

In East London most families lived in flats, whereas in the North an overwhelming majority lived in houses. This difference was overridden by the dominance of social landlords in all the families' lives, even when they owned their own home, by virtue of the social landlords' control over area conditions. The tenure mix with 30 per cent or less owning their own home was so different from the average area that tenure determined the types of families, incomes and other resources they could command.

Over 90 per cent of the families had lived in the areas for over two years, and half had lived there more than 10 years. Over a quarter had been born in the areas, so in spite of the changing populations, there was a strong core of traditional 'born and bred' families in all the areas. In East London, families from a minority ethnic background formed the majority. In the North the opposite was true, although in the Northern inner city, one third were from a minority background.

Married couples formed a minority of all the families, except in West City, where just over half were married. Overall half the families were headed by a lone parent and about one in five had an unmarried, and often not permanent, partner. At the outset, around a quarter of the parents had jobs, but by our fifth visit, well over half were working, with nearly two thirds of these in full-time jobs. Figure 1.1 shows the make-up of the 200 families at the outset and Annex 4 (available online at www.policypress.co.uk) provides summary information about the families.

**Figure 1.1:** Make-up of 200 families at the outset, 1999–2000

(a) Housing type (%)

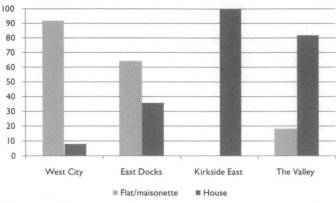

■ Flat/maisonette  ■ House

(b) Tenure (%)

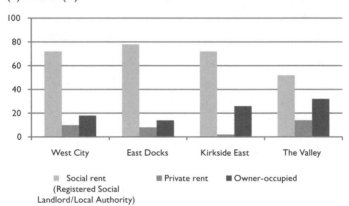

■ Social rent          ■ Private rent      ■ Owner-occupied
(Registered Social
Landlord/Local Authority)

(c) Ethnic composition (%)

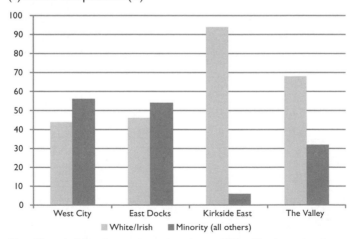

■ White/Irish   ■ Minority (all others)

*Note:* The ethnicity of parents was based on self-identification using showcards (see Figure 8.2).

## (d) Couple status (%)

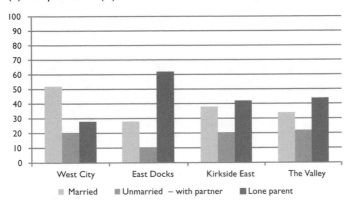

## (e) Time in area (%)

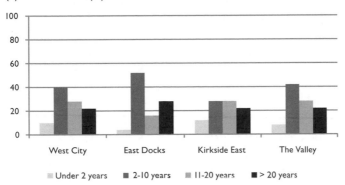

## (f) Parents in work (%)

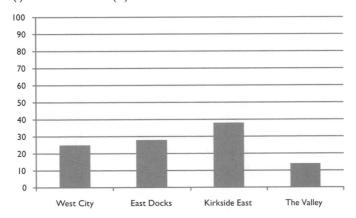

## A decade of targeted efforts

In late 1998, as we began to make contact with the areas where we planned to find the families we wanted to visit, the government announced the formation of the Social Exclusion Unit to 'bring Britain together' and 'close the gap' between the poorest area and the average.[11] Social exclusion was defined as the phenomenon of multiple, interacting and mutually reinforcing disadvantages concentrated in particular individuals or areas.[12] In its first report, *Bringing Britain together*, the Social Exclusion Unit in the Prime Minister's Office identified the dominant problems it found disproportionately concentrated in the poorest areas: poor schools, low skills, high crime, lack of job opportunities, high levels of benefit dependency and workless households, poor health, poor local environments and housing conditions, poor quality public and private services and general neglect of local community needs. After 10 years of close involvement through the families in what happened to the most deprived areas, we used our evidence to assess the value of government programmes in changing the areas through government-funded programmes. (See Annex 5 [available online at www.policypress. co.uk] for a list of special programmes targeting disadvantaged areas.) We used the families' own experiences collected during 2,000 hours of talking to them. This book is the outcome, showing how they struggled to overcome the concentrated problems that surrounded them.

We asked many of the same questions each time we visited in order to track parents' evolving views on such matters as: 'How has your family changed since we last visited?', 'And the area?', 'Have the area changes been for the better or worse or stayed the same?'. Our questions were all directed at understanding bringing up children in disadvantaged areas. We introduced new topics as they became relevant to the parents' experience. Other topics, such as schools, housing or work, came up every few visits. Annex 6 (available online at www. policypress.co.uk) sets out the topics we covered with the parents in the sequence in which they came up. As we followed the evolution of parents' experiences, so too we watched programmes and interventions unfold. On our last visit, we tried to capture, in the parents' own words, how far the areas were changing, what things had improved, what problems remained and what their hopes and fears were for the areas and for their children's future. We round up the parents' views in our final chapter, Chapter Nine.

As we visited the families, we observed the changes on the ground at first hand. Our evidence provides a unique perspective on the benefits and limitations of devising special programmes to improve conditions in disadvantaged areas. It is hard to sustain support for interventions for four main reasons:

- some spending is wasted on physical projects that do not tackle fundamental social ills;
- the wider community of taxpayers carries the main burden of these costs;
- social mobility is proving elusive so longer-term benefits for children are hard to identify;
- disadvantaged neighbourhoods are still falling behind today, in spite of progress.

Area programmes never last long enough to reverse completely long-run neighbourhood decline, but 10 years make up half a childhood in every family, so we witnessed significant changes affecting the childhoods of around 500 children. We show both how tantalisingly slow area change is, and how quickly we can lose the chance to help children through their formative years. Change has to happen quickly and steadily if it is to matter to families bringing up children today, and it has to stay in place for the long term to help children of the future. Clearly much remains to be done. Yet the new political and financial agendas raise special worries about neighbourhood viability.

## Outline of the book

This book begins by exploring local community relations and the ways in which families create social networks to secure their foothold in areas that otherwise might seem too harsh to survive in. We then look theme by theme at each aspect of area-based social exclusion and concentrated disadvantage as they affect the families in the following sequence: community links and community activity; schools and education; facilities and activities for young people; community safety and crime prevention; health and well-being, both mental and physical; work, tax credits, training and benefits; housing and regeneration; and how conditions changed over our visits.

Chapter Two examines why involvement in community activity and decision making matters to parents; what enhances or detracts from a sense of community; and how rapid change can undermine it. It ends with parents' views on what makes communities work and what needs to be done to make families feel part of what is happening, using Sure Start as a prime example of how interventions on behalf of families can work.

Chapter Three assesses the role of schools in family lives, in building community links and in helping parents and children. The contrast between primary and secondary schools and the special difficulties faced by parents of children with learning difficulties and special needs underlines how important schools are in family lives, and how much more help children with special needs require.

Chapter Four looks at one of the biggest challenges in low-income areas – the shortage of open space, low-cost facilities and safe, well-supervised activities for children and young people. This is the highest priority for parents and of crucial importance to young people's healthy development. The Olympics Bid injected new hope that poor East London communities would secure these goals and our families explain how this is playing out in practice.

Chapter Five is about the most dominant fears of parents: crime, drugs and anti-social behaviour. Several anti-crime initiatives evolved in the areas during our visits and parents report their impact and shortcomings. They explain how much more needs to be done to make families in urban areas feel secure.

Chapter Six is about family health and the role of health services in family lives, particularly where there is a disability or ongoing health problem. The most dominant health issue may be mental health, depression and anxiety, sometimes linked to area conditions but also linked to the struggles of everyday family life on low incomes in those poor conditions.

Chapter Seven explores the work histories and work experience of the parents, their ambitions and the role of training in helping mothers in particular into work.

Chapter Eight looks at housing and regeneration as two dominant influences on neighbourhood life. It examines the way housing, its history and ownership, its management and access routes can determine the way families feel about their neighbourhoods, and whether they will stay and work to improve them. It also assesses the impact of major regeneration programmes, particularly involving demolition on the viability of communities.

Chapter Nine collects the parents' views on how areas are changing, what is positive or negative, what improvements work and what more needs to be done; it ends by looking at the biggest hurdles facing families, communities and society as a whole today in an era of severe resource constraints.

Each evidence-based chapter opens with an overview of the responses of all the families. We then show how particular interventions affected parents, relying as much as possible on the parents' own words. Each chapter ends with a summary of the most salient points that parents raised, based on their lived experience. Parents had both positive and negative experiences of neighbourhood services and programmes; we try to reflect both, pointing to the conspicuous gaps still waiting to be closed.

## Mining the evidence

Making sense of the vast amount of information we accumulated over seven rounds – around 56,000 answers to 280 questions collected from 200 parents – forced us to identify dominant themes in what the parents said. Wherever possible we tabulated this evidence under these themes and each chapter presents the 'hard' evidence from 200 parents on these dominant topics and themes.[13] At the same time, our main aim was to understand the dynamics of family life within poor areas, and the detailed interactions between families and their surroundings. Many of the views we heard contained subtle observations, nuances and contradictions. To capture this rich source of knowledge about the inner workings of poor communities, we extracted as many illuminating and contrasting quotes as we could fit, under the themes and topics we identified, round by round, and in our chapters here, such as schools and crime. This unique source from 200 slowly evolving life stories underpins more general findings.

The direct quotations reflect as far as possible the different ideas and reactions of parents, based not only on different area conditions and programmes, but also on different family perspectives. The range of possible quotations to support each argument we make was so wide that it endorsed the value of reporting parents' opinions directly, although inevitably some parents were more articulate and more open with their views than others. Views from different areas were often mutually reinforcing. There were literally hundreds more quotes on each subject than we used.

During our visits we talked about what happens to families as a whole, parents, partners, children, other relatives and household members, even though in most families mothers play the dominant childrearing role and most of the parents we interviewed were mothers. In over 96 per cent of families in our study, the mother was the main carer and the 'most present parent', although during many interviews other family members got involved too. In nearly half of the families the mother was the only continuous carer for the children as a lone parent. Therefore, mothers are our main source of evidence and the quotes we use reflect this. We believe that their perspective on their areas reflects with striking insight the lived experience of families for several main reasons:

- they spend most of their time in the areas and depend heavily on local services, even where they are working;
- they are directly and continually affected by area conditions and are highly sensitive to these conditions because of their caring responsibilities with children;
- they act as 'community conduits and brokers', seeking out local contact, local activities, local supports, while attempting to overcome community troubles and disruptions;
- they have strong protective instincts as parents, particularly as mothers, and therefore 'watch out for' their children and for threats to them;
- the risks to their children's futures from the areas where they live are one of their highest preoccupations, so their ears are constantly attuned to what their children say and what they hear from other children and parents;
- they are in almost daily contact with relatives, neighbours and local services, particularly schools and doctors' surgeries, where they gather information on what is happening and who can help solve problems.

All these roles mean that in most families the mother is the main anchor. The dominance of women in family life, childcare and local communities is common to many cultures and widely accepted as a crucial part of community dynamics.[14] Mothers offer a grounded perspective that is too often unheard. This book is unique in its reliance, not on official statistics and academic studies, but on what the families themselves, particularly mothers, say about conditions, experiences, problems and changes. Did area conditions improve? Did families recognise and value the efforts being made? Did the interventions work? How many of the changes will stay in place and prove of lasting benefit?

Our whole society, over a generation, has been caught up in changes that are not easily influenced by government programmes, such as the growth in lone parenthood and in the elderly population, the increasing concentration of minority ethnic populations in poorer city areas and the changing nature of work. With all these changes, the weakest areas have come under the most intense pressure. The families tell us how they cope, as the social conditions of low-income areas have changed. We can learn a lot from this. A large majority of parents are optimistic about the future prospects for their children, but they are worried that the task of improving the areas is only half done. The future is hedged with uncertainty.

The Coalition government, committed to building 'the Big Society',[15] wants to put more onus on citizens, particularly families, to shoulder responsibilities previously born by the state. They argue that local communities will tackle local problems and help their communities work better. To achieve this requires a high level of local social and community resources, often referred to as social capital. But it also requires wider support and external resources.[16] The Coalition government is committed to 'localism', driving resources and control down to the most local level, explicitly accompanied by a drastic reduction in resources.[17] Education, health and policing are three examples of local services reliant on wider support. Many live experiments in tackling severe disadvantage show that community initiatives must be firmly underpinned by society as a whole if they are to work.[18]

Families occupy the shared spaces and participate in the shared activities that link families, neighbourhoods and the wider society. In hard-pressed times, society needs to find ways of capitalising on what poor areas can offer poor families, and what families can offer to the communities they live in and to the wider society. Therefore, behind our questions about bringing up children in low-income areas are much bigger questions:

- What future do families face in disadvantaged areas?
- Who shapes that future – the families themselves, the communities they live in or the wider society?
- How far is the wider society responsible for that future?

## Notes

[1] Hills, J., Sefton, T. and Stewart, K. (eds) (2009) *Towards a more equal society? Poverty, inequality and policy since 1997*, Bristol: The Policy Press; Jargowsky, P. (1997) *Poverty and place: Ghettos, barrios, and the American city*, New York: Russell Sage Foundation.

[2] Young, M. and Willmott, P. (1957) *Family and kinship in East London*, London: Routledge and Kegan Paul.

[3] Samson, R.J., Raudenbush, S. and Felton, E. (1997) 'Neighborhoods and violent crime: a multilevel study of collective efficacy', *Science*, vol 277, pp 918-24; Wilson, W.J. and Taub, R.P. (2006) *There goes the neighborhood: Racial, ethnic, and class tensions in four Chicago neighborhoods and their meaning for America*, New York: Knopf.

[4] Dench, G., Gavron, K. and Young, M. (2006) *The new East End: Kinship, race and conflict*, London: Profile Books.

[5] Power, A. (2007) *City survivors: Bringing up children in disadvantaged neighbourhoods*, Bristol: The Policy Press.

[6] Social Exclusion Unit (1998) *Bringing Britain together: A national strategy for neighbourhood renewal*, London: The Stationery Office.

[7] Blair, T. (1999) Speech on eradicating child poverty, Beveridge Lecture Series, 18 March; HM Government (2003) *Every child matters*, London: The Stationery Office; Sustainable Development Commission (SDC) (2009) *Every child's future matters*, London: SDC.

[8] Office of the Deputy Prime Minister (ODPM) (2002) *Living places: Cleaner, safer, greener*, London: ODPM.

[9] Department for Children, Schools and Families (DCSF) (2008) *The play strategy*, London: DCSF.

[10] Power, A. (2007) *City survivors: Bringing up children in disadvantaged neighbourhoods*, Bristol: The Policy Press.

[11] Social Exclusion Unit (1998) *Bringing Britain together: A national strategy for neighbourhood renewal*, London: The Stationery Office.

[12] Lupton, R. (2003) *Poverty Street: The dynamics of neighbourhood decline and renewal*, Bristol: The Policy Press; Mumford, K. (2001) *Talking to families in East London: A report on the first stage of the research*, CASEreport 09, London: LSE; Bowman, H. (2001) *Talking to families in Leeds and Sheffield: A report on the first stage of the research*, CASEreport 18, London: LSE.

[13] For a more detailed discussion of the methods used to conduct this long-run study, see Annex 3 (www.policypress.co.uk) and Power, A. (2007) *City survivors: Bringing up children in disadvantaged neighbourhoods*, Bristol: The Policy Press.

[14] Moser, C. (2009) *Ordinary families, extraordinary lives: Assets and poverty reduction in Guayaquil 1978–2004*, Washington, DC: Brookings Institution Press; Moser, C. and Peake, L. (1987) *Women, human settlements and housing*, London: Tavistock; Yunus, M. (1998) *Banker to the poor: The autobiography of Mohammad Yunus, founder of the Grameen Bank*, London: Aurum Press.

[15] Cameron, D., Rt Hon (2009) Speech given on 'The Big Society' at the Hugo Young Lecture, Tuesday, 10 November.

[16] Halpern, D. (2005) *Social capital*, Cambridge: Polity Press; Power, A. and Houghton, J. (2007) *Jigsaw cities: Big places, small spaces*, Bristol: The Policy Press; Power, A. and Willmot, H. (2007) *Social capital within the neighbourhood*, CASEreport 38, London: LSE.

[17] Hills, J., Le Grand, J. and Piachaud, D. (2002) *Understanding social exclusion*, Oxford: Oxford University Press.

[18] Hills, J., Sefton, T. and Stewart, K. (eds) (2009) *Towards a more equal society? Poverty, inequality and policy since 1997*, Bristol: The Policy Press.

# TWO

# Family roles in community matters

*I just liked the area from the moment I arrived for my interview at the school. I just walked up the road and thought 'I like it here', which was totally illogical, because it isn't a nice area to look at. It's tower blocks and mid-rise and litter. But I think it's something about the community feel that is what I've always liked about it and the fact that you see a lot of people that you know when you just go out somewhere. There's lots of people who you'll stop and just say hello to, and the friendly sense of it. Which I guess people might not expect to find in London.* (Jane, West City)

*Community spirit matters because it's really multi-cultural and families and people live together. It's nice walking round and you bump into someone and they're nice to you.* (Fatima, The Valley)

## Introduction: Community spirit

People have many views on what community itself means and why it is important. Parents identify a sense of community in a friendly atmosphere, a sense of trust and reciprocity, a link to neighbours and to local activity, a helping hand, mutual support and a sense of responsibility. It is these social links that reflect what families think of as 'community spirit', a somewhat ephemeral feeling about local social relations. Mothers often use the terms 'community' and 'community spirit' interchangeably.

This chapter explores how the parents we talked to feel about their local community, how much they can control or shape what happens in it, what efforts they make as parents to get involved and help the community work better, who else they rely on and what undermines the sense of community. It looks at the role of special programmes for parents and children, using Sure Start as an illustration of community support in action.

The existence of 'community spirit' was clearly important to families from our first visit and was a recurring theme in ideas about what would help families and children. Parents talked about their community and held strong views about it because for them it made where they lived succeed or fail as a place to bring up children. Community 'spirit' was most keenly felt through friendly, informal contact, such as exchanging help with children, other kinds of informal care involving neighbours, attending fun community events, frequent contact with friends and meeting people they knew on the street. Bumping into people, getting to know parents at the school gate and recognising local faces strengthened a family's sense of security and confidence. 'Community spirit' was a phrase often used by parents to reflect a willingness to help each other, recognition of small gestures of friendship, knowing there was someone to turn to. Feeling 'linked into' where families lived was central to the strength of 'community spirit'. Parents discussed many different ways of feeling connected, including formal links such as working locally, taking on a responsible community role, such as school governor, attending and helping with school activities, using local services, sending children to after-school clubs, and attending tenants' association and other local meetings. We start the chapter by examining the limits of parents' influence and involvement, then we show in what ways parents are involved and with what benefits. Then we look at problems and barriers, before discussing the special impact of Sure Start.

## Can families influence what happens?

In all four neighbourhoods at the outset in 1998, about half of the parents told us that there was a strong community spirit in their neighbourhood, and around three quarters felt that community spirit mattered. When we revisited the families a year later, even more of the parents said that they felt 'community spirit' mattered, almost nine out of ten. Annex 7 (online at www.policypress.co.uk) gives more detail on families' sense of belonging.

Community spirit helps families work together, yet most parents felt they had very little control over conditions. A sense of community did not readily translate into a sense of control over neighbourhood conditions. On our fourth visit, we asked parents whether they felt they could influence what happened in the area – over half said they could neither influence decisions nor had any influence over what happened in their areas, in spite of community consultation on many local initiatives. We asked parents *why* they felt that they had so little influence over their neighbourhoods. The most common reason was that they had 'no chance'. Half the parents felt that other more powerful people had greater influence over what happened in their neighbourhood than they did themselves because they didn't see their ideas shape what actually happened:

> *We are led to believe we can, but when it comes down to it, it doesn't make any difference.* (Joan, West City)

Figures 2.1(a) and 2.1(b) summarise the reasons why parents felt unable to influence what happened in their neighbourhoods. Interestingly a third of parents felt they had some influence.

**Figure 2.1(a):** Parents' reasons for lacking influence in their neighbourhoods, 2001–02

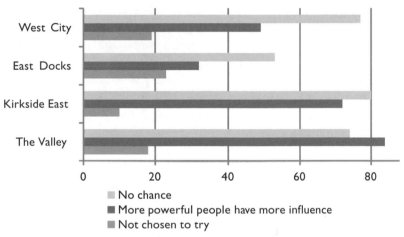

**Figure 2.1(b)** Parents who believe they have some influence in their neighbourhoods, 2001–02

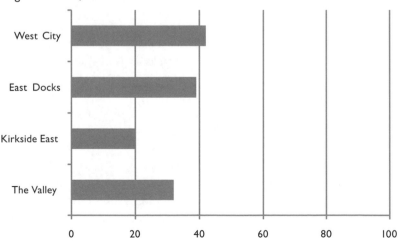

The minority of parents who were more involved believed that they made a greater input into decisions as a result and therefore exercised greater control over their surroundings. The issues they felt they influenced ranged from schools to leisure activities, the local environment, housing, other local services and community activities. In London, nearly a quarter of parents felt they influenced their children's education, by far the most significant input they mentioned. East Docks had more parental involvement in schools than the other areas, partly because it was an Education Action Zone.

Most parents explained that being able to influence what happened was important to them, reflecting their need to feel linked into the local community and also to make things work for their families. London families felt this need much more strongly than families in the North. A majority of parents in all neighbourhoods rated having influence as important. When parents were involved and had influence, they were more positive about their role in the community. It gave them a stronger sense of control and security. Certainly the parents we spoke to who were active in their community believed that they had real influence and directly made things better. This in turn strengthened their commitment to their community. According to parents, community involvement in local decisions and activity directly helps to build stronger communities:

> *That's where you get the community from, people being involved in what goes on.* (Liza, Kirkside East)

There were examples of parents feeling that consultation improved over time and therefore a community consensus grew that directly helped shape area conditions:

> *Community spirit, I think that's the way you get your voice heard, as a group rather than an individual. I'm talking to you and I don't know how far that will get all these problems. As an individual I don't think you can get far. Involvement helped. Generally they're involving tenants more, and now everybody goes along: families, refugees, they're listening to everyone. It's made a difference. We're all in on the community meetings. It used to be only senior citizens, only white.* (Cynthia, West City)

An area of community life that generates enthusiasm and support among families as well as actively strengthening community spirit is the organisation of community events. Popular community events included local events that brought community residents, particularly families with children, together to enjoy themselves. Nine out of ten parents in London thought they made a difference. We asked parents about their involvement in community events on our fifth visit. Participation in 'fun' community events played a big part in the parents' sense of belonging – nearly two thirds of parents told us that they attended such events. In Kirkside East only 40 per cent did, but in this estate family links were stronger among residents than in any other area, and many local community organisations existed. This may explain why bigger, more organised events seemed less significant there. In all the areas locally based community organisations were conspicuous, and over four fifths of parents thought they helped people feel more part of their community.

Parents drew a clear line between 'fun events' and formal community involvement. Participation in community public meetings and other more formal events was much lower across all four neighbourhoods, partly because they weren't usually 'fun' or child-friendly, but mainly because parents felt that their voice would not count, that others would make the decisions and have more say, so the feeling of 'why bother' was very strong. Even so, the efforts by public bodies to involve communities did lead to some involvement. Just one in ten parents in Kirkside East went to these more formal events, about a quarter of the numbers attending 'fun' community events. In The Valley a quarter had attended community meetings in their neighbourhood, partly provoked by the launch of New Deal for Communities in the area, but the numbers attending 'fun' events was three times higher. Attending public meetings was more common in London, just under 40 per cent in both West City and East Docks, because the major regeneration programmes in the areas worried the parents, and affected their own future in the areas. They were generally driven by fear that things might get even worse for their families if they didn't go, not by a feeling of optimism that they could change things. Overall, confidence in formal participation or in being heard was low, as Joan in West City explained:

> *It's all things that make you feel completely helpless and powerless to do anything about. You know, you cannot stop kids coming from another block. You cannot get the sewage fixed, nobody'll do it. You cannot change the congestion, the road congestion 'cos you're part of it yourself [laughs]. It's when you get into a situation that you just, there seems to be no way out.* (Joan, West City)

However, in East Docks, families sometimes got involved because of the threat of redevelopment, and the worry that otherwise they would be pushed out:

> *A lot of people have been uneased because you're not sure what's going to happen, you're always left wondering.... We were told these houses were part of the regeneration, so we were thinking we might have to move. We didn't want to but that's what I understood of it. They were going to knock these houses down. And now we're being told they're going to stay for the moment. Eventually we are going to want to move on but not before our time. You shouldn't be forced to move out.* (Annie, East Docks)

The feeling of lack of influence or control was countered by parents' involvement in local groups or activities, such as their children's schools. The more we learned about parents' activities and roles in the community, the more important these seemed, both to the parents and to the local community as a whole.

Parents' involvement in local organisations varied between areas – in two neighbourhoods, The Valley and East Docks, half of the families were involved with a local organisation, nearly 40 per cent were involved in West City and a third in Kirkside East. Parents often counted attending area events as involvement but many directly contributed by helping in schools, Sure Start or community centres.[1] Overall, the proportion of parents directly participating in local organisations by our fifth visit was a healthy 44 per cent.

Generally far fewer fathers were involved with local organisations than mothers, although in the North partners were more likely to participate than their London counterparts – roughly one in four compared with only one in seven in London. Mothers participated more because they spent more time in the area, were generally more socially connected and played more active roles in the community.

By participating, parents felt that they were adding something to their community as well as enriching their families' lives. It enhanced the parents' sense of belonging and helped the areas become more 'family-friendly'.

## Community involvement: *"Lots to do here"*

For parents, community involvement meant doing things, and many were involved in community groups. One mother was involved in Kirkside East community centre bid for Millennium funding:

> *Me and a friend filled in a form for a Millennium Award, £2,600, and we spent it on toys, a toy library for the community centre.* (Anita, Kirkside East)

An East London parent talked about applying for funding and getting it as her greatest achievement:

> *I put in a bid to the lottery to get the community hall refurbished for £123,000. We got £10,000 from a charity for our youth club. It was all done on the phone on a Sunday morning!* (Tracy, West City)

Officially children's special needs were being met, but parents often found their involvement made a difference to what actually happened. A West City mother described the support group for parents of children with special needs she belonged to:

> *I help parents in the local Primary, I tell them about tutoring. I'm involved in a support group based in a neighbouring area for parents with children with special needs. Parents have to do it and fight for themselves.* (Leah, West City)

Another West City parent had helped raise money for her son's school for valuable school equipment that was subsequently stolen. She felt upset and disheartened by this but had not given up:

> *In actual fact, in my son's school, I never told you this, they had new whiteboards put in, you know those electronic whiteboards. The second time now the school's had 'em installed, they've all been stolen, been broken into. So they can't have anymore. And they're like £3,000 each and they just can't have no more. It's definitely an inside job somewhere. It takes so long to get money for anything, you know. You have to keep applying and applying, trying to raise funds.* (Destiny, West City)

A parent in The Valley talked about the local events she and her partner helped organise at the local children's play area:

> *It is a lot better here than where I grew up, lots of things to do here, for example the adventure playground. Our children go all the time, and my partner and I do a lot there, for example at Christmas time, my partner does DJ-ing and I do food.* (Gillian, The Valley)

An East London mother described raising money for play equipment, applying for funding to refurbish the local park and organising a 'fun' social event to bring everyone together and publicise the upgraded park:

> *We raised money before I saw you last time, to do up the swings in the square that the council had left completely dishevelled, and burnt out. So we raised all the money for that, we got grants, and there was a little extra money. So last September we had a party for everyone living in the area at no cost to anyone, to try and get kids to come, and we're looking at another one in June.* (Leah, West City)

Parents' involvement was not limited to children's needs. For example, two parents, one in the North, one in London, were working on getting internet services for their neighbourhoods. A parent in The Valley was trying to develop wireless networking, which would benefit both children and adults, and another in West City was working on a broadband scheme in his neighbourhood.

> *We're launching a triple-play broadband scheme which will put the local area as the largest broadband community in the whole of Western Europe, which is providing cheap TV, telephony, our own local TV channel, and 8 meg broadband, all that for under fifteen quid a month.* (Alan, West City)

Sometimes community involvement was provoked by plans to 'regenerate' the areas, putting the local community under pressure. For example, community activists in West City were campaigning against large-scale new building in their local area because it would add pressure to already over-stretched local services without directly adding community benefits:

> *There's various community groups involved with campaigning against the building work. There's new building planned which*

*would mean 500 extra people, yet no extra doctors, parking spaces etc. We're all worried. Any little spot now, the council has a bad reputation for giving planning permission. With the local park they're thinking about building a coach park there.* (Leah, West City)

## Neighbours: "I actually try and help people"

The parents' feelings of security within their neighbourhoods were greatly influenced by the role of neighbours. We asked parents whether they could trust people in their areas and four out of five said they could call on neighbours for help when needed. In Kirkside East, the large Northern council estate where over three quarters of parents had relatives living on the estate and many of the mothers had grown up there, the proportion was even higher. In all of the areas close relatives played a surprisingly important role, with half of the families in London and the North having direct family in the area. Nearly three quarters said that grandparents played an important role in their children's lives. Three quarters of parents exchanged favours with neighbours, almost nine out of ten in East London, as Julie explained:

> *You see community spirit if someone's got a problem. People rally round and sort it out.* (Julie, East Docks)

Much of what parents called 'community spirit' reflects social capital, an asset like other kinds of capital, but one that is shared within communities, helping to foster social support and shared values, leading to cooperation for the common good. Local social relations and bonds help keep communities together and create positive social outcomes, a theme parents returned to many times.[2] Parents painted pictures of rich networks of friends, neighbours and relatives that they could talk to or turn to when they needed, and social capital had a dual function of countering feelings of insecurity among parents and creating informal lines of support. This led to families finding the areas far more friendly than average, with over 70 per cent finding them very friendly and only a tenth finding them unfriendly.

Annie, from East Docks, linked the sense of community to actual ownership, reflecting the link to real capital, bringing real value:

> *I think sometimes it's to do with ownership. If you feel that you're part of something, you're part of the community, you own the community. If you're part of what it is, then you're more likely to*

*contribute. Some people don't feel part, for whatever reason, so it's important to feel part. You look after something more if you feel it belongs to you.* (Annie, East Docks)

## Voluntary work strengthens community ties

Community activities involve serious commitments of time and voluntary effort. Many parents talked directly about their voluntary roles, involving a regular, 'work-like' commitment. These included: reading in children's schools; teaching arts and crafts to adults via Sure Start; and sitting on Parent Teacher Associations (PTAs) and school governors' boards, local management boards, Neighbourhood Watch committees and in one case a health improvement board. It also sometimes involved unpaid work in local community services such as credit unions; setting up and running tenants' and residents' organisations; being a church council or choir member; helping in a local hospital; doing sports coaching; or children's football. Most parents became involved because they had children, and neighbourhood conditions and services mattered to them. A few parents played several voluntary roles and worked many hours a week voluntarily, as the following mother from Kirkside East explained:

> *Last year I listened to Year 6 class, my 12-year-old daughter's, read. Now it is just those really needing it. And I do a reading club with four kids, Monday lunchtimes. Three more want to join. It is for kids whose parents don't listen to them. One is listened to at home but he just likes it. And I do voluntary reading Tuesday, Wednesday and Thursday for the last 15 minutes of school, to hear children read. I go to college and then straight to school after that. And I'm on the PTA at school.* (Kathleen, Kirkside East)

A West City mother explained why the more social aspect of volunteering appealed to her:

> *I volunteer at my son's school a couple of hours a week and do reading with the children. I enjoy it – probably for the interaction with other adults.* (Felicity, West City)

One mother from The Valley was involved on many fronts:

> *I got involved in things like being a school governor, and I work at a local pool, and I have set up a tenants' and residents' association for this estate.* (Phoebe, The Valley)

Often parents' main motivation was to help their own children. Several parents living in East Docks described how they helped to set up and run a community group specifically to support families in the local area. One group was still a strong presence after several years, and Annie explained what prompted her to become involved:

> *The school was running a group in my daughter's school, a parents' group, and I just went along to find out what was going on. I liked what they did, so I got involved that way. I like the way they helped local people. Before the help they now give to people, that support wasn't here.* (Annie, East Docks)

This mother then went on to help with children's reading and was eventually offered training by the school so that she could become a teaching assistant.

> *I was only supposed to fill in for six weeks but I did so well that they asked me to stay on. There's a really good feel in the school, lots of togetherness.* (Annie, East Docks)

Another mother explained how she helped with organising outings, making a big play of involving the kind of parents who might normally feel excluded:

> *I got involved five years ago. We're doing a steering group through the school. I'm secretary. That's been going since last year. We ask parents where they'd like to go, we arrange places, book them and give £5 towards an evening out. We're trying to get as many people as possible who don't get out or can't afford it.* (Rose, East Docks)

A mother in West City was active in a local community group and over time she gradually became a 'leading light'. The social networks that the group developed, which she referred to as 'word of mouth', were what accounted for her emergence as chair:

> *I was asked to be on the committee years ago, and gradually people moved away and no one was willing to take on the responsibility of chairing things. As I'm much better at that than administrative*

*things, that was how it happened. Word of mouth is the ultimate way that it happened. I was already using the group.* (Joanne, West City)

One mother in The Valley held a voluntary committee post in addition to helping with children in her housing cooperative. The cooperative where she lived encouraged shared activities:

*I joined the steering group for recycling, a friend and I run that. And I try to get to know the local kids, they spend days in the garden in summer. [The garden is four gardens knocked into one, at a housing cooperative.]* (Angie, The Valley)

The idea of mutual aid and cooperation is fundamental to human society, and in disadvantaged areas it is not surprising that parents find local involvement both useful and reassuring.[3]

## A helping hand: *"Something that touches us"*

Sharing usually implies reciprocal or mutual forms of support, but some parents voluntarily helped more vulnerable members of their community. Many parents worried about isolated and elderly residents. This mother in East Docks was particularly concerned about people with social problems, particularly parents with children in difficulty, who became isolated because of their children's behaviour. She had a very inclusive view of community and believed strongly in the need to build bridges. Helping people with problems to become linked into local services and support groups would integrate isolated families and help the community become more cohesive. People would cope better as a result:

*Some people out there are in crisis. Some people don't want outside help 'cos they think they'll be judged, you know. And that's because the community judges them as a parent because the child has these problems, and they get blamed, so they've become isolated. But I think the community that don't understand makes things ten times worse, especially friends and family. There's a lot of people that become isolated.*

*Some people don't even know about some of these services. There is so many support groups, I mean, even for single parents. I never knew all these things were out there. And there's a lot of people still don't know. I actually try and help people get to some*

*of these services that they didn't even know about, you know.*
(Julie, East Docks)

Sometimes mothers played an informal communication role in their community, helping to foster a sense of belonging and indirectly building social capital. Hannah in East Docks came from West Africa and had learned the hard way how many pitfalls there were for newly arrived and unsuspecting foreigners. She saw her informal community role as something of a lifeline. She felt sorry for people who were clearly at sea in a strange new world, and she became particularly clued up, after her own bad experiences of what could go wrong. She played several different community roles:

> *In the Ghanaian community – there's a guy with money problems – I had to advise him and his wife. There was a woman who's getting beaten up by her husband. They need advice. Some of them are illiterate. Some Africans are doing a scam, where they take you to a conference, but it's a hoax where they try to take your money, a money pyramid. I went to one, managed to leave and phoned everyone to say what was going on. Anything that they approach me with, I help them or refer them to the Citizens Advice Bureau. I help prisoners get in touch with their families back home. I speak our language with them so they feel at home.*
> (Hannah, East Docks)

Hannah experienced real kindness from her white neighbours, including protection from other, extremely racist neighbours who were harassing her:

> *In this area my next-door neighbour, she would leave money and chocolates in an envelope through the door. The people down the street, we call 'nanny' and 'granddad', and we don't even know their names. They are white people, not black people. The link between us and the neighbours is something that touches us. Sometimes we pop in and have a chat – the black boy with the white grandma and granddad! They stood up against the neighbours harassing us.*
> (Hannah, East Docks)

This powerful story of cross-cultural community bonds was not uncommon:

> *When I moved here it was mostly old people in this block. When I was going to work, I used to see them, you know, the old ladies who stand together in groups and chat for hours. One opens her door and one opens her window and they talk. I talk to all the old ladies. They look out for everyone.* (Cynthia, West City)

Another East London mother expressed frustration at the low level of involvement. She knew how much progress depended on people's commitment:

> *We have meetings in the local community centre but only a few come sometimes, yet everyone goes around moaning if they don't hear nothing. Lots of things have been achieved but it's down to every individual. It's my neighbourhood, it's where I live, I put an input into it. So when children are doing graffiti, asking them, 'do you live around here?'. Or everybody coming together when there's a meeting and putting their views on the table so the area can improve on a daily basis.* (Yetunda, West City)

## "Not paid work"

Sometimes voluntary activity helped parents make the transition into paid work. For example, one parent in Kirkside East explained that she had been working voluntarily as a learning support worker at a local adult education and community centre, and her tutors then asked her to work on a paid basis. A father in The Valley explained that his experience of working voluntarily for New Deal for Communities was a catalyst for him becoming self-employed. A father in West City had a similar experience. And many mothers took on paid childcare roles through their involvement in helping the school or a local play scheme.

A Northern parent explained her ambitions to get paid work following her volunteering, which helped her raise her sights:

> *I do two hours voluntary work at a local centre and my tutors want me to do it in a paid capacity. I'm really pleased. I really enjoy doing it. I saw a learning support post in prison, to apply via the University. But I lost the paper so I wasn't meant to have it. But the pay was very good. And it needed no qualifications. They wanted you to train and I've done it mostly. It was just before Christmas.* (Kathleen, Kirkside East)

Another parent saw volunteering as a direct stepping stone into work:

> *I've been trying to do a pottery class with some funding and I've done voluntary work at church for the Sure Start crèche, but not paid work, I think it'll be next year when I start work.* (Avril, The Valley)

Some parents talked less positively about voluntary work in their neighbourhoods. Lack of qualifications and limited experience were the biggest barriers to paid employment, including the fact that voluntary work did not pay while parents tried to build up experience.

> *I think most of these jobs are outside of the borough. So therefore you've got longer travelling time. But there are care homes in the borough. There's one that's not too far. But the majority of 'em, they're all fully staffed, or they just don't wanna give people the work experience, or you've got to have NVQs. You've got to have one or two years working in a care home environment. They say about doing voluntary work, but voluntary work doesn't really pay the bills.* (Marie, East Docks)

Other parents saw voluntary work as a choice which closed off other opportunities rather than helping them into paid employment. A West City parent saw the negative impact of local voluntary work on her finances, in spite of the satisfaction she derived from the contribution she made.

> *The things I've chosen to do, you know, always doing community-based jobs or voluntary jobs, rather than jobs that are gonna enable you to save a decent amount of money in order to move out of an area. If all your life, choices have been to do things that've been of use to the community, you get nothing to show for it at the end. But that's been my choice, you know. I wasn't forced into doing any of those things. And it's just when you get to a certain age and you think, 'Oh my goodness, I have nothing to show for this', you know, no pension plan, you sort of think, 'what have I done?'.* (Joan, West City)

## Problems with involvement: "Only looks good on the surface"

A few parents became disillusioned with their role and with the organisation they were working with. For example, one East Docks parent had been involved in developing a tenant compact, a formal service agreement between tenants and the council. However, she stopped when she began to realise the compact would not achieve anything concrete. The following extract captures her disillusionment with the council's approach to involvement:

> *That all sort of fizzled out. It's like everything with the council, it's stage-managed, it looked good, but I haven't been to a meeting since it was launched. They do all these things on the surface, but that's where it seems to have ended. I've distanced myself from it again, because I don't want to be part of something that only looks good on the surface.* (Joyce, East Docks)

Sometimes multiple factors combined to undermine parents' involvement. One London mother was caught between her involvement in the local tenants' association, and its ambition to deal with anti-social behaviour, particularly when it involved her neighbours:

> *I got asked to sign a petition to get rid of my neighbour. She used to be so bad, running around naked, different boyfriends coming in all the time. But I said I couldn't 'cos, what if she saw the petition with my name on it. I don't want hassle at my doorstep, I've got two kids.* (Destiny, West City)

## Troubling barriers to community spirit: "There's no longer that nice balance"

Parents identified some crucial barriers to community, particularly related to sensitive ethnic divisions. This East London mother talked about the priority accorded to certain minority beliefs and sensitivities, which could make the original local community feel excluded. She herself had a mixed-race son, and like many parents with mixed-heritage children, she wanted him to understand his whole heritage. Her views echoed what many parents told us:

> *We had a really difficult time this Halloween trying to find something to do. They sell the costumes, they sell the candy, but where do you go from there? You knock at people's doors, they don't*

*answer. You can't wear the costumes at school 'cos it offends certain people. So it's like, in order to cater for other people's religions and beliefs, we're kinda losing our own. And I don't think that's fair. I think it should cater for everybody, including us. So yeah, that would be nice, to have more of a Christmassy thing at Christmas and a Halloween haunted house, somewhere that people can choose to go to if they want to. There's no longer that nice balance. And it's like certain things, you can't sing 'bah bah black sheep' at school and I'm like, how is that racial? You're singing about sheep and they do come in black and white. And it's just gotten so extreme. It's like my son is mixed race, you know, he's half and half and I don't want him to be confused about a certain part of his heritage. It's kinda gotten just a little bit too politically correct, just a little [laughs].* (Beth, West City)

The pressures on the East London areas seemed particularly intense, diluting an already fragile sense of community. Local families sensed a loss of community that for many was now a distant memory. One parent described her feeling of isolation and exclusion, reinforced by the isolation she saw around her:

*I see nobody. We don't socialise with our neighbours. I do know there's a young Asian woman living across the road, brought over by an arranged marriage: 'They brought me a wife over', but I've never seen this girl. There isn't a huge sense of community. I may feel excluded but I don't think there's a huge inclusive group from which I'm being excluded.* (Ariana, West City)

Other parents echoed this loneliness:

*I'm not cut off because there's nothing to be cut off from. Neighbourhoods can isolate you. There's nowhere to meet people.* (Poonam, Kirkside East)

Another parent from West City talked about the loss of a sense of familiarity and therefore the loss of communication:

*That's what we were saying before. The community thing, no one knows each other. I said to you before, you could walk from one end of the area to the other taking two hours 'cos before you chatted to 18 people along the way. So that's what the shame of it is. Although we're all living in a community now, nobody speaks to each other.* (Natalie, West City)

A contradicting result of the forced sharing involved in local areas was the desire expressed by some parents for less 'community' and more privacy.

Many nuisances arise in dense urban neighbourhoods where people's habits and lifestyles are visible and in some senses shared. Those living at close quarters with neighbours can end up feeling oppressed by too much proximity. Conflict or friction with neighbours could make parents feel trapped. So weighing up the need for community against the desire for freedom and choice was often difficult for parents. There were built-in contradictions and dilemmas in the parents' need for community and desire for autonomy, and it was often a question of balancing pros and cons. Some families, particularly in blocks of flats, wanted more privacy, more private space and more personal control over what they shared:

> *I just wanted to get out of the estate, I weren't happy at all. 'Cos you lived in a block, you always met someone on the landing, in the lifts, always gossiping, knowing each other's business. No one goes to work round there, they've got nothing better to do, so I think that can cause trouble as well. Whereas here in my new flat, I've got my own front door.* (Megan, West City)

Changes under way in local services accelerated the disappearance of community as community bases were lost:

> *All the local pubs are going, you know where people used to build friendships, you know, neighbours. People are not neighbourly anymore. They go in of an evening, shut their doors and that's it, they don't wanna know. Community spirit, that's what they call it, there's no community spirit.* (Gillian, East Docks)

The withdrawal of front-line services such as caretakers, maintenance teams, park keepers and so on had compounded the decline, alienating people from their own community.[4] This much wider trend shows up in levels of environmental neglect which parents connected on:

> *I mean I've always lived in this area all my life. Very disillusioned with this area, in particular, like the way you're treated. People don't take pride in where they live, you know, they don't worry*

*about the outside of their place. I dread to think sometimes what the inside of their houses are like. And the area's, this whole total area, it's just, it's just really sort of – gone down.* (Gillian, East Docks)

## "Just so many different people"

A number of East London families suggested that living with change, diversity, new communities, brought special benefits. This parent positively favoured the fact that she lived in a mixed community because of the special community atmosphere it generated, although this did depend on the crucial 'linking in' that parents often referred to:

> *It is to do with where [you live], it is nice being in a mixed community. You are free to do what you like. Nice community spirit. Always parties, celebrations, somewhere.* (Petra, The Valley)

But an African mother we visited had a more jaded view of community integration and described the hostility between different minority groups. She believed more familiarity, more contact, more understanding, would help:

> *I think it's important to bring the people closer, different people, and to understand people's religions and where they come from. For example, you see the Asian boys, the blacks and whites, they don't get along, there's something wrong. West Indians sometimes don't like the black Africans. I realised the West Indians regard us as just Africans, all Africans together, whatever region, West Africans. They think they are better than the Africans. With knowledge they can understand, but when they don't, that's why those few people are like that.* (Yinka, East Docks)

A crucial barrier to better community relations, recognised particularly by parents in East London, was the continual rapid influx of newcomers from abroad into their neighbourhoods. Integration was difficult to achieve in such pressured and competitive environments. One African mother, a long-time resident, remembered the sense of community when she first came before the population swelled and changed:

> *It's had its highs and its lows. It's been good and bad. The good experience was when I moved in and we had older people and they were very community-minded, they'd watch out for your kids. Now the people who've moved in are totally different, they just say*

*'hi'. It used to be lovely round here, with lovely flowers outside. When it declined, it was just so many different people. You can't help that but with so many people there's no community spirit. I used to know the names of all my neighbours. People just seem to lock their doors and that's it. Before we'd knock on doors and say 'Hello, how are you?'. It seems calmer now, thank God. It's a bit more of a desirable neighbourhood to live in but that's how it started.* (Yetunda, West City)

Extremely rapid ethnic change in a matter of a decade had undermined the confidence of the traditional white working-class population.[5] People of South Asian and African origin were the fastest growing groups in the two East London areas;[6] the rapid rate of change was a driver for parents to move out of the neighbourhood:

*I like the neighbourhood, but it was changing too much, there's a lack of respect. It was becoming – it sounds strange – you can't get simple things from the shops, English food. The shops weren't catering enough for English food, they don't stock barley. I wonder, how do older people cope?* (Tracy, West City)

## "More of a community thing"

Another mother who had moved out of the East End stressed how community-oriented her new area was compared with what she left behind. She saw the London neighbourhoods as transient and unsettled, hard to put roots down, whereas her new neighbourhood, further out, seemed more settled and therefore happier:

*The area was a rat race really, weren't it. Where I'm living now, it's more a community thing though, d'you know what I mean. You can go out, you can talk to your neighbours, you can all sit out on the front on your street. It's much better, it's much more friendlier. Look out for each other. Someone goes on holiday, you watch their property for 'em. Much more, I don't know, totally different. The old area ain't a neighbourhood, is it? Where I was, that's not a neighbourhood, that's just people going in and out, in and out, temporary housing, get 'em in, get 'em out. Type of 'stop off point' weren't it. Where I'm now, it's like a proper place where you live, innit. Like, people've lived there for years.* (Rebecca, West City)

The feeling of transience and lack of commitment to the area damaged the sense of community, particularly in East London, intensifying the parents' feeling of weak control.

Another 'born and bred' local from the same area expressed similar sentiments. Her entire family had moved out and she was trying to find a way to follow them because she felt the community had been destroyed by development:

> *They've ripped the heart out of East Docks.* (Lesley, East Docks)

Parents' sense of loss of community in these neighbourhoods mirrored their own need for community. Gillian, from East Docks, had older children and could remember the trust and solidarity that developed when their community was rebuilt in the early postwar years. Then there was full employment and dock areas like hers were still flourishing:

> *Considering it's an area I've lived in all my life, it is very, very different. I was born in 1956 – this area was very heavily bombed. The house is newish. Going back and thinking when I was growing up in the sixties, the area was better then, even with all the waste ground. The docks were thriving. They say there's regeneration, but I think it's for the wrong reasons. There's no community spirit. People used to leave their back doors open with their keys in. People don't want to make a life for themselves. If you want things, you have to work for 'em. People have no respect. If you left your door open now you'd be cleared out.* (Gillian, East Docks)

A couple in West City were active in the local community regeneration initiative, New Deal for Communities, and saw clearly the need for community building. Community activists like Debra and Alan worked hard to secure the community and social benefits of regeneration. They saw community as a vital ingredient in turning around an area and bringing people together. This perspective on community renewal reinforces findings from other neighbourhood and family studies.[7]

> *Bricks and mortar is not regeneration because all they do is shift the problems elsewhere. So many schemes you can look at where the number of people who live there at the end of the programme compared with who lived there at the beginning, well, they just don't live there anymore. This street was one in ten which survived, you know. Nine out of ten have been shifted elsewhere and all their problems go with them. It's not good enough to just get rid*

*of problems, you actually have to deal with them and that's the tricky bit. How do you turn round, you know, people who live in multi-generation homes where nobody's ever worked? And you know, there's a whole subculture going on that's outside the norm of society. Now, you don't deal with that in ten years, so this whole generation's been signed off from normal society for ever more.* (Alan, West City)

## Overcoming the barriers: "Somewhere for people just to chill out"

A mother who moved out highlighted the strong sense of belonging that had arisen from families sharing communal spaces and tenants getting to know each other through sharing a block on a council estate. The extended family also played a big role in this, often traditional white working-class families. The community ideal she described harked back to an earlier era of settled extended families:

*Only the one thing I still miss after moving away and that's the community spirit, I always go on about that, always, but it's not here at all. But I think that's probably again to do with each place being owned, everyone's owning their own home and doing their own thing. Whereas when you live in a block and they're all council tenants and they're all, I don't know, just living the same life, all bringing up children together. And, you know, you would grow up with their parents, which is basically what happened in East London, you know, we all had children together, we all brought 'em up together. We'd go round to our mum's with our children and we'd been neighbours to start with. So when you were round with your mum, you know, taking her grandchildren round, there'd be three, four, five other families doing the same thing and you'd just be in the garden, they'd be in their garden. It was like a continuing thing through the generations.* (Marilyn, West City)

Some parents saw the need for shared communal spaces and shared local services as a way of bringing people into contact with each other. This mother talked in the same breath about the shortage of places that would bring people together easily, and the closure of simple local services such as cash machines, making the area 'poor':

*We need somewhere for people to just chill out, for everyone, like an adventure place. And there's no cash machines, things like that.*

*The petrol stations have gone. It's like you don't have a choice when you live in a poor borough. That's what concerns me.* (Sophie, West City)

Another mother saw the direct connection between local services such as street markets and the social atmosphere of a place. Like many East Enders, she harked back to the days when there was a better community spirit:

*What needs to be achieved is quite a lot, and I know they are trying but it's a bit slower than I'd like. I'd like to see the market bloom again, that would be really nice, just for social reasons as well, you know. It's a nice place to hang out and chat and see all your friends on a Saturday. And at the risk of sounding racial, which I really hope I don't, I'd like a bit of the old East End culture to come back.* (Beth, West City)

Shared activities in local streets such as street markets, stalls, even just local shops opening onto the street, galvanise community contact that can build a much greater sense of familiarity.[8] Parents' support for community spaces and community contact ran strongly counter to people's innate desire for privacy. Several parents argued that only by providing common meeting places would a sense of community among strangers form. This plea for more meeting places was particularly common among foreign parents and more recent incomers:

*I'd like to see more community cohesiveness in terms of we've got a lot of new faces there and that, it'd be nice if there was some way of people coming together more.* (Annie, East Docks)

A sense of 'community' could override the bad things people heard about:

*Where I live is not too bad. The neighbours get on, like. If you want anything I could run next door and vice versa. There's a good community within the neighbourhood. I don't know about the other block. The neighbourhood is all right. For me, I've lived here 11 years now and it's not too bad because I'm here, my mother's across the road, so it's not too bad for me. I mean, people say it's rough round here, there's this, and that going on, but I don't see it.* (Faye, West City)

Another mother who was critical of many aspects of the area strongly defended its core value of community:

> *It's a very community-minded, helpful area. People don't worry what you've got, but they'll share what they've got if you're in trouble – you can't say that about many places. So it's got its upsides as well.* (Trudy, West City)

## "More power to the community"

On our last visit, parents gave many examples of 'community spirit' in action in their neighbourhoods. It showed most clearly at events because these more than anything else made parents feel involved. Events took place in school halls, churches or parks. This often made 'community spirit' palpable, as this mother explained:

> *People have the opportunity to live in a nice area. At Halloween yesterday there was an increase in parents taking kids out. Real community spirit built up recently and I saw it in action on Halloween. Parents dressed up, it was lovely, no trouble.* (Amanda, Kirkside East)

A number of families saw younger people getting involved in neighbourhood events as proof that 'community spirit' was strong. One Northern parent was pleased that young people were helping in local festivals:

> *More young people are getting involved and helping people. I think it gives them a bit of a buzz to be a community steward or something.* (Cynthia, The Valley)

Another parent drew a favourable comparison between the level of community activity in her neighbourhood and where her sister-in-law lived because more things were happening locally. So even though she thought the community was declining, it was stronger than elsewhere:

> *The comparison I make the most is with where my sister-in-law lives in Tottenham, and I think that we've got a lot more going on in my area than what she has in her area. I mean, although I'm saying the community feeling is going down, there is a lot more here…. I've found it more accessible. I've done a lot more here than what she's been able to do there. I mean, she's more cut off and*

*she's found that she hasn't been able to access things more easily than what I have done.* (Janet, East Docks)

Meanwhile an East London mother argued that local people needed to take much more responsibility:

*I think what we're working toward is, particularly this community group, is people being more active in their own community and taking responsibility, so I think if we can have local residents, local shopkeepers, schools. We have community police officers here, housing officers, youth workers – we're trying to get them all together to look at how we can work together to help improve what's going on here, 'cos I don't think the responsibility lies in one place. It's about the community taking responsibility for itself.* (Andrea, East Docks)

One mother raised the need for fathers to contribute more to local community effort, alongside other things:

*The neighbourhood looks good, very green and mostly homeowners around here, so people are caring for their houses. But we need more recycling equipment for plastics. And men need to get involved in the community and in their kids' lives.* (Nita, The Valley)

Another mother talked about the proactive role her local authority was playing in backing the local community, bringing together what the council could do and what communities could contribute. This generated confidence in local community action:

*The community has rights. If there's anything going on, you report it. We're given a record sheet so you can report accidents, even if it's your neighbours. Whereas in the past, you wouldn't even approach the children. The council have given more power to the community, the tenants. Before, if you said anything, you'd have a brick through your window. Now, the community police are just around the corner. We have peaceful weekends…. The area is a better place now. Even if I won the lottery today, I'd look to buy a house in the area.* (Sasha, East Docks)

Families produced evidence of the need for community and the existence of 'community spirit' in many different places and ways. Voluntary efforts, local events, feelings of safety within the neighbourhood, links between different cultures and ethnic groups, social networks, children and young people doing things for the community, schools supporting and fostering community spirit, neighbourly contact and local council approaches all underpinned a sense of community. Numerous barriers, tensions and pressures ran alongside this, but community spirit could still be found.

## Sure Start and community involvement: "The Sure Start programme is absolutely wonderful"

Parents with young children often feel lonely and isolated, which can prevent them from securing the support they need. One special programme, launched in 1998 to help parents with young children in very disadvantaged areas, was particularly significant in galvanising community support. Sure Start's core goal was to help vulnerable, low-income parents with pre-school children. It relied heavily on parental involvement and as a result built great commitment and enthusiasm within the local communities where it operated. Sure Start generated great interest among parents with young children:

> *I would say the Sure Start scheme for under fives has probably had a big impact.* (Joan, West City)

Many parents positively benefited from Sure Start in their neighbourhood, seeing how it developed their community networks. In the two Northern neighbourhoods where Sure Start began in 1999-2000, over four fifths of parents said they knew about Sure Start. A lower proportion knew about Sure Start in East London, partly because the programme there started in 2001–03. Over one third of parents in the North were directly involved with Sure Start compared with one in ten in East London.

> *I think Sure Start have done a lot, lots of courses.* (Laura, The Valley)

Sure Start encouraged parents to take up training as well as helping them with their children, and Sure Start centres often ran training for parents, both in 'soft' skills such as parenting, family health, fitness and so on, as well as 'hard' skills like job training. It also sometimes led to parents finding employment. Many parents we spoke to were heavily involved in Sure Start, particularly if they or their young children had health problems. One Kirkside East mother found Sure Start programmes and the projects they generated very empowering. It led to her taking on a much bigger role as user representative on one of the local health boards. She continued her voluntary work with Sure Start, while playing a serious role on the health board:

> *I work voluntarily for Sure Start now, I teach adults arts and crafts and I'm a member of the Service Improvement Board for Leeds Mental Health. We ask all involved in services how to make things better and pass on information to those who can make changes, if we have good ideas. It got together in December. The official launch was in February. There are 11 potential projects.* (Lucy, Kirkside East)

Voluntary involvement with Sure Start sometimes led to parents securing paid employment, such as community outreach or support for parents with particular problems or disabilities. This mother from Kirkside East offers a remarkable testimony to a mother fitting all the negative social stereotypes, feeling worthless as a result, then discovering a new sense of worth because Sure Start draws out her potential, reinforces her talents and offers her a way forward:

> *Sure Start, yes, I was with them for over a year, doing voluntary work, before I worked for them. The voluntary work I did included boxing, the fitness side of things, and I did talks on how I got involved, on being a teen parent, and getting into boxing. And I ran a few behavioural courses and training classes for nursery staff too.... The feedback was good. I was a single mum, always on the estate, going to lots of groups, and then doing voluntary work and talks, et cetera, and it was a big turn around. It was a success to go from doing nothing, then to do all sorts of things, and sit in a room full of 'professionals' and talk. It was a confidence boost. I always was confident but I was defensive too. I'm not so defensive now. I know that just because I live on a council estate and didn't work, I now know I am capable. To see them, their reaction to that was good.* (Cheryl, Kirkside East)

A mother in The Valley had a similar experience:

> *I used to use Sure Start, then I became a volunteer, and now I work there. I used the Family Support Service. A worker would come and see you and take you out or just support you. Then I became a volunteer worker and now I am a paid worker. It has given me opportunities, and given them to others, that I wouldn't*

*have got. So many free things. And then the work experience.*
(Nita, The Valley)

Sure Start had helped parents and their families with a specific problem or worry relating to their children. The following examples illustrate the problems, from serious medical ones through behavioural problems and special needs, to a problem of acute shyness in both children and adults. Parents mentioned how Sure Start had helped them tackle seriously daunting problems, and to meet other parents too:

> *The main thing I will love Sure Start forever for is, they were brilliant about my son age four. They helped me to get him diagnosed with autism, for a speech and language therapist to see him, and that started the whole diagnosis process. I just feel they take parents very seriously. And it has been nice to meet other mums with kids the same age.* (Gillian, The Valley)

Another mother explained how Sure Start helped her child make the transition between home and school:

> *My daughter was so shy, I knew I needed to get her somewhere before school, to build her confidence, to mix and play with other kids. She'd go nowhere without me.* (Linda, Kirkside East)

Sure Start helped parents and children build their confidence and social skills, particularly where a family was isolated and small children weren't used to mixing, as this mother from The Valley told us:

> *It came at the right time. He wouldn't mix with other kids at all. I was at the end of my tether. They advised me to go to a parent and toddler group and I did. I was shy, so he suffered. But Sure Start got me to go to groups and to mix and he benefited from it.* (Deidre, The Valley)

## "Being part of the community, I suppose"

Involvement with Sure Start fostered a stronger sense of belonging, helping parents to feel part of the community where they lived. It created a virtuous circle between families, with families gaining confidence and in the process reinforcing the community. Sure Start's community role was widely recognised by parents:

*Well, I think it is nice to know what is happening in the community and to be part of the community too, to get your name recognised and be able to share your information with others. That is really important to me.* (Chandra, The Valley)

This mother from The Valley liked the training Sure Start offered, but she also liked the fact that it helped her feel involved:

*When I've done courses I will see Sure Start, or New Deal people. But I don't go to their stuff much, just the odd open day and the kids' library, being part of the community I suppose.* (Avril, The Valley)

The real strength of Sure Start seemed to lie in the support it offered parents, within their community, valuing what they, the parents, could contribute. Parents did not feel so isolated because it galvanised help for their children. One of the chief added values of Sure Start was the emotional support it offered, both through its activities and the way it linked parents in positive action. Typical comments from many mothers in Kirkside East showed this:

*You're not on your own. You've got someone to turn to.* (Amy, Kirkside East)

*You've got someone to support you, when friends and family aren't enough!* (Chloe, Kirkside East)

One mother felt that Sure Start was a real magnet for the community:

*It is helpful. No Sure Start, nowhere to go. Lots of support. Right friendly.* (Laverne, Kirkside East)

Laura, in The Valley, felt that Sure Start was a backdrop to the community, a sort of reliable mainstay of the community:

*I had a little bit of support when my son now age two was quite small. And I have done some of their courses, like First Aid. They do Christmas parties for kids too. It's another group of people you can go to and to a lot of extent it is just another group of people I know. You know they are there.* (Laura, The Valley)

### "They supported me"

Mothers sometimes credited Sure Start with preventing mental illness. Just knowing that Sure Start was there to help meant that this mother who had suffered serious depression was able to avoid it with her second baby:

> *I think it meant a lot because of not having a parent figure myself. And my partner being at work all day then. It meant I felt I had some support. I got depression with my first child and I knew I had the support when I had my second daughter so I didn't get depressed.* (Louise, Kirkside East)

It often helped set parents in difficulty on to a healthier, more self-reliant course:

> *I went to massage. And hypnotherapy for stopping smoking. And they've knocked on the door a few times in the last year, telling you what is going on. It was more for me than my son. It gave me confidence to get back into work, because I'd talk to the man who ran it, and when I was going through behavioural problems with my son, they supported me. Just a support network really.* (Rosie, Kirkside East)

This extensive support meant that parents could more readily manage their children:

> *I got support from Sure Start with my son's behaviour....* (Chloe, Kirkside East)

Mothers particularly stressed the value to them of personal support:

> *It would be a lot harder [without Sure Start]. Even before the baby comes you get £500 maternity grant. Then after, there's all drop-ins and stuff, and a really good support system.* (Angie, Kirkside East)

Many parents talked explicitly of Sure Start's 'support system'; through this they were drawn into wider support networks. Thus, Sure Start helped to build social networks, creating bonds that were a key component of community viability, and social capital.[9] Being able to talk through problems with other people was immensely reassuring:

*It means we meet lots more parents. If we've got fears or problems with raising children, you're not in a lonely world, there's a drop-in where they discuss their fears.* (Millie, West City)

*I accessed a lot of groups for my daughters [now aged five and seven] when they were younger. I attended lots of groups from when my eldest daughter was six months until she was five years old. With my second daughter from birth until she was five.* (Louise, Kirkside East)

For one London mother, Sure Start quite simply meant that she always had somewhere to go with her children:

*Sure Start's been brilliant actually. There's always somewhere to take the children now. Parent and toddler drop-ins, fun days, and music groups. There's somewhere to go every single day. Toy libraries, whatever. Before, we just went to the park really. Especially if it's a cold, rainy day, going to the park, it's hard. But now there is somewhere to go every single day.* (Destiny, West City)

The option to get together with other parents and allow children to play and mix is a basic need among parents, one that they could not take for granted. Their praise of Sure Start underlined the gap it helped to fill.

## "It's for younger kids"

There were some criticisms of Sure Start, but significantly, such criticism tended to be offered alongside praise for the programme. One worry was that Sure Start could run out of steam or become spread too thinly:

*… talking to other mothers, they say it's not very good. They say when it first started, there were all these activities going on, but it's dwindled and they don't keep in contact anymore. That's what I get, the feedback. They do in the summertime do a lot of things, they have outings and that. And they do give grants.* (Rose, East Docks)

Parents experienced a drop off in activity as their children moved beyond the Sure Start age, so another common criticism was the age limit:

> *It is a good service. But we need more for older kids though. They could do more for that age.* (Olivia, Kirkside East)

One mother questioned its focus on young mothers:

> *Sure Start has been good but it is for younger kids really. I wonder if there is too much help for young girls having a baby. It is easy, an easy way out. I did receive help with my second child [now age seven] but now I'm out of the catchment area for Sure Start.* (Jessica, The Valley)

We did also come across examples of Sure Start helping mothers with problems connected to older children as part of their community outreach and support. A parent from Kirkside East had even more dedicated help, which clearly reinforced her own special efforts to help her 10-year-old:

> *I have seen Sure Start for my son's behavioural problems. We go to a class together with Sure Start, once a week. I rang Sure Start and asked if they had anything at all. They were helpful. We've only just started last week. Second class this week. It is a six-week course. An experimental class. So they're not sure what the results will be. He took part.* (Kirsten, Kirkside East)

A few parents worried about Sure Start's image because its targeted approach on the most deprived areas might reflect on them:

> *There is a stigma to Sure Start, as something for deprived people. But good that they helped us with a bit of funding.* (Amanda, Kirkside East)

In spite of these criticisms, it is hard to dispute the popularity and community benefits of Sure Start. Put simply:

> *Sure Start has made a big difference.* (Rosie, Kirkside East)

## Summary and conclusions

Parents in all four areas believed that community mattered for their families' futures, and they wanted to be involved in order to help shape and control their immediate environments. However, only half of parents saw positive signs of community and only a minority felt that they could influence what happened. The stronger general feeling was of loss of community spirit over time and a lack of a sense of control over what happened in their communities. On the other hand, most parents were involved in some way and did draw satisfaction from this.

The fragile sense of community was influenced by many things: environmental conditions and general decay; the number of incomers and the over-rapid change parents saw in their areas; the presence of families with multiple problems and people 'who don't care'; and the threat of large-scale regeneration plans, undermining local social networks.

Conversely parents saw organised community-oriented activities and services such as Sure Start and other local supports as contributing positively to community networks, helping parents directly and offering a focus on 'community betterment'. Community events played a big part in bringing people together and encouraging families to take part. Their value was that they included all groups.

Voluntary contributions by parents were very important and often opened the door to training and jobs. Schools, parenting groups, IT training, fitness classes and local community training played an important community role, but so did voluntary work and the training that went with it. The more parents had the chance to play an active role, the more they seemed to benefit and progress, the more positively they viewed their local community and their local links to it.

However, we found significant barriers to the development of community, the most important of which was population change. Racial and ethnic divisions are intensified by the general instability of communities and ethnic scapegoating becomes a form of defence. Family ties and local claims on scarce resources can be overridden by the urgency of re-housing, and keeping schools and other services open to all.[10] Community ties are constantly weakened and undermined by the pressures on poor areas where there is more need than capacity to respond.

Special efforts can help to overcome community divisions and several parents argued for a stronger emphasis on 'traditional community values', meaning support for family ties. This view was particularly common in East London, where community instability is far more visible and where enough residents have a long history in the area to remember its well-known sense of community.[11] The need for spaces to meet and events to bring people together have become more pressing as community identity has been eroded, but clearly official public meetings have far less appeal than family-oriented events, and the former can deter parents unless they concern a life-and-death matter for families such as major demolition proposals.

The traditional working-class roots of these communities only a generation ago have gradually weakened, through the demise of stable, large, industrial employers, the devaluing of manual traditions, the outward movement of the younger generation and the rise of immigration to fill new, low-paid service jobs while fuelling conflict over resources.[12] The erosion of the extended family, the rise in lone parenthood and the declining patterns of marriage and fertility have changed the shape of traditional communities almost beyond recognition. Yet enough remains in local memories of the strengths of these communities to encourange families today of all 'races' to want to recreate their positive value and worth. Community ties are now built on more immediate, more unfamiliar and more unstable links with neighbours, often complete strangers. Because of this, community matters more and yet becomes more fragile. It requires organised events to buttress parents' sense of belonging, which is why parents like fun events. They quickly respond to interventions that support community and to invitations that include children. But community is only rarely completely self-organising in modern urban conditions.[13]

Community-oriented initiatives by government, local authorities and voluntary organisations made residents more positive about the impact of community-oriented efforts. These initiatives were usually organised and run by local community-based services such as schools, health centres, childcare services, regeneration programmes and other social organisations such as churches and charities, with the involvement of local volunteers. The more these bodies turned to the community and tried to involve residents, the more positive the response became. This underlines the importance of local services.

Sure Start's high stress on children's well-being and parental involvement genuinely fostered a sense of community that in turn enhanced community capacity. Sure Start was a model of family and community support in the eyes of parents.

Progress is reflected in the sheer numbers of parents who got involved, and the range of activities they supported. The high level of voluntary involvement by parents, the belief that being involved and having local links makes 'all the difference', should counter the commonly expressed view that people in disadvantaged areas are apathetic and 'don't want to know', that people are 'takers' rather than givers and that people who are not doing well do not have capacity to do more even though family responsibilities, work, study, childcare and sheer exhaustion all do limit involvement.

These communities can become more resilient if society and particularly public bodies recognise the value of involving parents and children, who are easily excluded from more formal consultation, making them prey to wrong decisions. Our evidence shows that families prefer to be proactive, rather than simply recipients of ready-made decisions. In advanced, post-industrial urban societies a sense of community depends as much on external as internal supports. In the next chapter we explore the role of schools as 'community anchors', grounding the findings from this chapter on community within the most powerful and influential community institution in family lives, the local school.

## Notes

[1] Mumford, K. and Power, A. (2003) *East Enders: Family and community in East London*, Bristol: The Policy Press.

[2] Halpern, D. (2005) *Social capital*, Cambridge: Polity Press; Sampson, R.J., Squires, G.D. and Zhou, M. (2001) *How neighborhoods matter: The value of investing at the local level*, Washington, DC: American Sociological Association.

[3] Birchall, J. (1994) *Co-op: The people's business*, Manchester: Manchester University Press.

[4] Power, A. (1997) *Estates on the edge: The social consequences of mass housing in Northern Europe*, London: Palgrave Macmillan.

[5] Dench, G., Gavron, K. and Young, M. (2006) *The new East End: Kinship, race and conflict*, London: Profile Books.

[6] Lupton, R. and Power, A. (2004). *Minority ethnic groups in Britain*, CASE-Brookings Census Briefs No 2, London: LSE.

[7] Tam, H. (1988) *Communitarianism: A new agenda for politics and citizenship*, London: Macmillan; Hothi, M., Bacon, N., Brophy, M. and Mulgan, G. (2008) *Neighbourliness + empowerment = wellbeing: Is there a formula for happy communities?*, London: The Young Foundation.

[8] Worpole, K. and Knox, K. (2007) *The social value of public spaces*, York: Joseph Rowntree Foundation; Minton, A. (2009) *Ground control: Fear and happiness in the twenty-first century city*, London: Penguin.

[9] Putnam, R. (2000) *Bowling alone: The collapse and revival of American community*, New York: Simon & Schuster.

[10] Denham, J. (2009) Speech to Policy Network, 1 December; Denham, J. (2009) Speech to Trades Union Congress, 30 November.

[11] Young, M. and Willmott, P. (1957) *Family and kinship in East London*, London: Routledge and Kegan Paul; Dench, G., Gavron, K. and Young, M. (2006) *The new East End: Kinship, race and conflict*, London: Profile Books.

[12] Power, A., Richardson, L. et al (2004) *A framework for housing in the London Thames Gateway*, CASE Brief 27, London: LSE.
[13] www.citizensuk.org/

# THREE

# Schools in communities

*I think the schools are improving. They get better and better each year, basically. There is much more profile on education than there was before. Nowadays you see, especially in this area, so many kids going to university. Well years ago, it would never have happened in an area like this.* (Barbara, East Docks)

## Introduction: Why schools matter

Families talk a lot about schools because they play such a dominant role in family life, and children's development, enriching the social life of communities, particularly in low-income areas. Schools act as anchors within the community in two main ways: first, they have long-term, stable functions, funding and roles which almost all families accept; second, they attract a constant flow of local parents and children through their doors and 'anchor' families over most of their children's young lives within a consistent, day-by-day network of contacts and activities. This makes them invaluable to parents, providing often under-exploited potential to help. In this chapter we explore the role that schools play in family futures, and their special contribution in anchoring communities, bringing families together and responding to rapid social and ethnic change, as well as helping children from disadvantaged backgrounds to learn.

In spite of many ups and downs, schools were the most dominant and generally the most positive local institutions in family life. For this reason, we think of them as the archetypal community anchors. On average children in disadvantaged areas achieve lower standards of education, including the four areas where our 200 families live. There is a wide gap in aspirations between families living in disadvantaged areas from poorly educated backgrounds and more typical areas, partly because exposure to opportunity is more limited.[1] But parents see schools as vital institutions which try to make good these shortcomings, serving not only as educators but as socialisers, and often as supports for families struggling with parenting responsibilities. Children's problems most often come to light in school and schools feel they must respond to the welfare needs of families, otherwise families will not cope with school.

The government over the last 10 years has put a heavy emphasis on improving local schools in disadvantaged areas, and there has been measurable progress in the most disadvantaged schools and areas.[2] The role of schools in poor neighbourhoods is under-estimated by the wider society because in 'league tables' of academic achievement and progression into high-skilled careers, these schools 'under-perform'. However, talking to parents about schools and their direct experience of their children's education offers a distinct perspective on their role, showing schools as a source of stability and discipline, acting as agents of integration and support, tackling severe disadvantage and helping children develop social as well as literate skills. Schools stand out as places where much is done to help anchor communities, families and young people, and to overcome barriers to opportunity. Wider evidence of progress is examined in light of parents' actual experience.

## Parents' experiences of local schools

The 200 parents overwhelmingly sent their children to local primary schools for fear of sending them to schools that were out of reach. Each area had two or three local primary schools, at least one of which was a church school. There was a main secondary either in or very near each neighbourhood, but secondary schools had far weaker local connections and a much lower local profile because their catchment area was much bigger and the schools were larger.

Almost all the families had a child or children at local schools when the study began, and the issue of schools was raised on our first visit. Parents' general view of schools was positive, in spite of some worries. Parents' own experiences often ran counter to the stigma that is attached to schools in poor areas with a poor intake. Around three quarters of the parents were satisfied with their local schools even though many still saw problems, and they praised teachers for the efforts they put into helping their children. Less than one in five was dissatisfied, as Figure 3.1 shows.

The proximity of schools to home was very important to parents, both because parents knew most about neighbourhood schools, but also because neighbourhood schools generated security and friendship. Parents often deliberately chose the most local school so as to keep a 'close eye on things' because they worried about their children falling in with the 'wrong crowd' if they were out of their sight. Chains of local information received from friends, neighbours and relatives were an important source of ideas about which schools might work for their children, underlining the links between the strength of community feeling, social capital and schools as community anchors. Schools with strong links to the community were the most popular because of the social contact and familiarity they offered. Their children's happiness and local friendships were important to parents.

**Figure 3.1:** How satisfied parents were with children's schools, 2006

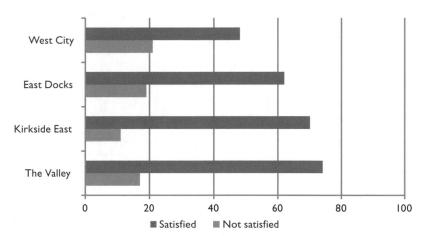

The physical condition and social environment of the school gave parents clear signals. Old, poorly maintained buildings, laid out to make supervision more difficult, signs of racial divisions and an unwelcoming atmosphere could put the parents off certain schools or make them feel more worried. In contrast, good school facilities helped a lot, including after-school clubs and social events involving parents. After-school clubs won praise alongside improvements to school buildings, new computers and better facilities. Changes in local schools, such as the re-introduction of homework and school uniforms, new headteachers to restore discipline and standards, attracted parents.

The approach of staff was important too – a welcoming attitude towards parents and frequent communication helped build cooperation, and a strong home–school link galvanised support for what the school was trying to achieve. Parents approved of staff who punished bad behaviour and rewarded children for small signs of progress. Parents wanted a disciplined environment with clear, set boundaries. They took seriously the messages they received from teachers, as long as they reflected a positive and supportive attitude, but they could react defensively to sharp criticism.

Schools had developed proactive approaches to the problems parents mentioned. Most parents spoke positively about helping children with their homework, but many parents had problems in understanding the homework once their children began secondary school. In some cases this was because of the way in which studying had evolved since their own time at school; often it came from their lack of experience of homework in their own school days. Several parents thought that the pressure of homework was 'too much', one of the biggest educational problem that parents highlighted. Working parents, parents with several children and lone parents struggled to find the time to help, and others spoke about the struggle to follow the work that their children were doing in schools. The older the children got, the more difficult helping them became. Some schools offered homework clubs, and some organised special support sessions for parents to explain what was being taught and how parents could help. For some parents, language was a problem too. Schools were becoming increasingly sensitive to ethnic diversity and responding with different supports, including outreach and special events.

Parents saw many problems in their children's schools, including a shortage of financial resources for extra teaching support, poor academic attainment, poor discipline, bad behaviour, bullying and language problems. Parents whose children experienced basic learning difficulties were often frustrated that the school could not solve their problem. A small number of children in the neighbourhoods had poor attendance records at secondary school, although they rarely referred to this as truanting; rather that their children weren't learning. Parents sometimes gave up at this stage, and their children 'dropped out'.

On our fourth visit we asked parents about changes to their children's primary and secondary schools over the previous year or two. In the North, about a third of parents felt that their children's school had got better but most felt that they had stayed the same, while almost none felt they had got worse. In East London nearly half the parents felt that their secondary schools had got better, and most of the rest thought they had stayed the same. By then all the London parents had at least one child in secondary school. The Education Action Zone in East Docks, the only one in the four areas, had a high profile and contributed to over half the parents feeling that all the local schools had improved, more than in any other area.[3]

Well over half of the parents in all four of the neighbourhoods felt that their children had *better* prospects than they did when they themselves were children. Only one in five felt that their children's prospects were worse, except in East Docks, where a third thought their children's prospects were worse despite big improvements in the schools. Schools ranked second in what worried parents most. The competitive job environment, the need for higher skills, the 'rough' local environment and the loss of apprenticeships influenced parents, particularly if their children were not doing well academically. Figure 3.2 summarises these views.

**Figure 3.2:** Whether parents think their children have better or worse prospects than they did when they were growing up, 2004–05

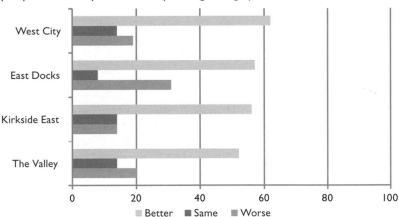

Therefore, while two thirds of parents were satisfied with their local schools and half were optimistic for their children's prospects, big challenges face both teachers and parents. We explore why the parents were so positive first, then the challenges.

## The benefits of local schools

Parents described the direct support schools gave to their children and themselves, explaining their mainly positive feelings towards their children's schools. In the following, lengthy extract, a parent praises her son's school for all the extra effort teachers were putting in:

> *At my son's school, he was pulled up at the age of six and they thought he was not performing as well as he should, and there's extra classes there for children and they get 'em up to the standard, and that's how they carry on, they're very good. The teachers've been there for years. They haven't got a high rate of supply teachers, they do a lot of after-school clubs. And leading up to the SATS he was getting an extra two hours a week after school, for 10 weeks. No other school I know of done that. It weren't compulsory, but*

> *I thought, well, you don't chuck education back, do you. And, he was doing Tuesdays and Thursdays every week for 10 weeks before the SATS exams to get him through because that's how good the school is. Teachers and everyone putting themselves out, you know. Could you imagine that, after work? You'd just want to go home wouldn't you? Not stand doing another hour.* (Alexa, East Docks)

Two powerful points reflected a more general view: letting a child 'slip through the net' could harm a child's chances far into the future; and taking up the extra help on offer was crucial to a teacher's morale and motivation, otherwise you were 'chucking an offer' back in their face.

A few parents worked as dinner ladies or teaching assistants in their children's schools; one talked about how reassuring it was to observe all the effort she saw being invested in children at her son's and daughter's school. In many parents' eyes teachers often 'go the extra mile', to offer children and parents stability, support, encouragement, advice, extra time. This mother felt that the teachers' efforts helped to anchor children, even when their family background was difficult:

> *I've actually had no problems, fairly satisfactory. Working at the school, I know from the inside that we're constantly working at our performance. Sometimes you can get disillusioned because it's all about results to please the government. You can see how much effort teachers put in. Recently we've been having interviews about my son and I feel they'll go that extra mile to help under-performing kids. At another local school, I've noticed the turnover of staff. Kids are coming from unstable homes and there's not the stability at school.* (Rachel, East Docks)

One innovative school helped parents over the hurdle of homework that they could not understand. This parent described the family learning programmes, which help parents help their children, that she had attended in her children's schools, as a way of proactively helping her children:

> *I'm very happy, with both children's primary and secondary schools. No problems. And I attend classes, like family learning, reading, maths, computers. You learn how they teach in school and then you can help them by teaching at home. I've learnt loads from it. I attend classes in both schools to help teach my kids. There is a good take-up rate. You get a certificate at the end.* (Poonam, The Valley)

Parents talked of the 'comfort and reassurance' schools offered. For example, one mother in The Valley explained how her children's school was "genuinely concerned about the kids", and another praised her children's school for taking so much trouble with different needs, coping with constant newcomers and outmovers.

> *It is very child-centred, looking at the needs of the particular population of children. It is a white minority school and over one third are special educational needs and a third leave during the year, because of being refugees and asylum seekers here, and people being short-term housed here.* (Louise, The Valley)

Another mother described the holistic approach of her children's school to educating children:

> *I'm very satisfied, it is genuinely trying to look at the child as a whole and the importance of the family and looks at the child's overall development, not just literacy and numbers but creative development too, that is the general feel at the school.* (Rosie, Kirkside East)

One mother became a parent governor because she was so pleased with the school:

> *The school has been marvellous. Since I voiced my concern they help. I'm now a governor because they're so committed to us I wanted to be committed to them.* (Amanda, Kirkside East)

Faith schools were generally popular with many parents including parents who could not get their children in or did not have a religious background, because they saw them as having high standards and strong discipline.[4] Although they often ranked higher in school league tables, some parents thought the focus could be rather narrow. This parent explained, based on her experience, that involvement with the community was not as strong as it could be:

> *I'm satisfied. It's a Catholic school and they're very up to date with the curriculum and learning. They make all the pupils feel valued and build up self-confidence. Education-wise, they do well in league tables. But because it's a Catholic school, they don't get all the funding. But I'd like to see the kids taking part in workshops or plays. Recently there was a Citizenship week and*

*they interviewed people on how they contribute to the community. I would like to see more of that. You hear about other schools and see pictures of the pupils and read about what they've done for the community — I see it through the local magazine. My daughter's school do stuff but only for the school, for school purposes, not for the community. We get frequent newsletters from the school on how you can extend learning in the home and with school trips. On trips it's just a teacher and assistants whereas before parents might go for support.* (Amber, East Docks)

In spite of so many positive views and a generally strong endorsement by parents of their local schools, there were many problems and pressures, often stemming from the home and neighbourhood environment. The biggest schooling challenges came in teenage years.

## Secondary schools: the big challenge

Parents' generally positive experience of local primary schools was not matched at secondary level where we picked up much bigger worries. By secondary age, children with less academic ability or aptitude were often becoming disenchanted with school. Secondary schools were invariably bigger, less personal and further afield. Children, as they grew into teenagers, wanted more independence and less input from their parents. Secondary school teachers seemed to have less time for individual children, and less close liaison with parents. However, there were notable exceptions, including the 'fresh start' school in The Valley:

*I'm very satisfied with the school that my son's been at for a year, because my son's quite timid and it was a big deal for him to walk to school on his own. They have a set-up where they have learning mentors. My son's been unwell and not keen to go to school so the learning mentor's been spending time with him, understanding his needs. They could well just help the naughty kids, not the quite unhappy ones. Now he's enjoying school, occasionally feels anxious, but not much.* (Jade, The Valley)

### "A history of failing schools"

Many parents, particularly in East London, began to worry early on about secondary schools because of the competition for the good ones:

*With my three-year-old son, I hope we're not here by the time he's at secondary.* (Lola, West City)

Parents were often driven to try and move out at the secondary transfer stage, even though they mostly failed to achieve this. This is regarded as a 'middle-class obsession', but many low-income parents shared this aspiration:

*I want to move. The schools aren't good enough. I'm not so bothered with primary schools but by the time they get to secondary schools it's not good enough. The eldest is 11, the local schools have poor equipment, buildings and standards. I look at the league tables and search for houses in areas with good schools.* (Delilah, West City)

One ambitious parent was not confident that the local secondary school would help her daughter get to college:

*She wants to be a scientist. She's very good at science and English. She was on the 'gifted and talented' list at primary but they don't seem to be doing anything to encourage it now she's at secondary.... I hope they can get access to a good education to get a good start in life. Go to college or university, get a good job and get out of this area; so they don't have to bring up their kids here.* (Carmen, East Docks)

One East London parent sent her children to school outside the area, but saw other parents ignoring failures in the local school:

*I think the biggest problem as a parent in this area is secondary education. Primary schools is much easier to deal with and I think maybe it's just about the size of schools or maybe it's just about the age of the kids and what happens when kids get to 13 and 14. So, you know, the area does have a history of failing schools and my kids don't go to school in the area. Now, that's fine and we're lucky that we were able to find a school that's right for us. I think a lot of parents here, I don't think they're even aware of these issues. I think they've just picked the local school, whether it's failing or not. I'm not even sure they know whether it's failing or not, or what failure actually means.* (Alan, West City)

Occasionally things went badly wrong at secondary level. One mother described at length how her son was excluded from secondary school during a very difficult and painful family break-up, leading to him losing almost his entire secondary education:

> *When I needed help with my son they just let me down, totally, from the schools, I know they could do better than that. Education's very important. If you don't deal with the cases when you're young, you just miss out. They messed him up. When my son was about 12, he got expelled for something really stupid, and then because he got expelled, all the rest of the schools blacklisted him which I think was wrong. From 12 years old, he's never had a proper education and he's quite bright. I got a phone call from the Education Authority saying 'yes, I've got a place for him', and I rang up, and they say 'no, they haven't got no place'. So I felt that they let me down. They were lying, somebody was lying.* (Sola, West City)

Sola's son was actually allocated a place in a special educational unit, but he couldn't bear the stigma attached – "he felt stupid". Sola, who was Afro-Caribbean by background, was convinced that black children fared worse in the system because of discrimination:

> *Once you're a black person in this country, they don't care nothing about you. And they've got to remember that black people put a lot into this society, our parents and grandparents put a lot into it. And now our children get treated like rubbish, it's just not right. You can see it happening. The same way it's happened to me, it's probably happening to other people as well. So he's never got a proper education really, and he's not stupid, quite a bright lad. And now he feels it too late, he hasn't got the confidence. I say 'No, it's never too late', he could go and do his 'O' Levels. I told him I'd give him a hand. They have failed me, they failed me bad and that gave me a lot of stress, not to see my child in school, getting an education, it's not easy to cope with.* (Sola, West City)

In spite of progress in reducing school exclusions, exclusion from secondary school is a big problem in poorer inner-city areas, particularly affecting black boys.[5] Sola's son ended up going to college after missing five years of secondary school and getting involved in drugs. Sola concluded that "in secondary schools they don't care about black boys", highlighting the serious consequences.[6]

Teenagers sometimes need more practical, more engaging, activities than classroom-based learning. Work experience through later years of secondary schools could help less academic young people into a job that they really want. This Northern mother, who had never worked herself and was determined her boys would succeed, was immensely proud of her son's work placement in a big supermarket:

> *He passed his exam with distinction. He's been doing work-related training. They've kept him on at ASDA. He knows what he wants and has it all planned. He wasn't paid for a year and a half which he accepted rather than go back to school. But he did two out of five days of college.* (Angela, Kirkside East)

The model of training linked to work experience was extremely useful, although not yet common enough to lever all children into a positive transition between school and work.

### "Like they're pushing you away"

Some secondary schools seemed rather remote to parents even if they were achieving academically. Security measures in inner cities can become harsh, and the constant struggle to keep control over large numbers of energetic teenagers can be alienating to parents:

> *At the old school, when the bell went he used to come out on his own but in this school you don't go in the building and I find it very strange. He's gone up a year, so I don't really know. If there's an after-school club you have to wait in a tiny reception. I find it strange, like they're pushing you away. At parents' evening, we're all waiting in the playground, going in the main entrance, whereas before you could go into the classroom. You can't even wait in the playground when they come out, all the mothers are queuing outside, but there must be a reason. I've never been to his classroom. With the other school, you never had that, you could wait outside the classroom and speak to the teacher. But he's learning much better. I've never had so many parents' evenings. But my son's not allowed to sit in on it, I'm not used to that. I'm not happy with that but I know he's doing well at school. All I've seen is the reception, I couldn't even look around when I applied. They're locked in for school and then locked out again.* (Megan, West City)

Another mother put it even more bluntly:

> *They seem to shut parents out, to me. They suggest you either ring up or email.* (Destiny, West City)

Overall, secondary schools seemed to have the opposite effect on parents to primary schools. The experience unsettled and worried them. Secondary schools in the East End had a reputation for poor achievement that most middle-class parents would not countenance. The schools were so large and difficult to manage that the sense of welcome and support was seriously diluted. This in turn undermined the confidence of some parents:

> *I was disgusted when I went round the secondary schools. We didn't apply for any in the area.* (Nadia, East Docks)

All the neighbourhoods had had 'failing schools' and local educational initiatives to 'fresh start' secondary schools. In two areas, bringing in a new head, revamping buildings and offering special support to children who struggled with basic skills won plaudits from parents. But the process of school closure affected parents directly and was extremely disruptive, as this father in West City, the worst affected area, explained:

> *They are closing this school, they are building flats. Doesn't mean getting better. We can't find a school for my son as well. They closed the local school, now two other schools. They closed the big secondary school as well. Three schools in the area. Three schools!* (Onur, West City)

Several schools were still awaiting upgrading during our visits even though other schools had received a big injection of funds and were much improved. There were long delays in the bureaucratic process of accessing funds and gaining approval. On cramped London school sites, it was often extremely difficult to deliver the improvements. One East London parent complained bitterly about the condition of the school. Her view of Sure Start stood out in sharp contrast:

> *You know, the schools've never got any money. I just can't believe it. Tony Blair, you know he was 'Education, education', and yet the schools are struggling so badly. He keeps saying he'll put more money into it, but where? I mean my son's school is in desperate need of remodernisation and renovation. You know the government have actually promised some money. It needs a new roof, it needs new windows, the playground's got terrible subsidence in it. All the*

*cladding all round the school is all falling off. I think it's unsafe but the kids play in the playground. The kids've got to have somewhere to play. One good thing we've had round here is Sure Start, that has been good, that has been good.* (Destiny, West City)

A few parents in East London were acutely aware of how inferior their children's education was. One parent felt angry because she believed that the new academies, rather than offering better opportunities, would simply take away from the ordinary schools.

*That's quite hard, the lack of funds. It's completely unjust and criminal, all these academies opening up and getting so much more money where the local secondaries get pushed aside, it's disgusting. Money governs everything.* (Charlotte, West City)

Another East End family deliberately chose the local 'fresh start' secondary school which had been classed as a 'failing' school, even though they would have preferred the church school further out. The school now had special measures in place. Annie, a mother in East Docks, had a lot of confidence in the new head who had introduced many positive changes, particularly more discipline, and therefore, she hoped, more learning. Annie wanted her children to do well, but she much preferred them to go to a local school where she knew what was going on and she thought they would be:

*Happy, healthy, and realise their potential. Now there's strong leadership in the school. Some parents don't like it, but here you need to be tough.* (Annie, East Docks)

Some parents in West City were desperate for more order and control in schools. Parents coming to London from other countries generally wanted more discipline. They remembered much more respect for teachers then they were seeing in London:

*The teacher couldn't understand because of the noise. I felt as if there was some kind of a war going on! In Turkey and Cyprus there's more discipline and respect for teachers. When you go to school, there's a dress code for teachers as well, whereas here one teacher has bracelets, tattoos and piercings so they're maybe not getting respect. My son says no one listens to the teacher. When I was younger, I would look up to teachers whereas now they don't look up to them. I went into the class once, the teacher has no*

> *control or discipline. Children learn everything when they're young*
> *so if there's no discipline they won't have it later. Even if my son*
> *has homework he won't do it as they won't check it afterwards.*
> (Hulya, West City)

Discipline was a big challenge. A West City parent explained her
worries over the combination of her son's basic writing difficulties
and the problems the school had controlling him. Behind this parent's
concerns lay the widespread problem of behavioural problems, difficulty
in concentration and hyperactivity:

> *I've always been dissatisfied with his school. They've just got a right*
> *load of crap teachers in the last couple a years he's been there. The*
> *other day, we had big trouble – they just can't control a 10-year-*
> *old anymore. Weird. They got the police out and everything. I am*
> *a bit worried. His writing is atrocious and he just can't concentrate*
> *and he gets bored too quick. He's bright in his mind.* (Natalie,
> West City)

## "Bottom of the league table"

Parents were much more aware of schooling problems in East London
than in the North, partly because schools were affected by more intense
pressures of change. Parents in West City were aware of the borough's
poor record in education:

> *It's been well documented again this year we are the bottom of the*
> *league in the country. We're in the worst borough for education.*
> *And it'll never change, it will never change.* (Destiny, West City)

Parents saw their children's natural curiosity and keenness to learn let
down by their poor basic skills. This problem applied to many children,
particularly boys:

> *He's inquisitive you know, 'Why's that? What's that?'. He asks*
> *some interesting questions. He's good at maths but the writing bit,*
> *he's going to suffer.* (Natalie's partner, West City)

Some parents felt that they were being 'told off' by the school because
their children were not performing to average standards. One parent
felt that the school was harsh on parents because of the pressure to

perform well on attendance, punctuality and so on. This overrode individual problems:

> *The local primary school, my daughter is there, and is getting on very well. But the school had quite a patronising attitude to parents. For example, they wrote to us once about her attendance, it was 90-something per cent and they said it can hold her back, et cetera. I wrote and said she had had an ear infection! And she is one of the top in her class. If you had spoken to her class teacher you'd know. I got no reply. I spoke to them in the end. And they said, okay, forget about it. I'm not impressed by their treatment of the parents.* (Jenny, The Valley)

Some parent felt undermined by judgemental teachers' attitudes, leaving them feeling that the school did not understand their difficulties:

> *The school was extremely patronising and wouldn't listen, dishing out penalties and being very elitist. When we had problems, I was gob-smacked at how they treated the situation because my daughter was crying nearly every day because they kept giving penalties over really minor things, instilling fear rather than encouraging them.* (Charlotte, West City)

## "In trouble"

Behavioural problems were common. A recurring theme that illustrates this was bullying, which almost half the parents said their children experienced, mostly in schools. One parent claimed:

> *There is a bullying issue, low grade bullying is allowed among boys, my son is being bullied, been going on for years. The school doesn't address it.* (Avril, The Valley)

Generally parents found their schools very proactive in dealing with bullying, in most cases resolving it. A parent whose son was the source of the bullying was particularly aware of the school's constructive response. This perceptive parent put her son's bullying down to his sense of failure over his school work, which the school was helping him overcome:

> *My son's high school's a really good school. He has been bullying and been on report for it, so they are dealing with it very well. Very*

*good there actually. He has a learning mentor for his reading and writing. Probably why he is having trouble, in trouble.* (Laverne, Kirkside East)

Another parent explained that for her children, bullying had not been a problem because the school was so proactive in responding:

*They have never had any problems and you can go if you need to speak to school. Like, my younger daughter was teased and I spoke to the teacher and then she dealt with it the next day.* (Liza, Kirkside East)

A troubled social and learning environment surrounded many children that teachers were constantly trying to manage. They are heavily reliant on parental support and they work hard to secure this, but through lack of experience and the need to exert authority, can misjudge their response. A lot depended on the head, as Flowella in East Docks explained:

*The new head has lots of schemes for dealing with children who are being disruptive, making them more involved in things, concentrating on their behaviour. And you see a change in the children. He's out there every single morning and afternoon watching their behaviour.* (Flowella, East Docks)

In most cases schools responded to parents' troubles and worries. Parents liaised with their children's schools over children's difficulties as they arose, including behaviour and 'attitude' problems. In some cases, a parent had approached their children's school, and in others the school had approached the parent. Many parents praised their children's schools for handling these problems well. When a parent approached the school, a positive two-way relationship could develop:

*I was dissatisfied before. But that wasn't to do with her learning, that was the fact that she had two teachers in the class but one was on maternity leave, and through the year they went through 30 teachers. So I complained because I just felt that children need stability, they need to have that one person there all the time. But now I'm happy with her school. If there's any issues at school, the teachers will let me know and they will call me and say, 'Well, you know, this incident happened today, blah, blah, blah'. And I*

*know what goes on, and I do go in their classroom and look and
see if they've done any work.* (Faye, West City)

Another mother managed to sort out her boy's special reading
difficulties:

*It's not bad – the school itself. I did have an issue with them once.
My older son was in reception and they swapped books everyday
and he couldn't read them, so he should have been finishing a book
and then starting a new one. And they get older kids in the school
to hear the little ones read and I don't agree with it. Children need
proper tuition and the older kids need to spend their time on their
own work. I complained about the reading and helped my son
read myself. So it was ok. Got sorted.* (Poonam, Kirkside East)

## "Disruptive in class"

Parents recognised that sometimes their children needed 'pulling up'.
Parental reinforcement was very important to the teachers when a child
was in trouble. If handled tactfully, parents were immensely grateful. This
parent had to explain to the teacher that she would back the school in
reprimanding her daughter for bad behaviour:

*I'm quite satisfied. I mean, if there is a problem, like once I got
called in because she was being a bit of a shit, and the teacher had
found me abrupt before and had an idea of me when I was going
on. But I said, 'I don't accept it from my daughter'. I think she was
taken aback at my attitude to my daughter's bad behaviour. And
they've been good since. It was a team effort.* (Patsy, Kirkside East)

One mother directly asked the school to 'tighten up' on her daughter
because she was starting to cause trouble in the class:

*When my daughter started secondary school, she started off really
well. She goes to an all girls school. By the time it got round to
October, November time, she started hanging around with certain
girls in her class. They started being silly and talking in class.
There was one little incident, she'd been getting told off in class,
and I was horrified. I was like, 'What!' So basically I went down
to visit the school and they told me what had been happening
and I said 'Can she get put on report?' and they was like, 'We
only do it in extreme cases'. I said 'It's extreme enough for me'. I*

> *said, 'I can teach her and show her and I can keep an eye on her when she's at home, but when she's not in that environment, I can't do that. So the only way I know what she's doing at school is if you keep me updated'. And what happens is, when they're on report, the school informs you straight away. The school gives you updates, so if they've been late you'll get a letter, or if they've been disruptive in the class. They have a planner and every single day the teacher will write a comment in there, and you check the planner.* (Flowella, East Docks)

A Northern mother explained the school's response when her 15-year-old daughter became pregnant, and her opinion of the school changed in the light of their helpful response to what this mother saw as a critical event:

> *The secondary school, I didn't think much to it, but now she is pregnant, I see how well they have dealt with it, very supportive, that has been good. She can focus on childcare, English and Maths if she wants to. Her choice is to do childcare. She can go for a lie down if she needs to, et cetera.* (Liza, Kirkside East)

A seemingly intractable problem was 'rough behaviour' among children. Parents wanted tighter discipline so that their children would not be affected by bad behaviour or get involved in bad behaviour themselves. Many parents articulated worries about their children being easily influenced and about peer pressure:

> *My son could do very well but at the moment he comes under the influence of lots of naughty boys at school. He is a follower and the school don't tackle that. I've wondered if I should get him into a slightly stricter environment, as he is quite boisterous.* (Maya, The Valley)

Sometimes bad behaviour got out of hand and children's schooling started to suffer. Some children simply could not cope with disruptions in the classroom.

> *I am fairly satisfied with the primary school, because my daughter is fine. My son there, his class this year has been very unruly, very noisy and he has not wanted to go and the school doesn't seem to have been able to deal with it, not improved it.* (Kerry, The Valley)

Another parent, exhausted by her son's bad behaviour, had some sympathy with the teachers:

> *I get a bit tired. I don't know how these teachers cope with all these hyper kids.* (Zoe, West City)

One mother talked about her friend's experience of her children simply getting left behind because of the pressures:

> *They haven't picked up that she can't read or write properly, she's about to leave school. So, you know, her school let her lapse and let a child slip through a net.* (Alexa, East Docks)

The idea of including children with behavioural and learning problems in neighbourhood schools represents a positive attempt to help children in difficulty integrate. But it creates added pressure on teachers, particularly in struggling schools in these disadvantaged areas where children with special needs are concentrated.[7] This is a very difficult area with many different attitudes to solving it.[8] Parents often articulated the view that the most disruptive children who couldn't be controlled should not be in a normal classroom:

> *It's very sad. You get a few disruptive children. This is the hard line but take them out of the room and let the others learn. I do understand and appreciate that there may be something going on in their lives. But it's difficult, leaving them in the classroom ... most children, my own son will come home and say 'didn't get any homework, didn't get through the lesson' because so-and-so did this, did that. You just know, reading between the lines, the teacher's standing there and it only takes one.* (Rosemary, West City)

## "They keep changing the teachers"

The concentration of problems made the teacher's job much more difficult, leading to teachers moving on more frequently, setting in train a vicious circle, with discipline and learning problems stemming from teacher turnover, particularly in London:

> *I'm not really satisfied. In a year these children could have five different teachers. It's not right because if you keep changing staff, they don't know what they're doing. My younger boy complained throughout five years of secondary school. It distracts a child, makes*

> *them not concentrate. To make a child really concentrate and do well at school, the teachers shouldn't change. It did contribute a lot because when the child is always complaining it's not right. He said, 'they keep changing the teachers and I'm not getting things right, it's the third teacher in the term'.* (Gloria, East Docks)

School heads have only limited control over wider problems yet they have to deal with everything that happens within the school. The reality of supply teaching generates many of the discipline problems. Parents always found stand–in teachers, however nice, disruptive for their children, and a cause of trouble:

> *He's had a few supply teachers, then he gets hit or kicked. It's not dealt with properly. The class is madness, they don't learn nothing that day with the supply teacher and that's when he had his bullying, when he never had a proper teacher.* (Megan, West City)

Another parent explained the impact of supply teachers on her son's work:

> *You need stability. One whole year my son had supply teachers. 'What did you learn?', 'Nothing'. They said he hadn't done his homework but he'd given it to different teachers.* (Gabrielle, East Docks)

The unstable social fabric of inner-city schools with a constant stream of supply teachers and pupils from many different cultural backgrounds meant that parental hopes were often thwarted, reducing parental aspirations and putting their children behind in a competitive and skilled economy.

## Segregated schools: *"No community mix"*

A particularly worrying, recurring theme ran through parents' views on their local schools. In the culturally and ethnically diverse East London neighbourhoods, and in the Northern inner city, the problem of racial divisions within the schools came up. Some parents from minority backgrounds talked of language and communication problems relating to cultural differences, including making simple mistakes, but also detecting bigger ethnic barriers and prejudice. One active father found the school's approach to ethnic differences and cultural needs a bit insensitive:

> *They are alright, but they've not improved in terms of cultural and religious needs. Like they can't even get my children's names right. And they assume things like because they are Muslims and Asian they have certain needs. They are ignorant on this sort of thing.* (Kamal, The Valley)

Most white parents were concerned not to sound racist as they felt it was such a delicate subject. But some families talked openly about their children's schools being divided rather than inclusive. It seemed a bigger issue at secondary level. Parents highlighted the lack of integration and togetherness within local multi-cultural schools. A Northern white mother conveyed quite delicately her dislike of schools that had an overwhelming minority intake. Gillian wanted her children to mix, but the fact that the local secondary school had very few white children alienated her:

> *I am concerned about secondary schools in the area. The interplay between the ethnic minorities in the area is not good, for example. And the aspirations of kids there are not good. Unless things change significantly, I won't want my kids at the local secondary school. This is not something I am comfortable with because I want multi-culturalism to be present and to work but it isn't in the secondary school and it is a shame.* (Gillian, The Valley)

Most schools seemed unable to confront this problem directly, so it became self-fuelling as more white people withdrew. Many parents from minority backgrounds also disliked this separation, as a Sudanese mother explained:

> *When you look, a lot of them aren't white. Most are Asian and Pakistanis. It should be more mixed. There aren't many whites. You can see one, two or three whites. If there were more whites maybe they'd behave better. It's 90 per cent Asian at the school, it's not good, and behaviour is very low there because of it.* (Kali, The Valley)

Another parent suggested actively mixing intakes to avoid segregation in the secondary school:

*Re the secondary school, having brought up kids in a multi-cultural area, it is hard to raise this issue without sounding racist, but there's only four white pupils at the secondary school, there's no sleepovers and I can't go to Muslim houses to collect and drop off the kids if a woman is on her own in the house. The school promotes ghettoisation. I think they need a more even mix. My daughter didn't get into the secondary school and will go to one with more white children which will be okay, good staff, and a good approach. They need positive recruitment to mix the cultures up.* (Adam, The Valley)

One couple stressed the urgency of integrating schools, echoing each other's concerns about the fast changing population, and the threat posed by segregation:

Tina: *Living in the neighbourhood prepared us to be a foreigner. That's not racialist, it's a fact.*

Husband: *The people that have moved have not wanted to mix. The Bangladeshis and Jews don't want to mingle for cultural or religious reasons.*

Tina: *They are so suppressed. The children in the swimming pool. They let off so much steam. They have no social skills out with their own community.*

Husband: *Integrated schools are the way forward – look at Northern Ireland.* (Tina and her husband, West City)

A Northern white parent reluctantly sent her girls to the predominantly Asian secondary school on the edge of their large almost all white estate, but both she and her husband were pleasantly surprised at how well the children got on and how integrated the school was in practice:

*At first I thought, 'There are too many coloureds'. Peter would say I'm being racist but there are only three white girls in her class. But we went to the open day and it far outshone the other schools. We were impressed. The teachers seem more interested in the child. They have more going on. The head is doing very well to bring the different cultures together. They're in a bad area and they're making a go of it.* (Margaret, Kirkside East)

In an extreme case, one Northern school was already so completely segregated that local people thought it might only take Asian children:

> *The primary school … there are rumours that it's an Asian school,*
> *focused on them, that worries me. I don't think my son age seven*
> *suffers from racism, being white, but it is an Asian school.* (Jessica,
> The Valley)

Parents talked of school divisions where ethnic and religious divisions were inter-mingled:

> *I just put her name down for nursery. There seem to be big divisions.*
> *One school is C of E [Church of England] and another is Catholic.*
> *It's so divided. It's mainly black in the C of E one and mainly*
> *white in the Catholic one. It is Muslims at one and Catholics at*
> *another. So no community mix in either school. That's a shame. A*
> *big division. It leads to a division among the children when they're*
> *older.* (Cynthia, The Valley)

One particularly contentious issue was admission to church schools. People regularly attending church are normally given priority, sometimes leading to more Africans than 'local' white children being admitted. Competition for places in church schools within the four areas has greatly increased in recent years, mainly because of the greater discipline and the explicitly moral ethos of these schools.[9] Lesley, from East Docks, had attended the local church school herself, but had trouble getting her children in, in spite of this. She was worried by the growing share of places going to children from minority ethnic backgrounds:

> *I don't want to sound racialist. When my little boy started school,*
> *there were six or seven ethnic minorities, all nice people. When my*
> *little girl started three years later, she's a minority in the class. I*
> *know people who've lived here all their lives who can't go to that*
> *school because they don't go to church.* (Lesley, East Docks)

Several Muslim parents said they found it hard to get their children into faith schools. Fatima, in The Valley, was desperate for her children to go to the church school, even though she was a practising Muslim:

> *I don't want to send my children here. The children are wild,*
> *swearing, aggressive. I've just been putting it off. I haven't filled*
> *in the application form. I'll put the church school down. If I got*

*a place there, I'd move as soon as I got my wages. I'll look for a property. I think it's depressing, thinking 'Where will my child go?'.* (Fatima, The Valley)

Nadia explained why she and her Muslim husband opted for a religious school:

*He got into a strict Christian school but my children are Muslim even though they're not practising. I always said I wouldn't be a hypocrite and get baptised just to get into schools, but then we went round and saw the schools, my husband agreed.... Behaviour is better. He [her son] needed to be more organised and he can do that now.* (Nadia, East Docks)

One East London mother felt completely alienated by the 'foreignness' of the school:

*The bit I actually live in I like, but I don't like it here at all. I wouldn't have it. I would move tomorrow if I won the lottery, I'd move away. Because it's more for the kids as well. I don't particularly want my kids growing up in this area where they have to go to school and they're in Bangladesh.* (Kayla, East Docks)

The problem has become self-fuelling, with white parents trying to move to avoid majority/minority schools:

*With white children, sometimes it's a case of 'spot the white'. In lots of schools round here there's not a lot of balance. My son has taken his child out of the area to prevent this.* (Trudy, West City)

### "There's a shift in the community"

Schools were trying to respond to these difficult changes as this parent who became a school assistant explained:

*I think anyone new coming into the school, any mix of people will change the dynamic. We're very diverse here, we've got more than 48 first languages, so we do have a very culturally diverse community in the school anyway. And we do a lot of work around that. We do cultural diversity projects, celebrate cultural harmony, the way different cultures actually are. So we try to celebrate all that stuff and recognise it but I wouldn't say that it doesn't cause conflict from time to time. Where there are people there will be things happening.* (Andrea, East Docks)

The interaction between the schools and neighbourhood change was clear:

> *I think in terms of the school, the most significant change is the cultural mix. We've been quite a culturally mixed school for a while but always predominantly white, which means there's a shift in the community in terms of the transient community coming in. There's a lot of shift in the area, and I think that underlying shift is influencing the stability of the area. So it's definitely the mix, I think that's the biggest thing we've had.* (Andrea, East Docks)

In contrast to these worries, parents from abroad were often grateful that their children could receive the education this country offers.

> *Here, we have advantages, like education. Back home in Africa if you don't have money your children can't go to school.* (Becca, East Docks)

Schools are having to act as community anchors in this whirlwind of change, responding to every child's needs, meeting parents, keeping order, organising events, covering core curricula, compensating for home problems and coping with behaviour difficulties. Only with extra resources to compensate for all the extra burdens they are carrying can they match the educational needs of so many pupils.

## Special learning difficulties: *"He's in his own world"*

Parents of children with special educational needs spoke positively about how their children's schools were responding to these needs, including autism, dyslexia, anxiety, behavioural problems and attention deficit hyperactivity disorder (ADHD). They praised the special facilities and services, the mentoring and extra support that schools offered them. One mother described the immense care the school invested in helping her son:

> *I would say I am very satisfied with the secondary school that my son has been in for a year. My son is quite timid and it was a big deal for him to walk to school on his own. And they have a set-up where they have learning mentors, and my son has been unwell*

*and not keen to go to school and the learning mentor has been spending time with him, understanding his needs. It's particularly good because they could well just help the naughty kids, not the quiet unhappy ones. Now he is enjoying school, and occasionally feels anxious, but not much.* (Kerry, The Valley)

Mentors for older children with particular problems in coping with school can help counter challenging behaviour, where only one-to-one help works. This parent was hugely appreciative:

*My son doesn't look up to anyone as he's in his own world. He's diagnosed with ADHD and dyslexia. But at school he's got a mentor, he does look up to him. They're like guidance teachers. They're trained in a different way from teachers – teachers shout, whereas mentors talk to him. He stays with him all the way through. I have his mentor's mobile number so I can contact him.* (Clare, East Docks)

Parents described the remarkable efforts schools put into helping them and their children cope:

*My son's secondary school, fine, no problems … they have been excellent, he has come on loads there. He is dyslexic, he is statemented. They have a dyslexia base there, that is why he went there, and he gets transport to and from school too, and there's only four such places a year.* (Jackie, Kirkside East)

Another younger boy with behavioural problems also got a lot of additional support:

*My son's primary school, very satisfied, my son is supported with his behavioural problems, they give him extra support.* (Chloe, Kirkside East)

One mother with a pre-school autistic child was already receiving help from the local school before he started:

*I plan to send my four-year-old son there, he has just been diagnosed as autistic and the school were really good, I had a meeting with them and they work with a local special school and I have spoken to them too and they help with the transition from nursery to school. So I'm very happy at the moment.* (Gillian, The Valley)

A mother with a disabled son praised the local primary school in general, as well as highlighting its strong support for her son who had cerebral palsy:

> *The local primary school is a really good school. My five-year-old does the work of a seven-year-old and she has extra lessons too. They accommodate all kids. And they will be able to support my three-year-old son too. And I want him to go to a normal school.* (Louise, Kirkside East)

One of the families who had moved out missed the caring atmosphere of the inner London school her son had gone to:

> *My son was diagnosed with dyslexia in London when he was small and the school was just brilliant – not just helped but really helped. Now, the secondary school here has offered help but they haven't followed it up.* (Joanne, West City)

We spoke to many families where children had been tested and shown to suffer from dyslexia. Children with dyslexia, concentration problems or other learning difficulties sometimes seemed to parents to get lost in the classroom. They rarely received as much help as parents wanted, even though schools tried to help. Resources within schools to tackle special learning difficulties were rarely adequate and sometimes special help ended long before the children had caught up. Children who are slow learners need continual long-term consistent help if they are to progress in school and not simply drop out with poor literacy:

> *At my son's school there's not much help for dyslexics. My son gets some help but not enough. If you're good at Maths and English and Science you're ok. If not you're not helped.* (Chandra, The Valley)

Resources were sometimes stretched between foreign language and other special needs. But children who received special help with English language progressed quickly, while children with dyslexia and other learning and concentration problems continued to struggle. The problem was more common among boys in our study, and some statemented boys with special needs did not receive the extra help their parents hoped for. This mother was quite upset about it:

> *My 16-year-old son is at the local high school and I'm not happy at all. He is statemented and his first year was fine but since then*

*his statements have not been met at all. He leaves next Easter. We need to keep him in school and help him at home as much as possible.* (Kathleen, Kirkside East)

When teachers could not give children with educational difficulties all the individual attention they needed, they behaved worse in order to attract attention. This led to all the children faring badly because teachers simply could not manage a big class and dedicate sufficient time to a child who continually disrupted the class. A few parents reached a point of despair when this happened:

*The local high school, it is the worst school I've ever known. And I'm trying to get him out of it. They don't want to know. They just don't want to know. He is badly behaved and has learning difficulties and they don't help. I'd go in every day in tears. I told them he needs help and they didn't want to know.* (Cath, Kirkside East)

Another parent felt extremely upset because her son was only diagnosed as autistic and her daughter as dyslexic after she'd reached the point where she couldn't cope:

*I never had none [help] at all until my daughter got diagnosed with dyslexia, where I literally had to go to a solicitor to force the council to give extra help. Diagnosing my son helped everyone else. Sometimes that was what I was more angry of, how could I deal with an autistic child? I was very angry within my family, friends and the system. I'm angry at how I was treated. If he was diagnosed earlier, we wouldn't have had all this trouble.* (Julie, East Docks)

Parents often felt they had to take the initiative and fight for their children:

*We've had zero help with the children despite them all being dyslexic. The eldest is dyspraxic…. It's all been pushed through by me.* (Leah, West City)

There was a tension between the focus on academic progress and special needs. This parent articulated the lack of more hands-on, practical learning in her son's school:

> *At the local secondary school there is not so much help for dyslexics;*
> *my son gets some help but not enough. In schools generally, if you*
> *are good at Maths and English and Science, et cetera, you are okay.*
> *But if not, you are not helped. They need more practical learning*
> *at school.* (Chandra, The Valley)

Parents had many different needs and our conversations left us with the strong impression that schools in these areas were coping with extreme pressures:

- some families could only cope with their children's schooling difficulties thanks to intense inputs over long periods of time by the school;
- some parents felt their children's schools were failing to help with their children's particular educational needs;
- some children with dyslexia, physical disabilities, autism, behavioural problems and other learning difficulties received too little help, or it came too late;
- a few parents faced such extreme difficulty that they simply felt desperate, and the school did not have sufficient capacity or resources to respond;
- behavioural problems seemed remarkably common and secondary schools were struggling to maintain order and discipline.

In spite of parental praise for their efforts, schools, particularly at secondary level, struggle to cope with the scale of the challenge. The size of secondary schools, the movement from class to class between lessons, the drive for higher achievement and limited physical outlets within school for teenagers' irrepressible energy all work against containing problems easily.[11] Often problems moved beyond the capacity of the average secondary school teacher. Schools cannot do it on their own. Parents tended to accept limitations on schools and value the extraordinary efforts they saw schools making, a constant juggling act between needs:

> *The local school does the best it can given the difficulties. I don't*
> *think it's the best school that could be found. But given the situation*
> *and circumstances of the area and different ethnic groups, they do*
> *quite well really. Far more than they have to. I'm really happy for*
> *them to be there.* (Phoebe, The Valley)

## Summary and conclusions

Schools play a dominant role in family and neighbourhood life. In this chapter we have focused mainly on the direct interactions between parents, children and schools, which impact on the daily lives of families (see Annex 8 [available online at www.policypress.co.uk]). Only a minority of parents focused on higher education and the majority seemed satisfied if their children completed GCSEs and then worked, with some training alongside. The performance of schools in these areas rose rapidly in the past 10 years, faster than the national average and closing the gap somewhat even though it remains significant.[12] The numbers going on to further education and colleges were rising and several parents talked of much higher ambitions, but most did not expect their children to go to university. All parents had a great deal to say about schools, about supporting parents and preparing children for a much tougher world than the parents felt they faced themselves in their youth.

Parents usually chose local schools, even at secondary level, in spite of knowing the shortcomings and in spite of knowing better schools in neighbouring area, a bus ride away. Parents who tried often failed to get their children into better schools outside the area. The only way to realise their ambitions for their children's education was to move nearer to better schools, yet most failed when they tried. Parents saw the efforts to help many children that schools made. They wanted their children to be happy and end up with a job, rather than aiming for university. Many more talked positively about college courses, training and work experience, as a supplement to education and jobs.

Schools acted as powerful social magnets, constantly bringing together parents who were strangers to each other before sharing the intense years of schooling, the confined social space of school gates and playgrounds, or parents' meetings and school events. Parents often relied on local schools as a way of getting to know other families, ensuring that their children had local friends and protecting their children from the wider, local environment which they saw as threatening their children's safety. Schools are embedded in local conditions and family circumstances, carrying responsibilities far beyond teaching, trying to meet diverse family problems. Children with special educational needs such as dyslexia were conspicuous in most local schools and schools were often failing to match the extra help these children needed.

Schools in poorer areas were constantly looking for extra resources to provide the wider supports, so vital to the families and children themselves, and to the overall attainment of the school. Many schools tried to meet other community and family needs such as after-school activities, sports clubs, drama, fundraising and cultural events. All schools do some of this and parents rate these events and activities highly. They made a big difference to their confidence in the school and their children's ability to integrate.

Discipline and control in schools is a constant challenge where three or four hundred primary school children are kept together in a confined space for six-and-a-half hours continuously, with very little opportunity to release physical energy. At secondary level the problem is even more serious, with bigger numbers, longer class sessions, bigger more boisterous teenagers and more discipline problems. The issue of classroom control arose frequently in discussion with parents. The surrounding environment often influences the behaviour of children and young people outside their parents' sight. An environment that militates against control builds up problems for schools and frustrates parents in their hopes for their children to 'be good' and resist peer pressure.

If teachers aren't supportive and are judgemental towards parents who struggle with discipline, behaviour control and simple coping, then the parents feel rejected and can become disillusioned with the help that the school is offering. On the other hand, if the school is firm, disciplined and supportive, parents will have confidence to respond in like manner.

Yet many local schools in difficult areas are forced to recruit inexperienced teachers and lose them very quickly as they gain enough experience to work in less challenging environments, escaping the extra demands of special needs in low-income areas. Parents therefore sometimes face a disrupted and discontinuous relationship with their child's teacher, reducing confidence and making control more difficult. This seems to apply less to church schools, where a stronger ethos of discipline is accepted by teachers, parents and children, and tighter controls are in place. Parents are admitted on the understanding that they support this more restrictive approach and it is one reason why many 'non-practising' parents said they wanted to get their children into religious schools.

The government's relentless emphasis on school performance puts a lot of pressure on under-performing schools and low-income parents. Families with more highly skilled, more highly educated, more professional parents can respond with a combination of parental support and school activity. In struggling areas, the parents' more limited education and work experience does not match the demands of the present educational system. Nonetheless, over the last 10 years the educational gap has closed somewhat, confirming the parents' overriding feelings of progress, underlining the value of direct parental involvement, attending special learning sessions, brushing up on required homework and liaising with teachers when asked.

An issue that looms large in three of our areas was the extent to which schools had become the melting pot for the local community. Beyond the school, parents often found it difficult to come together from such diverse backgrounds, but in school their children accepted each other and were learning to live together. Parents praise schools for this, but the growing separation of children from diverse minority ethnic backgrounds into almost exclusively non-white schools is accelerating the exodus of white families. This makes the remaining white families feel alienated and sometimes bitter. The problem of integration and alienation is partly countered by the fact that the vast majority of white and minority parents accept that it is better for their children to learn to mix. Their idea of mixing is based on roughly equal numbers of minority and local children, whereas in practice many schools have become 'majority/minority'. Parents from a minority ethnic background often feel as strongly about ethnic segregation as white parents.

Unless we respond to the urgency of helping children to integrate in schools and communities, we will, in maybe less than 10 years, have intensely segregated schooling in key inner-city areas of the country, simply because white parents will succeed in moving their children away from majority/minority schools.[13] The growing reality of segregated schooling was a constant pre-occupation of parents. Once racial separation reached a certain critical mass, it seemed to accelerate rapidly as schools in all of our areas showed. The tensions that result, particularly at secondary school level, can be severe, and this is an outcome that all parents were anxious to avoid.

Two other issues dominated: the importance of education for future jobs, even low-level jobs; and the modest ambitions of low-income parents for their children compared with more affluent groups. Educational failure seemed more serious among boys, while practical subjects, work placements and vocational training seemed undervalued by most secondary schools and the wider educational system. Where job links and apprentice-style training were encouraged, they seemed to help immensely – this surely needs to be massively expanded as an option for all young people.[14]

Low aspirations and expectations beset children's futures. Schools coping with intense social and behavioural problems also have to juggle the conflicting demands of mainstream targets and special needs. Going 'against the grain' of local culture is difficult and this is where religious schools have an advantage. Parents have signed up in advance to the higher aspirations of the school. The all-pervasive influence of the family and local 'peer pressure' on children's attitudes and behaviour make countering the 'rough' environment through a disciplined school environment difficult without devaluing or undermining local communities and parental self-esteem. One way of tackling this problem is to create more constructive out-of-school activities and more family support and outreach that would strengthen and extend the work of schools, as a way of counteracting other pressures.

Schools exert a positive influence, on the children and on family life. They play multiple roles alongside their main purpose of educating children. As a result, they generally win parental support. With some imagination, schools can take on a wider community role to improve the life chances of the children growing up in these areas. Playing this wider role in helping children and young people would make schools extremely useful to families in ways that reach far beyond their direct educational role. Schools cannot meet all family needs, but the more support they offer to families, the more likely children are to be able to learn.

In the next chapter we explore young people's need for space 'to let off steam', places to gather and have fun. The need to release energy constructively is particularly clear to parents living in cramped flats and on isolated estates, set in an environment they regard as unsafe. Families are desperate for outdoor spaces, local community facilities and activities that allow them and their children to reach outwards and flourish.

## Notes

[1] Prime Minister's Strategy Unit (2008) *Getting on, getting ahead. A discussion paper: Analysing the trends and drivers of social mobility*, London: Cabinet Office.
[2] Hills, J., Sefton, T. and Stewart, K. (eds) (2009) *Towards a more equal society? Poverty, inequality and policy since 1997*, Bristol: The Policy Press.
[3] Power, A. (2007) *City survivors: Bringing up children in disadvantaged neighbourhoods*, Bristol: The Policy Press.
[4] Power, A. (2007) *City survivors: Bringing up children in disadvantaged neighbourhoods*, Bristol: The Policy Press.
[5] Hills, J. et al (2010) *An anatomy of economic inequality in the UK – Report of the National Equality Panel*, CASEreport 60, London: LSE.
[6] Power, A. (2007) *City survivors: Bringing up children in disadvantaged neighbourhoods*, Bristol: The Policy Press.
[7] www.dcsf.gov.uk/performancetables/
[8] Ofsted (2010) *The special educational needs and disability review*, London: Ofsted.

[9] Power, A. (2007) *City survivors: Bringing up children in disadvantaged neighbourhoods*, Bristol: The Policy Press.

[10] www.dcsf.gov.uk/performancetables/ ( Note: the Department for Children, Schools and Families monitors schools for special education needs.)

[11] Department for Children, Schools and Families (DCSF) (2009) *Delivering the behaviour challenge: Our commitment to good behaviour*, London: DCSF.

[12] Hills, J., Sefton, T. and Stewart, K. (eds) (2009) *Towards a more equal society? Poverty, inequality and policy since 1997*, Bristol: The Policy Press; www.dcsf. gov.uk/performancetables/

[13] Burgess, S. and Wilson, D. (2004) *Ethnic segregation in England's schools*, CASEpaper 79, London: LSE; Power, A., Richardson, L. et al (2004) *A framework for housing in the London Thames Gateway*, CASE Brief 27, London: LSE.

[14] Apprenticeships, Skills, Children and Learning Act 2009, London: The Stationery Office; Conservative Party (2010) *Invitation to join the government of Britain: Conservative Party manifesto 2010* (www.conservatives.com/Policy/ Manifesto.aspx); Labour Party (2010) *A fair future for all: Labour Party manifesto 2010* (www.labour.org.uk/manifesto/); Liberal Democrats (2010) *Change that works for you: Building a fairer Britain. Manifesto 2010* (www.libdems.org.uk/ our_manifesto.aspx).

# FOUR

# Young people, space, facilities and activities

*The residents' committee at the moment are trying to get all kinds of football teams, youth clubs and stuff but I think they'll find it hard to get premises from the council. I think all that's kind of disappeared really. There were loads of clubs and groups for children but that's all gone now.* (Sinead, West City)

## Introduction: *"Letting off steam"*

Children are naturally energetic, noisy, playful, boisterous and therefore exhausting to adults. If they cannot explore and expand their horizons, their progress into the wider world will be constrained by insufficient 'free play', making it more difficult for them to weigh up risks and cope with unknown dangers.[1] Schools in deprived urban neighbourhoods cannot provide the space or resources or time that children need. Therefore, children and young people in confined urban areas need public open spaces where they can play, discover and develop their informal social skills. This chapter examines the families' experience of the outdoors, parks, play and sport facilities. It explains the problems of too little space and too costly facilities. The issue of the 2012 Olympics that are sited within the East London neighbourhoods raises many relevant issues for parents in these areas.

'Letting off steam' was a phrase commonly used among the families to reflect the pressure that builds up inside children to release pent-up energy. The home is obviously the starting point, but most families we visited live in small, sometimes crowded homes and nearly half have no direct access to a garden or open space. Therefore, parks, play areas, clubs, community centres, leisure and sports facilities and swimming pools all become extremely important.

Families had little money to spare; most did not have a car and very few went away on holidays. So they were more dependent on their local area and cheap or free local provision than the average family.[2] They needed open but supervised outdoor space, safe streets and indoor facilities. Yet the local environment militated against parents letting their children out to play or to the local park without an adult – it seemed too risky or too far away. Parents therefore struggled to give their children the freedom they wanted, or to pay for the activities they dreamt of, or to join things that might help. Parents wanted to keep their children constructively occupied, sometimes using local parks, swimming pools, after-school clubs and sports facilities. But television, PlayStations and computers played a bigger, more accessible, seemingly safer role. This chapter reflects different views on what activities and spaces children and young people need and how those needs could be met.

## Children and young people's need for space and leisure activities

Over 90 per cent of parents believed that young people needed to release their physical energy and around 90 per cent thought sport would help young people in the neighbourhood 'let off steam'.

Parents' top priority for their neighbourhood was more local parks, facilities and activities for children. Over half of the parents in the two Northern neighbourhoods put these among their top priorities. A third of London parents said they would do more for young children if given the power, and 90 per cent wanted local parks for children above all else. Fewer London parents called for extra community facilities and activities, because there was more provision already. Parents in London also felt more 'connected', closer to amenities and to good public transport links, living in the capital. On the other hand, their worries over neighbourhood conditions, crime and anti-social behaviour were pressing, while their need for outdoor space was acute. Figure 4.1 shows this.

**Figure 4.1:** What parents say children and young people need, 2002

Local parks

More facilities and activities for children

Proper supervision of local area

A majority of families used parks, although far fewer did in the two Northern neighbourhoods. The lack of a local park in Kirkside East explained the very low proportion of parents using local parks (8 per cent), with two thirds rarely using a park. In London neighbourhoods, over half the families used local parks, and four fifths used parks either in their neighbourhoods or further afield. Figure 4.2 shows these differences.

**Figure 4.2:** What parents do with the children – activities outdoors, 2002

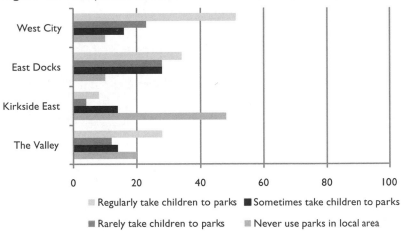

Parents told us about young people's leisure activities on our second visit. Parents said they most enjoyed outdoor activities, seeing their children play sports and going to parks. Two thirds of the parents felt that their neighbourhoods were badly provided with leisure facilities. Nearly 70 per cent of the parents said they most enjoyed outdoor activities, sport and going to the parks with their children, even though many of them were not able to do this.

Just under half of parents let their children play out in the street and local area, and around 43 per cent confined them to their own garden or balcony. The main barriers to children playing out were the combination of poor supervision, poor facilities, poor access and fear of trouble. Around half the parents only let their children out when an adult was with them. The lack of safe outdoor play areas, activities for teenagers and inadequate facilities made parents anxious over safety, peer pressure, drugs and other dangers:

> *Teenagers need something to do. It's so built up here ... they come out on to the street causing trouble, fighting, throwing bottles over*

*the wall. It can be threatening and intimidating – shouting, pushing, girls screaming.* (Ellie, West City)

## "Sports would help"

Parks and sporting opportunities for children and young people mattered to families in low-income areas. Some parents encouraged their children to get involved in sport and were overwhelmingly positive about the benefits of structured physical activity. Football was often linked to building confidence in boys:

> *They've just finished building a community centre. It'll get children off the streets when it opens. That's why I was very keen for the boys to play football. It gives them confidence.* (Kate, East Docks)

A London parent was glad her children were into sport and fitness.

> *The youngest likes playing football. He goes regularly to training and goes to the gym.* (Gloria, East Docks)

Another parent explained her conscious decision to work longer hours to pay for her children to join in sporting activities and have fun. She underlined the struggle to make the money stretch and finding the time to fit everything in:

> *It is hard, both working full-time and having kids, it takes its toll on them and us, but the benefits are a higher household income, so we can do nice things with them, like ice skating lessons, football season tickets, et cetera.* (Polly, The Valley)

On our last visit, we wanted parents' views on whether young people in their areas needed more organised ways of physical activity. All parents in the North and the vast majority in East London (over 90 per cent in both East Docks and West City) told us that young people needed exercise 'to let off steam' and that sport would help with this. And in some families, particularly with boys, the children simply *had* to find physical outlets for their energy.

*"Keep children on the right path"*

Some parents made a clear connection between organised physical activity and keeping 'on the right path', arguing that sport helped children keep out of trouble:

> *Well, I think sport would help. Or they are easily led into crime. They have taken the local sports centre away, it is a very bad thing, kids will turn to crime.* (Laverne, Kirkside East)

One parent thought that young people could too easily behave in negative ways instead of turning to sport:

> *It is not about barriers, it is about them letting off physical energy in bad ways, not via sports, kids, today.* (Laverne, Kirkside East)

> *Yeah sport would help. It's a constructive way of doing it, because otherwise they let off energy and usually end up in trouble, so sport's constructive, it's a good direction for kids to go.* (Barbara, East Docks)

One London mother mentioned the multiple benefits of sport, keeping children away from drugs and helping them meet other children:

> *They need all the help they can get to let off physical energy. Any sports for youngsters, it helps with the drugs problem, to keep them interested. For young boys, football and boxing, they've always been very important in this area, boxing in particular. Years ago this used to be a poor area and you do find boys go into boxing. Once a boy likes his body he's not going to get into drugs, is he! And it's sociable.* (Trudy, West City)

Parents often linked sport, physical activity and 'letting off steam' with the needs of boys, but they did also apply this argument to girls, as we show later. Sport could take up 'idle' time that otherwise might be turned to bad use:

> *It's keeping yourself busy. There's an old saying, well not an old saying, an old-fashioned view − if you're keeping busy you're keeping out of mischief. It's true isn't it, really.* (Peggy, East Docks)

Many parents stressed the social benefits of sport for children, as an outlet for aggression particularly among boys:

> *My three certainly benefit. My middle one can be a bit aggressive and [judo] is an outlet.* (Tina, Kirkside East)

Sport also directly countered behaviour problems and helped parents as well as children if the activity was engaging enough. This East End parent described her son's bad behaviour, his concentration problems and the value of organised sport in calming him down:

> *My personal experience is, looking at my son – someone who has huge problems concentrating in class and being a total nightmare most of the time – sport, for him, I think, has just totally focused his mind, which is why I'm still so keen that he continues. Because it does, it burns off his energy and he is far calmer and more focused because of it.* (Debra, West City)

## "Letting off steam"

Play and sport were not only important for older children, but could also help younger ones:

> *Yes, especially the little ones. I think it teaches sharing and fitness and self-control and enables them to let off steam. So yes sport would help.* (Denise, Kirkside East)

Young people often displaced small children in parks, so a common worry was how to make sure there were enough play areas for younger children:

> *I still feel that there needs to be more play spaces for the younger kids. It's like, yeah, there's a basketball court and I think that's great 'cos there's a lot of teenagers here, but there's still not really that much for younger children. I mean there's like a little piddly park downstairs that none of the kids want to go in 'cos it's boring. And the only local park is small. And then you've got a large number of kids there, so a lot of the time you don't get to go on the swings because – it's like one space for a bunch of kids. So it would be nice to see a few more, younger kids' park areas.* (Beth, West City)

Sport helps develop life skills, and the value of physical activity goes far beyond the activity itself. This parent favoured sport as a way of wearing her children out and burning off their excess energy:

> *All young people should be spending three hours a day running around. Lessons of endurance, competition and working hard, it's all great. I've got kids who respond to sport really well. My son has a knee injury and he's totally mischievous whereas if he plays sport he's knackered.* (Ariana, West City)

One mother encouraged her son to do sporting activities, which contrasted with her brother's attitude to his son:

> *There's got to be a sport a child likes. My brother said to me 'How do you cope, taking your son training four days a week?'. But he spends all his time in the pub and his kid's got an ASBO [Anti-social Behaviour Order].* (Alexa, East Docks)

One London parent connected the benefits of exercise for children with adults' need for exercise. She also noticed how a new basketball court had transformed the atmosphere among local children:

> *I think most people do need to let off physical energy. It's got to be good, wherever you come from. It'll probably make people a lot less aggressive. 'Cos I know after I've been to the gym I feel quite refreshed and in an 'up' mood. I don't come out all burned out and it probably works wonders for a lot of people. I think it's definitely a positive thing. Actually I must say it's been a lot quieter as far as the outside here, 'cos the kids used to sit outside and scream and yell at each other and make lots of noise. But since the basketball court's been put up it seems quieter. I don't know if it's 'cos it's gotten colder. But, no, it seems to be less manic outside.* (Beth, West City)

One parent blamed the cultural pressures on teenagers for putting them off, as it had her as a teenager too:

> *All young people do – kids aren't kids anymore. Sport can't help them let off energy – it's all crime now, cars, et cetera. Like when I was 14 and 15, it was going around in cars with boys and drinking cider, not playing a game of rounders!* (Amy, Kirkside East)

It was often difficult to take children to organised activities if the parent worked, and letting them go on their own seemed too risky. The fear of the local environment, of venturing beyond their reach, that persuaded them to send their children to local schools, also deterred them from letting their children go on their own to do sport:

> *When my son was young, I paid £15 a week to go to martial arts. I had to take him there and pick him up. But then I couldn't do it because of my job. If there was a mini-bus – my sisters in Canada and America say they have this, they participate in all these sports. We don't have the support, resources and organisation – I wouldn't think of asking my son to get on a bus to a neighbouring area for fear of him being bullied or something happening.* (Hannah, East Docks)

## Why informal outdoor play and activity are difficult in disadvantaged neighbourhoods

At our last visit, we asked parents about barriers to children's involvement in sport and leisure activities. Parents listed multiple barriers, including: shortage of local provision; lack of money; too little encouragement offered to local children; and limited government support.

Less common factors were: age limits on activities; lack of transport; lack of school sports facilities; sport being seen as 'uncool'; gangs and anti-social behaviour getting in the way; lack of confidence and time; oversubscribed waiting lists for activities; cultural and racial divisions; and laziness or lack of discipline. Parents in more affluent areas faced somewhat lower barriers and had more resources to overcome them.[3]

### "It's not safe"

Neighbourhood conditions contributed significantly to lack of participation in organised activities. Since general neighbourhood conditions troubled parents, organised supervised sport and leisure activities for their children were more important, yet simultaneously more difficult to achieve. Parents highlighted factors that clearly made normal outdoor games and informal play difficult.[4]

Fear and lack of confidence drove half of the parents to hold their children back. In three of the neighbourhoods a quarter of parents worried most about drugs. Drug abuse in communal spaces, including play areas and parks, prevented parents from letting their children play out. A West City mother described this problem:

> *There's a playground there but my daughter doesn't play there
> as it's not safe. She just goes to school. It's not even safe to take
> the lift. There's all sorts of people around we don't know. They
> [caretakers] clean the lifts regularly but they pee in them. They're
> coming to the stairwells to drink and do drugs at night. The staff
> fix the security door and it gets broken regularly. Usually it's the
> outsiders that are doing this.* (Yonca, West City)

Another West City parent described the takeover of their local park:

> *We have a park in here, and teenagers use drugs and smoke. We
> find condoms, there's swearing — F-words.* (Ece, West City)

Another parent explained why the local football pitch was abandoned:

> *There's an astro-turf pitch nearby but it's taken over by people
> in their twenties with drugs, making noise, so it was shut down.*
> (Leah, West City)

In all cases the lack of direct on-site supervision led to the loss of
valuable open space.

Growing up in areas where drug abuse is common, and where 'hard',
class A drugs are openly dealt on local streets, means young people
are exposed to drugs at an ever lower age. One mother in West City
explained how the area was affecting them. Her husband worked with
young people and had seen drugs changing hands between some of
his pupils.

> *The way the area was becoming, more drug problems. The changes
> in the area were getting more to my husband than me, being out
> in the community. He could see drugs changing hands. Some of
> them were his pupils. It's getting worse, rising crime, through drugs,
> kids as young as six!* (Tracy, West City)

This mother was desperate to move away because she felt she had to
keep her boys locked up:

> *The drugs and fighting worry me 'cos they're boys. I feel like putting
> bars on the windows and not letting them out. I don't want to be
> here when they're older. I want to be a lot further away. I think
> drug testing in school is a brilliant idea as it scares the kids into
> not doing it.* (Elaine, East Docks)

## "Influenced by his friends"

Parents worried about peer pressure. As children reached adolescence, this worry grew, with the fear among parents that friends would have a negative influence and lead them down the wrong path. So the restrictions on outdoor activities and 'joining in' got stronger as children got older just as their need for freedom and outside activity grew. This seemed a much bigger issue in East London than the North. One lone mother in West City struggled constantly to keep her son away from the pressures of outside the home:

> *My older son is more affected by his friends. But he's not allowed out after 6pm and he asks why his friends can and he cannot. I say 'that's how we live, what will you do outside?'. He's so influenced by his friends – the way they speak and dress. They buy expensive clothes and he asks why he can't. I explain we have a limited income so I feel depressed. It's difficult for me and him.* (Hulya, West City)

Parents worried most about their teenage children as they felt they could no longer fully control them:

> *Last week I was worried about fireworks night. They're mostly teenagers. I would like to move my daughters out before they become teenagers and are being influenced.* (Faye, West City)

The older the teenagers, the more uncertain the parental influence and the more powerful the wider influences:

> *The main risk I think is, because of their age. I see it all the time round here, they hang around in cars, which they do, it's typical of that age group, and I think it's peer pressure. You know, whatever their friends are doing, they're more than likely to get roped into.* (Barbara, East Docks)

Another mother felt that the street culture was so dominant that she had to battle constantly to counter the pressures on her children, particularly the boys:

> *There's some sort of culture going on in the street at the moment.*
> *It's worse for boys – I don't know who they're trying to be, in*
> *gangs, on a video. It's difficult for the good ones to get anywhere.*
> *A lot of weapons are used. For boys, you either go that way, or get*
> *beaten up or get left on your own. There's a lot of peer pressure....*
> *I'm afraid of the violence, the fighting. They don't argue nowadays.*
> (Carmen, East Docks)

Many parents were extremely protective and kept their teenagers on a tight lead:

> *The streets in general are a dangerous place to be around. She's not*
> *allowed outside the block. She's got a mobile, she phones me when*
> *she gets on or off the train.* (Flowella, East Docks)

### "Stepping into the road and getting hit"

Worries over traffic and road safety affected children's freedom, particularly among Northern families, even more than in London. Traffic seriously curtailed children's and young people's outdoor activities in their neighbourhoods.

> *For little children, road safety is an issue, they can't play out the*
> *front on their own so they can't go out on their bikes. When they*
> *grow up a bit, there's nothing for them to do, they go out and you*
> *don't know what they are doing, that is a worry, dangers.* (Jenny,
> The Valley)

Another parent explained how a busy main road ran right by her home on the large Northern estate:

> *I worry about them stepping out into the road and getting hit.*
> *It's just the nature of where the house is.* (Becky, Kirkside East)

In London, traffic moves more slowly due to congestion and in both London neighbourhoods the large estates had limited internal traffic. In any case, very few London parents thought it was safe to let their children 'play out' unsupervised. But the East Docks area was dissected by a busy main road that parents found threatening:

> *I control what my children do quite a lot. That might sound horrible*
> *but, I don't let my son play out. We have the back garden and we*

> *go to parks. So he's never been allowed to play out on his own. I don't feel comfortable with that. Mainly because of the traffic and because…. I wouldn't know who he would be mixing with. And I think I'll probably do the same for my daughter….* (Erin, East Docks)

Another mother in East Docks explained her double anxiety about traffic on the roads and the fact that parks are unsupervised and cut off by the busy roads:

> *I don't like them to go out of my sight. I wouldn't let them go to the park on their own because that road is so busy to cross and it's quite an isolated park.* (Nicola, East Docks)

One consequence of the level of traffic everywhere and the accompanying fear of letting children play out was the lack of informal activity on streets and open space. Very few street games happened and therefore very little informal supervision either.[5] One parent thought traffic fears were confused with bigger, more remote threats:

> *The roads. People perceive the risks of being abducted, but it's a fear, not a risk. Everyone thinks there are far more kids being taken away than there really are.* (Joan, West City)

In some places, traffic calming measures were helping:

> *When we came here, the bus drivers were speeding along the road. Then they put up speed bumps, I was so happy. There used to be more rubbish, but I always see the guys cleaning the road and less cars being dumped.* (Hannah, East Docks)

### "He can't play outside"

Fear of crime acted as a major deterrent to allowing children to play outside. This mother related a very scary encounter:

> *… when I was last in the park there was a man, startled me asking to buy cigs off me, and asked if a kid had gone missing in the park, and said he thought he knew where the body was. I rang police that night and they must have had a similar call from him, they talked of that.* (Nina, The Valley)

One nasty incident stopped another mother from letting her children play out:

> *Danny used to play with the kid opposite on the landing with the [front] doors open. We can't do that now. He can't play outside on the grass. There was a man with his leg bleeding. Danny is quite happy indoors. He can't go out on his bike unless you're watching him.* (Megan, West City)

Some of the incidents parents reported showed how unsafe local streets were for children to play out in. A London mother was upset by all the negative things happening around her. She saw young people's provision for activities shrinking leading to trouble in parks. Yet challenging bad behaviour could lead to reprisals:

> *The park over there, it was all done up but the kids wrecked it. There's nowhere for them to go. The kids stay out till 10.30pm – I had to be in at 7.30pm when I was little. I was threatened with stabbing by one of the boys who took my son's cap in the park. They play in the park where the kids are, the places where there's shelter. There's no youth clubs like when I was young. I used to play badminton.* (Kerry, East Docks)

As children became increasingly independent, pursuing their own interests and forming their own social ties with peer groups, parents' fears for them gained momentum. These fears were invariably based on real experiences within their environment. London mothers mentioned many different fears:

> *Children fighting, they walk around with things in their pockets to hurt somebody.* (Clare, East Docks)

> *Muggings, getting mobile phones stolen.* (Andaiye, West City)

> *Violent crime, my main worry as a mother. The worst thing for a mother is to hear your son or daughter has been killed.* (Hannah, East Docks)

> *Threat of intimidation from other children. Threat of one person who's a paedophile on the estate. There's crazy people round here. Dirty areas, dog poo. Hygiene, health and safety, well-being.* (Charlotte, West City)

Yet an East London mother took a much more cavalier approach, but tempering this with avoidance strategies:

> *I don't worry about dangers. My children grew up here. But if they look at someone eye-to-eye, you don't know what might happen. They stay in.* (Selda, West City)

## Pressures on space: *"All been built up"*

Pressures to create more 'mixed areas', build more attractive buildings and create revenue for local councils, was putting added pressure on space and facilities in the face of limited resources. Parents sensed that profiting from land values might replace investing in the community, and particularly in its families. Space was a huge issue in East London, as this mother explained:

> *The council keeps selling the land and the property. There's no place – they're not giving great big areas over to football pitches anymore. It's all been built up, so children have a lot less.* (Sinead, West City)

Zoe, from West City, described what had happened to the play space by her block of flats:

> *They've pulled all the swings down. The kids have nowhere to play. We tried to fight the council to stop them taking our play area away but they sold it to private buyers. They should be doing more for children, for example on that green there. But then you'd get old people moaning, you could have a time restriction. Say 8 o'clock.* (Zoe, West City)

Even where space is provided, local children from less well-off families are sometimes excluded by the design and enclosed layout of new facilities, fitted into new developments:

> *Before, there was a grass area where the children could play but now they're building there. A playground has been built but it's private to those people as the indoors face onto the areas, so my children won't be able to use it. They have nowhere to play.* (Hulya, West City)

Parents wanted more priority for organised children's activities and less for buildings and cars. The sense of losing community space was very strong:

> ... *there should have been places for social activities for kids after school. There used to be a library here, now we have to go all the way to the college. So not just the parks, but places for social activities.* (Hulya, West City)

## Too few, too expensive facilities: "There's a huge need"

The lack of activities and safe spaces stopped children from exploring and experimenting with new things:

> *At school, they have a day when they can do sports, they have somewhere to play, but at home they get bored and there's nowhere to play nearby. The other day, my son said he was going to play outside. I looked out and saw him climbing over a wall to another area, but I thought it was too quiet and unsafe so I brought him back. Also, the children get fed up of everything very quickly. They get bored of computer games. Because there's no opportunity to play in the area they're always restless.* (Hulya, West City)

The restlessness this mother referred to had much bigger implications as children became teenagers.

In East London, children's development was particularly bounded by an acute shortage of space, with over 70 per cent of families living in high density flats and tower blocks, making it even more important to have free access to space and organised facilities:

> *Most people round here live in flats, there's a minority in houses. You know, great, grown, hulking teenagers – they need to go out and run round. There's a huge need for swimming and football pitches, that sort of thing. Tennis and tennis courts are very popular, people are there for hours on end.* (Jasmine, West City)

Many of the local facilities were too expensive for local families:

> *Young people can't afford it. It's lovely to have the sports centre on our doorstep but it don't benefit normal people, kids whose parents are out of work.* (Ellie, West City)

Parents were aware of the poor facilities on council estates, compared with richer areas. The poor facilities made it difficult for parents to organise play provision directly on estates. Everywhere supervision was a problem:

> *I don't really know that there are enough good places around. I mean there is this adventure playground down by our school, by the local area right now. I think the problem with that is it's not — how should I say, supervised. We have an after-school club. You have to pay for it, a lot of parents now will send their children instead to the adventure playground which isn't supervised because they think it's cheaper. There aren't really that many parks to go to and I think they're not properly maintained, most of them. I mean the local small park for the little ones was only re-done because people in the area put up a fuss and said it had to be done and they funded it. They found the funding for it. Now if that small park had been in the middle of a council estate, it might not have got done. But middle-class people can make a fuss, and they also know where to get money from.* (Kathleen, West City)

## "One on every estate"

Youth clubs often proved difficult to run because of their open door approach and loose controls. Children with disruptive behaviour were sometimes excluded as one of the few sanctions youth leaders had. In some clubs rough groups took over and deterred more placid, shyer children. One result was the closure of many youth clubs and a loss of regular activities for young people as they entered their teens. Everywhere parents were crying out for more youth clubs. One parent saw a link between youth provision and more positive behaviour. But she also saw the more general decline in authority, among teachers, youth leaders and parents, as an underlying problem.

> *When I grew up there was six youth clubs where young people could congregate, one for every day of the week. This is why the 40 pluses are more sort of level-headed. You don't get that now. They've got one in Prince's Lane. My aunt works there, and last Thursday they just trashed the place. In school now, this age group from nine up to 15 are so disrespectful to adults. You get a mouthful of abuse and you can't talk to them anymore.* (Gillian, East Docks)

The controls that some clubs felt they had to exercise could put up barriers for young people. Getting the right balance was difficult:

> *There's no youth club or big hall. The community centre, they've got a club in there where you go, from 12 years old. But before you register, you have to bring a parent. When my son went they wouldn't let him register. He got upset and went to take his dad. Sometimes they won't go if they have to take a parent.* (Naomi, East Docks)

Some children were afraid to go to the clubs in the area, even if they were well run, because of the general bad behaviour and peer pressure:

> *I couldn't tell you. Even if there was, I couldn't tell you because my children don't go to anything like that. Like my daughter, I was saying 'cos she's hanging around with her friends, and I said to her, 'Why don't you get involved in a youth club or something'. The community project runs a lot of stuff, I was happy to phone 'em up and find out what stuff they've got going. But she said a lot of disaffected attend and so sometimes there's trouble, although they're laying on really good things. It could end up them sending your child where they're going to get into trouble.* (Annie, East Docks)

One of the teenagers explained:

> *If there was a youth club I'd be scared to go there because of the people there already.* (Tina, West City)

Other parents looked back to the different sports they enjoyed in their youth club and puzzled over their decline. Youth provision had clearly been standard on council estates, but not any longer. Parents believed it was lack of provision that caused problems among young people, not the other way round:

> *We used to have youth clubs. You could play table tennis, badminton, tennis, basketball. They stopped doing youth clubs for whatever reason, I can't remember. Most things kids go to now, they need to have an adult with them. We need more things for the younger ones. The older kids play in the park and intimidate the younger ones.* (Kerry, East Docks)

> *They used to have one for each estate, but there doesn't seem to be any anymore.* (Marilyn, West City)

> *Young people on the streets are dressed up as troublemakers but only 10 per cent are. Sport will happen when there's facilities for them to use.* (Tina's husband, West City)

## "Street-cred kids"

Rough behaviour put many parents and young people off. Racial divisions often became stronger in teenage years and following the pattern of school, white teenagers were often unwilling to join a predominantly black youth club. One mother felt that a big part of the problem was 'attitude', and the pressure to act 'big':

> *To be honest with ya, unless you wanted to pay for the facilities – I know there's the Boys Club and there's a place called The Centre. My kids have never been – this isn't being discriminative, but most of 'em are black boys, big black boys, swear and you know. They're all street-cred boys, and I don't want my kids being like that, you know? They promote children to go to these clubs, you know, so they're not congregating on corners, but when all these clubs close, the street-cred kids, you see 'em at 10, 11 o'clock at night, hanging around the streets causing trouble.* (Alice, West City)

Parents compared the dearth of activities for young people with the benefits of Sure Start for young children. Many parents wanted something equivalent for older children, particularly as so many youth facilities had been lost:

> *There used to be a youth centre up the road but the council shut it down. We've got Sure Start, and it's good if you've got children up to age four. But the youth get forgotten around here.* (Destiny, West City)

One Northern parent managed to borrow Sure Start equipment for her older children. She found it hard to let her children do activities such as a bike rides:

> *There's nothing available in the neighbourhood so I'd borrow sports equipment if I wanted to do anything like that with my eight-year-old daughter. I work for Sure Start so I can borrow stuff. There is*

*nowhere for kids to go and do stuff like this in the neighbourhood.
It is a long way to go to the park for a ride.* (Patsy, Kirkside East)

A London parent specifically highlighted how important free supervised
sport was in built-up traffic-bound areas where children were trapped
between confined space and dangerous surroundings:

> *Talking about sport, keeping 'em off the streets, they're like caged
> animals if they're kept indoors. They'll get into mischief, they need
> more things out there. The government needs to fund more free
> things for 9 to 10 years old. I wouldn't let my kids out on the
> street at that age. I need to make sure they're safe and looked after.*
> (Kerry, East Docks)

## "I want to be in the Olympics now"

In a flurry of progressive decision making, the Olympic Committee
favoured the East End of London because it would help to regenerate
the surrounding areas, and provide much needed sports facilities for
local children. The East London families live within reach of the
Olympic site, and in the run-up to the games, have had to live through
the noise and dirt of giant building works, while funding was diverted
away from local provisions into the Olympic site itself. The Olympics
have underlined the need for play and sport in deprived areas.

The location of the Olympic site close by has inspired many children.
A mother who was a teaching assistant talked about the impact on her
children and on local schools:

> *My sons used to do gymnastics and now they're both talking about
> going back to the gym! 'I want to be in the Olympics now.' Had
> they kept it up, they probably would've been. If they want to aim
> for that, not that they're gonna get there, but if that's what they
> want to aim for, the world's your oyster, go for it. Because it's in
> the East End of London, it's in their home town, it's down the
> road from them. They can say they can go and watch this or see
> this. They're really excited about it.*

> *Since we got the bid, I've found a lot more children are now
> becoming more involved in sport. They want to be active now
> because they've set their sights on being a part of that when it
> happens. It's a good thing because people'll get fit and healthy
> and they're doing something constructive. Football, gym, track*

*and field, and now even basketball. They've just set up a scheme in school where we teach our children how to play professional basketball. We've got a coach coming in now that's doing that for us. We also do cricket. We do quite a lot of sports. And most of the tournaments that happen within the borough, our kids attend.* (Nora, East Docks)

## "Not for the like of us"

Other parents were more doubtful about whether the Olympics would really benefit their children and their area:

*That's going to be a very, very hard one because the local council and all the other councils, they never really have much money to spend on kids, to be able to bring the kids through, like maybe do special programmes for them. They're always short of money, aren't they. So I really don't know, I don't think the 2012 Olympics is going to be any good for East London. It will be for the big business people and all, but not for the likes of us. I don't think it's going to make much difference around the local area. I'm hoping I'm wrong, but....* (Niamh, West City)

One parent realised quickly that the 'locals' were going to lose some football pitches as sites were taken over and developed for the games. The pressure to take space away for car parks and roads might not be matched by benefits for local families:

*Oh, the Olympics will definitely have an impact, let's just hope it's positive. I mean I was very positive about getting the Olympics, I thought it was terrific. I'm not sure if everybody thought it was terrific just 'cos we beat Paris – that's a bit of it, no doubt. But everyone was very, very excited. The worry is that the local area's going to get the dregs of it; the bulk of the money will go into neighbouring areas. We'll get the car parks and so on and the worry already is, there's lovely football pitches, they play Saturday and Sunday football and there's lots of very local leagues. Some of that's going to be built on for the Olympics. I think people want to be sure that the area gets a good deal out of it, and they don't see the area as ever having negotiated a particularly good deal for anything. I think the local leisure centre is a perfect example. We want to get some benefits from it if it's going to be – 'cos we'll certainly have to put up with congestion and traffic and noise no doubt. I hope local residents at least get some tickets and some lasting benefit. I think most of the sporting facilities in the area are pretty dire at the moment, so certainly they could be improved.* (Kathleen, West City)

In a Northern school where sport was actively promoted, the Olympics had a galvanising effect. But several Northern parents expressed doubts that the schools would pick up the Olympics message:

*My eldest, his school is also a sports college and it is gearing up for the Olympics already. Something about using the sports college for training, for training some of the kids for the Olympics.* (Holly, Kirkside East)

*I hope the Olympics will, but don't think it will, I hope it encourages the schools to be more involved in sports, but it's wishful thinking, I feel.* (Amanda, Kirkside East)

*The Olympics should do eventually, but nothing seems to be happening at the minute. I'd have thought the schools would be into it.* (Linda, Kirkside East)

*I think sport will be pushed more, or it will mean schools push it more. But if there's no local facilities to do it, what is the point? Kids will drive parents mad asking and there's nothing locally to do around here. This is definitely the case.* (Denise, Kirkside East)

## "I hope it encourages the schools"

Two thirds of the East London parents thought the Olympics would have an impact on their children's sporting activities and on access to them. Parents thought schools played a pivotal role in introducing children and young people to sport, and in 2002 the government set ambitious guidelines for exercise in schools. The amount of sport and Physical Education (PE) offered and its take-up have increased significantly as a result.[6] In practice, the efforts of local schools often fell short, as the following parent showed:

*Just the fact that my daughter, she hasn't had any PE this term at all, nothing, not anything. Last year she did swimming the first term, and PE the second two terms. But this term they've done nothing, as far as I can make out. I don't really know why. You get a letter saying what's going on and there's been no letter saying what they're doing this term. You know, they say 'PE's on Wednesdays, please bring your PE kit'. Her PE kit has sat in the cupboard since September doing nothing. Fortunately I'm able to take her myself to gym and swimming and stuff like that. If she didn't have that, then there would be no other exercise.* (Joan, West City)

One parent felt that schools were doing even less now than before:

*In our primary school we used to do gymnastics, we used to do the Coca Cola badges, weren't it? These people nowadays, they haven't got the staff in the schools or anything like that, to do it. Or the facilities.* (Natalie, West City)

Another London mother thought national guidance narrowed down the physical activity that was possible. She was scathing about the priority given to play space, sport and exercise:

*Sport isn't part of their lives, it's no surprise is it, look at the national curriculum, the sport, you know, yeah you've got a swimming lesson a term or whatever it is. Most schools hate doing swimming as it takes loads of teachers, it takes out two hours of the day, it costs them a stack a money, you know, it's all about minimum provision. Or they've had all their playgrounds flogged off, you know. It's a bit late now to suddenly think, 'Oh, perhaps sport was quite good for them'.* (Debra, West City)

Schools were caught up in the vexed problem of competitive sport and handling failure. One parent hoped the Olympics would help to build a more resilient attitude:

*What I've noticed, at school, when they have sports day, years ago, they used to have competitive sports, but now it's non-competitive where all the children come out in their classes and they do a range of activities, fun activities but there's no competition. So what I would say is it'd be interesting to see now with the Olympics, the Olympics is about competition isn't it? It'll be interesting to see now how schools are going to get children involved in things. Our children need to feel a bit of competition. Out there in the real world it's competitive isn't it? Whether we like it or not, that's what it is. If we shelter our children all the time from anything we think*

*might knock their confidence, it's against them building resilience.*
(Annie, East Docks)

Debra and Alan in West City were critical of the over-egalitarian attitude in local schools that avoided competitive team sports and failed to recognise children's abilities and successes. They wanted their children to learn cooperative skills and to become good losers as well as sporty:

> *Yeah, I think school sport should be compulsory, and there should be a lot more of it. And that's not just about the health of the kids, and fitness and everything else. It's about teamwork, and all that cooperative stuff and actually getting used to that. You know, there are winners and losers, and competing's important. And actually, you're not always gonna win, whether you think you're the best high jumper in the school or not. Sometimes it's gonna go wrong. I think they're great life skills. For too long school sports've not been seen as good things, you know. But people lose! You can't just divorce that from the experience of our children. I just think it's outrageous actually that for so long we've put these things off. We're all winners for taking part, well. We're actually all losers as well then!* (Alan, West City)

Being overweight deterred some children:

> *I ain't got fat, lazy kids, I've got skinny, active kids. A lot of their mates though, they've got quite a few of their mates that are just fat and they sit there all day, these little fat kids. I s'pose they'd need a bit more energy, but then that's to do with their fat parents I s'pose, isn't it.* (Hailey, East Docks)

Some parents felt that schools could help build confidence and participation among children normally reluctant to take part. One mother has seen sudden progress in the attitude of schools in East London:

> *In the last couple of years, the last year, it's been more geared towards sports. And even children who thought they weren't able or capable of doing sports are now doing it. In schools now, at least two or three times a day we have fitness. It's basically running round the playground, doing a few stretches. You've got children with weight problems, and that, 'I can't run 'cos I'm fat'. It's not about that, you're all equal. But if you can't run, you jog, or you walk you're*

*still exercising. And then once they become relaxed in themselves and feel that self-confidence, they then start to participate and become more active.* (Nora, East Docks)

This new emphasis on physical exercise clearly helps children in lots of ways:

*It's more or less there for them actually, by getting experts coming into school to do cricket sessions. At my children's school we've had cricket and tennis coaches coming in. It tends to have a knock-on effect. If they see that activity, they want to take it up outside the school.* (Rachel, East Docks)

## Facilities are far too expensive

The Olympics made sport more topical in East London, but there were many limits to access:

*Round here, there's an ice skating rink, there's ice skating lessons, but you have to go in and ask them, they don't have any posters. The Saturday school didn't have any posters either. I found out through the local school. This year you have to pay for it, last year we didn't. I think there's not enough.* (Helat's daughter, West City)

Money was a big barrier in all the areas:

*Most of the kids haven't got the money, they're getting up to mischief, nicking bikes and all that stuff. It's a deprived area, perhaps their parents haven't got the money, they haven't got jobs, the parents can't give them what they need or want.* (Ellie, West City)

Organised provision was often too expensive for local families and this West City mother thought the upgrading of local sports facilities was a way of excluding local kids for the benefit of 'city types':

*I think the facilities are too expensive, to be honest, they're far too expensive. They want nearly five pound for a swim and things like this. It's just ridiculous. I don't swim anymore because there's no lane pools, they're all kidney-shaped pools and you can't swim. Some of the leisure centres that are around in the area are for the children, they're very expensive because they're catering for the city folk and they're catering for the 'you know', the hi-tech gym equipment.* (Rosemary, West City)

High up-front payments deterred parents because children need to try out activities first and find their own level as they often lost interest or simply could not do the activity. Advance payments acted as a deterrent when money was short:

> *There is a sports centre very nearby. The only obstacle is money, because of the sports centre itself. You used to be able to pay for a session, now it is in terms, 12 weeks at a time. It is not helpful. Kids need to try it and see if they like it first.* (Holly, Kirkside East)

Parents with several school-age children struggled to pay even low fees, particularly if the children wanted to do several different activities:

> *With sports it's money. Because there's two of 'em, I can't afford it. You'd like to do dancing, wouldn't you? [speaking to daughter] They do after-school clubs. You've got drama and activities on a Thursday. And computers. But other things, if they want to do dance, then it's difficult.*

> Daughter: *And gymnastics.*

> *Oh yeah, and gymnastics. And they're very good at it. They want to do it. It's money worries.* (Rose and her daughter, East Docks)

Activities were strongly linked to family resources to fund extra-curricular activities and special facilities:

> *We took the kids to the council sorts centre and my son got chicken pox, so we didn't go back. I am a member of the local gym and I swim. My husband goes every night; if I can, I go once a week. We became members for the kids especially, for my seven-year-old son's coordination problem and we thought it was a nice atmosphere for the kids. That sounds snobbish. So all the family are members of the gym.* (Amanda, Kirkside East)

Both parents working, even in low-paid jobs, opened up more possibilities. Amanda, from Kirkside East, explained how they managed to pay a family membership:

> *Money and a car. It's a drive to get to the gym; we work hard and earn a bit extra so we can get a take away and watch a film on a Friday and attend a gym.* (Amanda, Kirkside East)

Parents had to prioritise sport and paying activities over other competing demands:

> *There's lots of facilities around us but they all cost money. The boys play Sunday League football – that's a cost – it's expensive to participate. They can't come to ask me for pocket money because they've already had it on sport. They've been doing it for four years – you can't take it away from them. But now my daughter wants to do other things.* (Kate, East Docks)

Swimming lessons which many parents were keen on for their children were often too expensive, but also too much in demand from parents who could pay:

> *Very expensive, it's not enough for this area, for example, for my child. They are waiting three months for swimming classes, all my friends are waiting three months. Before we had a nice swimming pool. They take the taxes and the money, the council just want the money.* (Onur, West City)

Some parents simply don't know what's on offer and don't have the confidence to join in. Cultural and language barriers play a part in this. This parent talked about what would help participation:

> *I don't know, I s'pose just knowing what's available, when you live for long enough in a place and you know what's available. Also, having enough money to pay for things, the gymnastics classes, they're not cheap. And things that are sort of culturally acceptable, like my friend at number one, she won't take her little boy swimming because she won't put on a costume and get in the pool. That's not acceptable in her culture. If I don't get into a costume and in the pool, it's because I don't like the size of me! [laughs]*
>
> *Knowing enough people that sort of say, 'Ooh, there's so and so, such and such going on, have your heard about this, have you heard about that?'. That helps. And there are lots of, well two or three free local publications that come through every so often and there's a lot of information in those. It's all in English, so people who can't read English would find it hard to access things 'cos they*

*wouldn't know what's on. And also, having the internet – I'm not computer literate but I can go on the internet and look up activities. If my daughter wanted to do them, I can find it out. I guess there's plenty of people who wouldn't have the first idea how to go about looking for what they need.* (Joan, West City)

## "There's an attitude of anti-exercise"

Lack of interest in sports among children and young people was in itself a barrier. The counter-attractions of gadget games was strong. Children could be put off by bad facilities, poor instructors and a boring approach:

> *We have things in school, but lots of young people in school just don't want to do PE I think there is an attitude of anti-exercise and anti-PE – not from everyone, but from a lot of the young people. It all fits into the whole idea that young people just wanna sit and play PlayStation and watch telly and things like that.* (Andrea, East Docks)

Some parents tried but failed to get their children interested. This father explained his own high expectations that clearly put his son off:

> *To be truthful I'm a sports man, I always have been. So, when he was younger I tried to get him into everything. He's never been interested. Never. You know, he's never wanted to go and play football – when he did wanna play, he wanted to play it his way, and his way was not the right way! So I would say to him, 'No, you don't play it that way'. He's just not interested in sport at all.* (Rosemary's husband, West City)

Another mother described the loss of interest among teenagers compared with the good work her children's school now did in pushing sport:

> *... the older kids, like primary kids, they get a lot of activity in school during the day and after school, 'cos we do a lot of after-school clubs, sporting activities. So they can stay behind two or three nights a week and do a sporting activity. So the facilities are there for them. And a lot of the parents have taken up on this.*
>
> *But you've got the teenagers – they're the ones that are sort of, out in the cold basically. That generation has missed that 'cos, sort of, at the end of their time, half way through their secondary, all*

> *this come about. They're like 'Can't be bothered now'. I think had it been there from primary, they'd've seen it through to where they are now. Because there wasn't such a push on exercise and keeping fit, it just wasn't pushed a lot, but now it is.* (Nora, East Docks)

When parents did not themselves like sport, they found it harder to encourage their children, and much harder to get them involved because children draw a lot of their motivation from parents:

> *Swimming – I don't know how to swim so I can't go with them. And I think unless you've got that sport ethic almost built into you from quite an early age, it's very hard to engage and get kids of 14 to suddenly think 'yeah, we're gonna go off and play sport', more than kicking a ball around. For a lot of them, they don't even do that, you know.* (Alan, West City)

Some parents simply did not have the energy or enthusiasm to help their children:

> *I don't know. I mean they are very young kids, so they are dependent on their parents sort of guiding them, aren't they, and if their parents just kick them out the door and let them play till 10 o'clock at night, then I would say it's definitely a lack of motivation on the parents' part to guide them into more constructive activities. As long as they're out their way, it doesn't matter what they do.* (Joan, West City)

Other parents talked positively about what was possible:

> *There is so many little clubs, perhaps a lot of people don't know about them. But I mean, certainly if you was looking for any club that held your interest, all you have to do is look in the local paper, the local magazine, there's promotions everywhere, so yeah. They done martial arts for about six years in the area, they don't do it anymore. And then my younger son switched from that to football which he done for a few years. He isn't doing that anymore. My daughter, she likes swimming, so she would go there when the fancy took her.* (Barbara, East Docks)

## "There's no girls' teams"

Girls and young women needed special encouragement as sport often appealed most strongly to boys:

> *It's more about what the providers want to run, you know, there's lots of old, traditional boys clubs here which are based on boys only. Yes, there's a sporting focus but it's boxing. It's kind of all those traditional things. Trying to get them to open up and engage with girls. Actually it's young girls as well, who need access to stuff, and they ought to be looking at a broader range of sports. I think for a lot of kids, unless those facilities are offering the things they want, there's no interest in engaging with them and they'd rather just hang around on the street. We are getting somewhere though.* (Alan, West City)

Girls who like 'boys' sports' such as football also found it difficult to join in:

> *My daughter wanted to play football from an early age but there's no girls' teams. She'd have to travel to Bromley, Crawley, Warwick, because girls in this area doesn't seem to have a lot going on. Even now there's not a lot of girls' teams. With me not driving it costs an absolute fortune in cabs and trains.* (Gillian, East Docks)

Most parents did not find it easy to keep their children active. A more sedentary lifestyle, the loss of local clubs and pools, high costs and lack of appeal acted as big barriers. But the Olympics has definitely raised the profile of sport, and schools and parents alike were picking up the message.

## Helping children and young people get involved

Parents told us what made access to play and sport easier for their families. There were many other factors besides facilities: money to pay and low charges; having your own transport, or a lift; good public transport; group activities and after-school clubs; family support and childcare; and good advertising. Some factors related directly to parents' attitudes such as willingness to travel, knowing where to go and what was on, and having enough energy and enthusiasm.

Ironically, low pay could create a higher barrier than benefits because working parents weren't eligible for free activities such as after-school clubs or other activities:

> *I can afford it but there's people that can't. It seems ridiculous, being in the middle of London. There's lots of people who work but are on a low income, don't have a car, don't go on holidays. They're not on all these benefits and it's very hard to make a low-paid job go round.* (Trudy, West City)

Parents coping on their own could not meet the conflicting demands. This could be particularly hard for a child:

> *My son wants to play football but it's me again, I can't take him after school. I have to help with his sister's homework. Being alone with them, I can't do it all. Their priority is their studies.* (Desiree, East Docks)

## "Time and effort"

Another mother explained how much effort, as well as cash, was involved in children becoming serious about sport:

> *In the holidays at the local sports centre the kids do sports. And my son plays football through a league run by the local Junior Football League. And the local football club will sign him on when he is done with the Junior League. My sons do judo locally. They had to stop when my husband was on sick pay because of the costs. Grading costs £10 each a time. Having the money makes it possible and we put ourselves out on a Thursday, so my son can go to football, driving around for that. So money and time and effort are needed for the kids to do sport.* (Tina, Kirkside East)

Media images of top-flight sports sometimes pushed young people's expectations far beyond what was possible. One 17-year-old explained that he and his friends liked games, but they needed more organising:

> *Yeah, where I work in the holidays, they wanna go out and play football and stuff all the time, you know. Because like, after school, they go there, but all they do is play a match or something. And then they get bored of that. They wanna do some training and games and stuff but they've got no one to help. And they got like,*

*no equipment or anything, you know. So they need a coach but there's no coaches about. So that's why they're usually playing outside.* (Destiny, West City)

## "You can play anywhere, it's really cheap"

Sport England in a nationwide survey showed how popular informal street games still were, how much potential there was for developing more child and play-friendly streets, and how much lower-income areas and families would benefit.[7]

We asked parents about informal games. If there were spaces, children would willingly play:

> *Wherever boys are, they always seem to be kicking a football around. You go into any of the parks and there's boys kicking footballs around.* (Andrea, East Docks)

Given the space constraints and children's irrepressible urge to play, any available space could be used:

> *It's true what they say, no matter where you are in the world, give a group a kids a football, don't matter, they can make a game out of it. And football is a street sport, I think really.*
>
> Son: *You can play anywhere, it's really cheap.*
>
> *You can play anywhere, but it's more kids from very deprived areas that are more likely to play football because they can't afford to go to like rugby, tennis, things like that. Although round here, if you can afford it, they do do tennis and rugby and cricket, but it's very expensive.* (Destiny and her son, West City)

A mother from East Docks thought that the most important things were more encouragement, cheaper access and more dedicated help:

> *It would help if the swimming was cheaper or free in the holidays. And it should be more advertised. My daughter hardly sees any of the staff in the gym. She's got no idea about programmes or what she should work on as there's no one around.* (Jackie, East Docks)

Some families in East London lived near a badly run but relatively modern and expensive leisure centre:

> *There's a leisure centre but it's a dirty, horrible place. It is, it's an awful place. So run-down now.* (Destiny, West City)

One of the children in another family bore this out:

> *It's dirty, it's free but only in the summer holidays. The water was really dirty so we only stayed 45 minutes. I think there's not enough facilities.* (Helat's daughter, West City)

Since 2006 conditions in this recently built leisure centre have greatly improved as new managers came in. The pool has been upgraded and another pool has opened. The government has helped fund free swimming access for all children in public pools during holidays and at weekends, although one of our Northern cities did not implement this.[8] The other three have free swimming for all children up to 16 in the local public pools, although this is one of the proposed cuts under the Coalition government.[9]

## "I wish there were more cycle ways"

One recurring interest for children and parents was cycling. When children had bikes, it was potentially a free sport. Most at some point had bikes, but many parents were then stuck. Not only did traffic make it dangerous and unpleasant, but parents also worried if it was not very local.

One family went outside the area for activities, including taking their children biking:

> *Well, all we really do is we go swimming. We've bought two new bikes for the summer and we do cycling. But any of the things we do, we do away from here. We go to other areas and we do our things out there. Lots of nature stuff, but it doesn't involve this area, it involves leaving the area. So I wouldn't really know about the local facilities.* (Sinead, West City)

Another parent would like to see a local cycling club, but couldn't see how to get it to happen:

> *A lot of them just cycle round there, you know. It may be if there was some sort of cycling proficiency club. The thing is, with things like that, the kids aren't gonna go somewhere else to do it, it has to be brought to where they are. It's almost like, if somebody came*

*around and found all the kids cycling out the front here and said,
'Ooh, come up onto the area, and once a week we'll do cycling
proficiency', they would do it. These youth outreach workers, it's a
job for them, isn't it, but I don't know who pays for projects like
that.* (Joan, West City)

One parent talked about the government's 'green agenda' and linked
it to cycling. Wider action was necessary to make cycling a cheap, safe
and accessible sport for children:

*I wish there were more cycle ways, like abroad, like in Holland.
I wish the government would spend money on that sort of thing.
They want us to be greener, but don't help us. My husband takes
the children on the canal cycle path.* (Kathleen, Kirkside East)

Some parents were even more ambitious and wished they could run
a club themselves. This mother felt that youth activities needed to
combine local know-how and real talent in working with young people:

*It's got to be something that looks exciting to them to want to get
involved and something that, I don't know, you could start a youth
club or something. Sort of run by people who understand young
people.* (Annie, East Docks)

At the end of the day, the spaces and streets where people live need
to feel safer and look more welcoming. The ultimate solution to the
problem of 'letting off steam' had to be more family-friendly, child-
friendly neighbourhoods.

## Summary and conclusions

Playgrounds and parks, youth clubs, sports and leisure centres, organised
activities outside the home and free play in the open air are vital to
families in low-income areas. Yet many low-income parents cannot
access these things freely, nor can they allow their children the
independence to enjoy them. They fear crime, drugs, violence, bullying,
peer pressure and 'getting in with the wrong crowd'. Parents use parks
when the parks are local but many parents do not take their children
to parks when they are further afield. Parents see organised sport as a
constructive way of using children's energy and developing physical

and social skills, but they find cost and organisation big barriers, and most do not find enough being done in schools to encourage exercise.

Policy makers and educationalists have increasingly emphasised sport and physical activity as ways of improving health, behaviour and learning.[10] These ideas are filtering through to schools. The schools where sport was promoted generated positive attitudes among parents, as well as real enjoyment for children. Parents and their children benefited greatly. However, the surrounding environment was a big deterrent to sport, particularly the fear of trouble, even within established sports centres. At the same time, the parents' fear of their growing teenagers getting involved in drugs and crime made sport and organised activity attractive if they could afford it.

Many parents bemoaned the closure of youth clubs and the lack of adequate local provision for young people. More space, facilities and activities for children were their foremost priorities across all the areas. There was more provision in London, and more London parents used local parks, but the environment was more threatening and many facilities and activities were too expensive.

Traffic and unsafe environments were big deterrents to free play, in spite of parents knowing how important this was. They were upset to see building on spare land and even school playgrounds, local play spaces and areas of local parks, feeling that making money had overridden young people's needs.

The Olympic Bid provided a big boost to the profile of sport, and East End families particularly hoped it would create more access, more school activity and more enthusiasm. But they were not sure how much their families would benefit.[11] They complained bitterly about the closure of youth centres, as well as the poor quality and high cost of local sports facilities.

Some parents admitted that their own lack of enthusiasm, energy or capacity was part of the problem. Many of the things that would help related to social as well as physical conditions – such as help with childcare, lower costs for siblings, more free, after-school activities, safer streets and more local clubs. Weak parental supervision with children just 'roaming around' made it more difficult. Many parents simply wouldn't let their children out as a result.

Parents also worried about weight problems, and this fed on itself – the harder it is to play and use up energy, the greater the problem becomes. It is an accelerating problem particularly among low-income families.[12]

There were three popular sports where simple, direct action could help. First, swimming was universally popular, and is now free for children in most areas. This helps where there are local, well-run swimming pools. The radical policy supporting free swimming for all under-16s makes a very big difference in deprived urban areas and threats of cuts make very little sense as a real saving over time. Smaller, more local pools should stay open, rather than be replaced by big expensive leisure centres. Second, football was particularly good for boys, easy to organise, cheap and popular, as long as there were free pitches. But football pitches are being reduced in the East End and street football can be dangerous. Girls find it hard to join in. Meanwhile scrap land that allows casual play is fast vanishing. Open spaces including school playgrounds in deprived urban areas should be strictly protected, maintained and supervised, so they can be used fully, during and after school. Third, cycling is an activity many parents liked and wanted their children to do – but they generally found it too dangerous. This is the biggest tragedy of all. Cycling, if safe, would be the cheapest, most equalising and most accessible form of local transport since virtually all children want to do it and know how to do it. It is valuable socially, economically, and environmentally.

In the eyes of most parents, the lack of youth clubs and other children's facilities was a major cause of youth misbehaviour, disrespect and crime, yet breaking through the barriers to attracting young people to clubs, offering counter-attractions to computer games and television, holding young people's enthusiasm while controlling their behaviour was one of the most difficult challenges. For this reason, organised sport and well-supervised, accessible, attractive local parks and youth centres seemed to offer answers. At the same time there is no escaping the need to make streets more family-friendly places and to encourage far more use of already available spaces such as small parks, school playgrounds, local football pitches and so on. It seems a great injustice that without money to buy these privileged supports, parents in low-income areas could not give their children the chance they needed to develop – particularly in the light of the fanfare around the Olympics.

## Notes

[1] Sport England (2002) *Participation in sport in England: Sport and the family*, London: Sport England; Sport England (2002) *Participation in sport in England: Trends 1987-2002*, London: Sport England; Sport England (2005) *Understanding participation in sport: A systematic review*, London: Sport England.

[2] Department for Children, Schools and Families (DCSF) (2008) *Play strategy*, London: DCSF; Power, A. et al (2009) *Strategic review of health inequalities in England post-2010 (Marmot Review): Task Group 4: The built environment and health inequalities*, London: The Marmot Review.

[3] Department for Children, Schools and Families (DCSF) (2008) *Play strategy*, London: DCSF.

[4] Dyson, A. et al (2009) *Strategic review of health inequalities in England post-2010 (Marmot Review): Task Group 1: Childhood development, education and health inequalities*, London: The Marmot Review.

[5] Rogers, R. and Power, A. (2000) *Cities for a small country*, London: Faber & Faber; Gehl, J. (1996) *Life between buildings: Using public space*, Copenhagen: Arkitektens Forlag; Gehl, J. and Gemzøe, L. (2001) *New city spaces*, Copenhagen: Danish Architectural Press.

[6] Department for Education (DfE) (2002) National School Sports Strategy; DfE (2006) School Sports Survey.

[7] Sport England (2005) *Understanding participation in sport: A systematic review*, London: Sport England.

[8] www.leeds.gov.uk; www.newham.gov.uk; www.hackney.gov.uk; Sheffield City Council (2010) Cllr Jackie Drayton, Full Council Meeting, 3 March.

[9] Hugh Robertson (2010) Minister for Sports and the Olympics' announcement on 17 June 2010 that free swimming is to be scrapped.

[10] Department for Education (DfE) (2002) National School Sports Strategy; DfE (2006) School Sports Survey.

[11] Davidson, R. and Power, A. (2007) *Families and children's experience of sport and informal actiivity in Olympic areas of the East End*, London: LSE.

[12] Foresight (2007) *Tackling obesities: Future choices – Project report*, London: Department for Innovation, Universities and Skills; The Marmot Review (2010) *Fair society, healthy lives: Post-2010 strategic review of health inequalities*, London: The Marmot Review.

# FIVE

# Preventive policing, community safety and community confidence

*Growing up around here is a big problem for parents because of the crime rate and the drugs. I've seen 10-year-olds who know about drugs. I heard this boy saying to his friend, 'Your mum's a crack addict'.* (Linda, West City)

## Introduction: Crime and fear

Crime is a big worry for parents everywhere. Although the fear of crime far outstrips the level of actual crime, it is understandable, particularly in poorer neighbourhoods where crime and anti-social behaviour are far more common than in more average areas. For parents it is a particularly acute problem, and in the urban areas where the 200 families lived, crime is a dominant reason for parents not wanting to stay in the area or bring up their children there. This chapter sets out the crime problem as seen through parents' eyes, then explores what interventions made a difference and what the overall impact on crime and on families' security was of the measures that were introduced, particularly, neighbourhood wardens, community policing methods, Anti-social Behaviour Orders (ASBOs) and neighbourhood crime prevention.

The neighbourhoods where our families live were deeply stigmatised by their occasional bursts of violent crime. The two inner-city areas in East London and the North had become 'crime hot spots' while we were visiting families early in 2000, involving gun battles, murders and drug wars, but the two outer neighbourhoods also experienced serious crime, including drugs. The underlying problems were pervasive: frequent trouble with young people hanging out on the streets and in stairwells; abandoned cars; vandalised, poorly maintained environments; and a barely visible police force. A strong police presence followed extreme incidents but often crime seemed ingrained in these neighbourhoods because of its recurring nature; their poor reputations reflected this conspicuous and disturbing problem.[1] Often parents' anxiety was heightened by anti-social behaviour and smaller problems of disorder.

The new Labour government in 1997 set itself ambitious targets to reduce anti-social behaviour, increase street supervision and cut actual crime. New Labour had come to power with the slogan, 'Tough on crime, tough on the causes of crime'. Crucial to doing this was winning community confidence and persuading local residents, particularly families who have strong reasons for vigilance and constant 'eyes on the street', to help the police prevent, as well as detect, crime.

The families freely recounted their experiences of crime, their fears and their views of progress. How had government initiatives to reduce crime and fear worked? Had they increased people's sense of security and confidence in the neighbourhoods and in the police? What worked from their perspective and what made them feel better about bringing up their children in these areas? What still needed to be done? What role could parents play in community-based approaches to crime prevention? And what were their limits?

In Chapters Two and Four we looked at parents' fears for their children's safety as a barrier to outdoor play, particularly in sport, and the pressures young people were under when they wanted to join in youth activities. The lack of a sense of control over conditions undermined parents' confidence in their ability to sort out bigger problems. It deterred them from using what spaces were available for play and turned public spaces into magnets for anti-social behaviour, drug abuse and crime. A sense of foreboding drove parents to follow their protective instincts and hold their children back from their surroundings, which then became a hostile environment in which to bring up children. Their fears became more explicit, more directly linked to local incidents and to local policing. Parents, fearful for their children, made tackling crime one of their highest priorities.

## General crime and safety in the neighbourhoods

We did not directly broach crime when we first visited, yet as the families talked about their neighbourhoods, they highlighted their worries about crime and safety as strong drivers of neighbourhood dissatisfaction. Figure 5.1 shows that a large majority of parents found crime a problem.

Nearly half of the London parents (47 per cent) said they were dissatisfied with their neighbourhood as a place to bring up children and a third felt this way in the North. All the areas we visited had crime rates significantly above the national average and it is not surprising that four fifths of parents found crime a serious problem in all the areas.[2]

The problems were more intense in London, but the North was also seriously affected. A London mother explains her fears:

> *A child was stabbed and killed. My son's 14, so when he goes out, I tell him not to get involved in fights because I don't want him to get stabbed. It's scary.* (Naomi, East Docks)

**Figure 5.1:** Parents who felt that crime was a problem in their neighbourhood, 2001–02

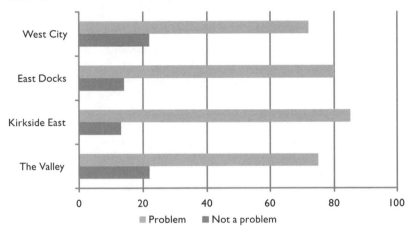

Parents' worries about bringing up children in these high crime neighbourhoods were strongly linked to the pervasive problem of drug use, drug dealing and related gang activity. In The Valley virtually every parent made this connection. Overall, two thirds of parents said drugs were a serious problem. Faye from East Docks put it this way:

> *Round here they have lots of crack houses. Drugs is a serious issue. I don't want it to be in my children's faces so they think it's the norm.* (Faye, East Docks)

Figures 5.2(a) and 5.2(b) show the steady fall in general levels of crime in all the areas coupled with a steep rise in drug-related crime in the two East London areas. However, drug crime only formed a very small proportion of all crime, even though it often dominated parental fears, reflecting its steep rise. While Figures 5.2(a) and 5.2(b) give the detailed figures for the four local authorities, Annex 9 (available online at www. policypress.co.uk) shows more detailed figures on crime trends in the local authorities.

**Figure 5.2(a):** Total offences and drug offences (per 1,000 population), 2002–09

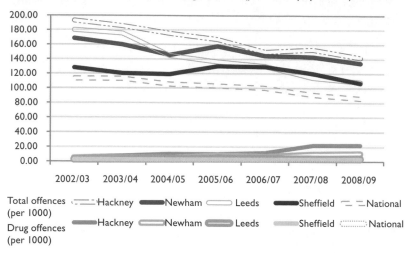

Total offences ⌐￣￣Hackney ━━Newham ◯ Leeds ━━Sheffield ￣ ￣National
(per 1000)
Drug offences ━━Hackney ◯━━Newham ◯━━Leeds ◯━━Sheffield ⌐┈┈National
(per 1000)

*Source:* http://rds.homeoffice.gov.uk/rds/soti.html

**Figure 5.2(b):** Drug offences (per 1,000 population), 2002–09

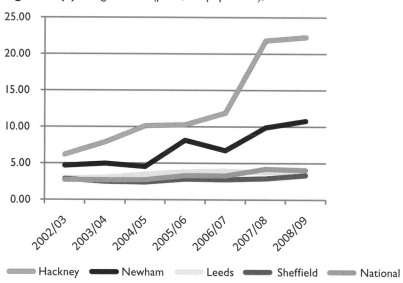

━━Hackney ━━Newham ━━Leeds ━━Sheffield ━━National

*Source:* http://rds.homeoffice.gov.uk/rds/soti.html

Figure 5.3 shows that by 2010 although all the neighbourhoods had above-average crime, the two inner neighbourhoods had less crime than their surrounding local authorities, while the two outer neighbourhoods were still well above the local level.

**Figure 5.3:** Total crime rate (average number of crimes per 1,000 people per month), 2010

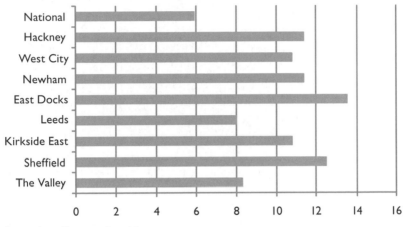

*Source:* http://maps.police.uk/

Parents saw many different types of crime as problems in their neighbourhood, ranging from car damage, vandalism, theft, burglary and muggings to gangs, drug-related crimes and violence. In Kirkside East, half the parents knew about or witnessed car stealing, joy riding and car burning. In both The Valley and Kirkside East, house and garden shed burglaries were common, and everywhere parents knew directly about incidents locally. A majority of London parents thought that crime was so pervasive that more minor crimes were somehow linked to other more serious violent crimes. This mother with four children and several foster children lived in constant fear because of the continuous reports about crime:

> *Crime, you're always hearing about people being broken into. I'm scared.* (Ellie, West City)

At the same time, a large majority of parents in all areas, 85 per cent, felt safe walking around on their own during the day. This fell to 73 per cent in East Docks which had a much more 'threatening' atmosphere because of the dual carriageway that cut most of the area off, and the blighting of large parts of the area through the pending demolition of some blocks of housing. Considerably fewer parents felt safe going out at night, and the same applied to many young people:

> *My son worries about gangs so he doesn't go out.* (Alice, Kirkside East)

Around one in five parents in all areas explained that they rarely left their home, especially alone, after dark: 20 per cent in Kirkside East, 28 per cent in The Valley, 16 per cent in West City and 21 per cent in East Docks. Most parents were afraid in the dark but in winter at least had no choice, especially if they worked. This reflected an instinctive response to darkness itself; it also partly reflected the division of activities between day and night, day being more outward turning and sociable, night time being more inward turning, and more home-bound. There is less street activity at night and therefore streets feel more threatening. Fear of going out alone in the dark was much stronger in Kirkside East, the large Northern council estate, than the other areas. There the general fear of crime was lower and most parents had relatives in the area. But the withdrawal from the streets at night left space for unsavoury activities to emerge. The council's re-housing policy of putting especially difficult cases in unpopular estates fuelled this problem. There were some long-run and deeply entrenched social problems connected with a few of the extended families that lived there. The high concentrations of lone-parent families, invariably headed by mothers, also made the community feel more vulnerable because there were fewer stable male partners around to offer support. Becky, a lone parent from the Northern estate, described this feeling vividly:

> *When you walk through the estate at night, you can feel friction between people, someone calling someone else. I have to try not to let it bother me but I fear for my safety.... I wouldn't get involved.* (Becky, Kirkside East)

## Families witness crime

Around a third of the families we spoke to on our second visit had experienced crime directly in the previous year. Parents worried about the sense that the streets could be taken over, particularly by 'guns and gangs', so they felt strongly about more supervision. But on our fifth visit, when we asked parents about whether they reported crimes they experienced, about one third of those who directly experienced crime said they failed to report the incident.

Parents in one inner London neighbourhood, West City, reported a big drop in their direct experience of crime between our second and fifth visits, while parents in the other areas reported a small increase in their own experience of crime between these visits. We asked again about crime in the areas on our last visit. Parents' views on crime showed that in their eyes crime levels were no longer rising, but were still high. The large drop of 16 per cent among parents in West City stood out against the overall pattern and was explained by intensive policing to tackle gun crime, which had much wider impacts on general conditions, as we show below.

One parent described the violence her sons encountered on the street in her Northern estate shortly after they moved in:

> *The first time Johnny went out, he got battered and couldn't see him protecting himself in a fight. Violence frightens him.* (Becky, Kirkside East)

Mothers who grew up in these areas felt that the atmosphere had changed a lot from a friendly, 'community' feel when they were younger to something much more threatening. The problem of drugs and its visibility on the streets was a big influence on parents' attitudes and fears:

> *My mum's road used to be beautiful, she's got people living there now, new men continually coming in and out and all women live there – it's a brothel. The woman that lived next door, she's only 24, she's got in with the wrong crowd. She used to be quiet as a mouse but now it's music all the time. She's got into drugs.... In the last four years it's got bad. People are on crack, there was a crack house on the local street near the supermarket. They used to have the door open – you look everywhere – you see someone I used to be at school with and they're on drugs.* (Kerry, East Docks)

One East London mother gave a vivid account of what happened to her daughter, age 11, stopping her from going out:

> *The crime, big crime risks. My daughter was mugged when she was 11, at the end of the road, for her phone, she'd just got it. She won't carry one now. It was two young women with a baby in a buggy and they hid her phone in the buggy 'cos I actually was there, I was going up to meet my daughter. She used to phone me to say 'I'm on my way'. I would walk up to meet her when it was dark, as she was only 11. As I got there she was screaming, she'd just*

> *been mugged, and I saw the girls and I knew they had the phone and they'd stuffed it in the baby's coat or nappy or whatever, and of course, if you're a mother yourself you're not going to pick up a baby and shake it to find the phone. They just ran away. The two young women were probably 17 or 18. They'd followed her off the bus, they'd targeted her. She doesn't want to talk about it even now.* (Kathleen, West City)

## "Obviously buying and selling drugs"

In open areas, drug dealing often happened in front of children, who quickly got to understand what they saw happening:

> *Cars slow down, a hand goes from one window into another. They're not affecting us but they're obviously buying and selling drugs. My kids know what's going on – maybe because it's a cul-de-sac.* (Leah, West City)

Drug dealing had many negative consequences in the area, which parents linked directly with crime. Sola, in West City, had a very bad time with her son who was excluded from secondary school at the age of 11 and developed such a serious drug addiction in his teens that he even stole from his mother:

> *I had a drug problem with him and his friends.... After he was expelled he was outside a lot. He had a lot of freedom which he shouldn't've had ... because he draws a certain kind of friend ... he's stopped a lot by the police in his car.... My son's friend wanted to kill him. Nothing came of it. There's nothing to keep them out of trouble – there's a lot of suicide, drugs, crime.* (Sola, West City)

Another West City parent felt that the police were constantly eluded by the drug dealers in spite of their efforts to protect children:

> *More drugs, it's more open dealing. People hanging about. I'm sure someone's dealing drugs in the block. I've seen a lot of police on push bikes and wardens in the last three to four months. They're a waste of time because they're in the wrong place at the wrong time, like they're in the schools at 3.30pm.* (Tina, West City)

Yet another West City mother said:

> *It's getting better, but the drug addicts are still the same ... they're always asking you for money. Five friends died in a car crash in 1991 and since then its spiralled, them all getting into drugs. After the funeral my brother started taking. He died last year.* (Sophie, West City)

In fact, during our visits, drug offences, unlike other recorded crime, became more serious, particularly in London.[3]

Not all parents were as disparaging about efforts to tackle the all-pervasive problem of crime, drugs and the fear they generated. In London, by our fifth visit, over three quarters of parents in West City and two thirds in East Docks saw beat police regularly in the areas and a third thought they made a significant difference. Policing was much less visible in the Northern areas.

## Neighbourhood wardens

Over the course of our visits many crime reduction initiatives were introduced with the goal of tackling crime itself and at the same time making places feel safer. As a result of these initiatives parents' views of crime and its prevention changed, although the range of different views was very striking, as we show below. Many parents talked openly about their fear of crime and their personal experiences of it, so they were keen to say what they thought about recent government initiatives to tackle crime. These initiatives included neighbourhood wardens who were introduced as part of the government's national strategy for neighbourhood renewal in 2000, a little before the introduction of Police Community Support Officers (PCSOs).[4]

The philosophy behind neighbourhood wardens was that active supervision of the streets and open spaces would generate confidence while directly improving conditions. They would reintroduce some of the roles caretakers had traditionally played in flatted council estates, supervision, contact with residents, reporting problems and carrying out minor remedial work, including removing rubbish and graffiti, fixing lights and locks. Above all they patrolled streets and estates of houses as well as flats, acting as a continuous, uniformed, recognised presence, visible in the areas they were responsible for, and overseeing local conditions. They could trigger targeted actions to solve local problems quickly before they got out of hand. They could only do this successfully if they befriended local families, young people and children, while maintaining authority. They generally helped build confidence in parents. One London mother saw it this way:

> *The wardens are a start. There are children hanging around and setting cars on fire in groups. But with the wardens it's better.* (Delilah, West City)

The central function of neighbourhood wardens is to provide eyes and ears on the ground, reporting problems and if possible dealing with them directly, looking and listening out for signs of trouble in the neighbourhoods, picking up these signals, liaising with and building up contact with community residents and in particular, young people. Wardens referred problems on to the services responsible for tackling them, but sometimes they contained problems locally through swift action. Local rapport with residents, particularly children and young people, was helpful in tackling and preventing trouble:

> *A friend is a community neighbourhood warden actually. If they see kids messing about, graffiti, et cetera, they deal with it. They are good, they are.* (Rachel, The Valley)

The neighbourhood wardens were in place in all four neighbourhoods by 2003. However, wardens often had too little visibility and patrolled too infrequently. Therefore their role was often unrecognised, which in many ways defeated the main purpose. Apart from West City a majority of parents did not realise that their neighbourhood had neighbourhood wardens – two thirds in Kirkside East and East Docks, and nearly nine out of ten in The Valley. However, where the parents did know about the local wardens, they believed their presence helped, at least to some extent. Their awareness of the work of wardens grew over time. Some parents praised neighbourhood wardens for their approachability, thinking that local people might favour them over normal policing:

> *I've seen neighbourhood wardens, no extra police though. I think they make a difference as people feel their presence and can approach them. Some may do so more readily than the police.* (Liz, The Valley)

## "Absolutely brilliant"

One or two parents praised their work in the neighbourhood with children:

> *The neighbourhood wardens go into schools and talk to kids too. They wear purple jackets and say to children to look out for*

> *'Ribena Berries'. They may introduce a Junior Wardens scheme to teach kids about being a neighbourhood warden. They can go out with them and understand the problems and causes. It may happen. Neighbourhood wardens are 'dirt busters'. You report to them, for example, needles, and they get 'Streetforce' to come and clean it up. It is part of the council's cleaning service, known as the 'Neat Team'.* (Maya, The Valley)

A West City parent talked about the impact that neighbourhood wardens had in preventing children from 'hanging out' in places where they could get into trouble:

> *… But the other good thing now is the wardens, coming around the estates now, which is absolutely brilliant. Because we don't see the groups of children that used to be on the stairs anymore.* (Niamh, West City)

Another West City parent explained how the introduction of wardens helped her family decide not to move, although she still worried about crime. But she felt this was being combated:

> *They've improved the local environment a lot, they have wardens now. With graffiti and vandalism it's got much better. The area looks cleaner and the rubbish has got better. Crime had got worse – I've seen a lot round here. I see more police around the shops, that's where all the trouble is.* (Cynthia, West City)

Parents underlined the limitations of the new initiatives. Confusion often arose not only over their powers but also over their actual role, compared with PCSOs:

> *I see wardens walking about but I don't know what they're supposed to do, what they can do. I can distinguish the uniform but I don't know if you make complaints to them or go to different people for different complaints. Once I was going to park in an area and I came across a warden and I asked 'Can I park here?' He said 'I don't have a clue', so he wasn't very helpful. If they were improving the area, pieces of my car wouldn't be broken off every few weeks….* (Hulya, West City)

Neighbourhood wardens brought intangible benefits through their familiarity with neighbourhood problems. Parents explained how responsive they could be to local needs, praising them for their caring attitude and the key role they played in preventing trouble:

> *I think they make a difference because they cycle about in summer, people know who they are, they chat to them in the street, they are a link really, aren't they? And less of a threat than if a policeman is on the beat.* (Becky, Kirkside East)

> *...the street wardens are really good. They escort the elderly around and they're around the school.* (Alice, West City)

One mother had extremely negative views about neighbourhood wardens:

> *The neighbourhood wardens hide in my work place and pick on people. They nicked someone at my work for parking on white lines, a jobsworth. They haven't made the neighbourhood safer because they're not here anymore, they've been scared away.* (Tina, West City)

A big limitation on wardens was their inability to intervene in more difficult situations. They were more an arm of neighbourhood management than a crime prevention measure, even though the two roles overlapped. Neighbourhood wardens, although useful in many ways, did not seem to make a big enough impression to overcome the more fundamental problems of crime in the areas. Wardens were responsible for general neighbourhood conditions while community policing targeted crime prevention, even though both approaches had a clear community liaison and crime prevention remit.[5]

## Police Community Support Officers

The more easily recognisable Police Community Support Officers (PCSOs) played a much higher profile role than wardens had been able to do in the neighbourhoods by virtue of the fact that they were a recognised part of the police force and that they also patrolled the streets.

PCSOs, introduced nationally in 2002, represented a shift towards closer supervision of neighbourhoods among local police forces, reflecting a desire to operate directly within communities rather than intervening from outside or carrying general responsibilities without regular beats. The police, in the face of public worries and strident press publicity over rising violence on the streets, recognised the need for more security and more visible patrolling, to offer a stronger front-line presence within communities.[6] Police officers and crime prevention bodies realised, very slowly, that local patrols needed to be highly visible, concentrated, consistent and frequent if they were to work.

PCSOs provide a new and different kind of local police presence, in some ways akin to neighbourhood wardens but with a clear preventive policing role. They have limited powers compared with fully fledged police officers, and they rely on their contact with local community networks to stay 'tuned in' to local problems. Their role includes intelligence gathering, crime detection and responding to immediate local community problems that have the potential to escalate. Because of their direct role in the police force itself, restricted though their direct powers are, they can generate a faster response to calls for help. By our later visits, all four neighbourhoods had PCSOs, although different police forces gave them somewhat varying roles. In West City PCSOs patrolled and handled all non-urgent police response work, with each officer covering a small dedicated beat. In East Docks the PCSOs were based in a local office. In The Valley and Kirkside East, the PCSOs also had a 'beat management' role. Parents' views on this new approach were far from uniform, and evolved over time.

## "Someone's out there"

Parents became quickly aware of the new and reassuring role of PCSOs, who were introduced to back up and reinforce mainstream policing. They informed, and patrolled the streets to help prevent trouble, report incidents and call for help:

> *You do realise that the gun crime and the gangs and all that, there just seems to be more and more in London. Really and truthfully, just to know that them people [PCSOs] are plodding around, maybe no one would take much notice of 'em, especially young children or teenagers, but just the fact that they're there on their radio and if someone was destroying something, they might be concerned – even if they just radio'd it through and someone else was aware. It does give a little bit of a, not exactly protective, but someone's out there.* (Marilyn, West City)

West City stood out from the other neighbourhoods, not only in the active role of wardens, which was more visible there, but also in its strong PCSO structure. Over one third of the parents in this neighbourhood felt that PCSOs made a big difference to their neighbourhood, while only a quarter felt the same in the other London neighbourhood, East Docks. About one in ten parents felt the PCSOs and wardens made a significant difference in the Northern neighbourhoods. Indeed, in the Northern neighbourhoods, the majority of parents could not see the difference that local PCSOs were making in their neighbourhoods.

Overall, by our fifth visit, West City parents said they were benefiting from both local community policing and warden initiatives. In the other three areas parents felt that they were having only limited visible impact on the neighbourhoods, partly because they were spread too thinly. West City was a high priority for crime reduction because of several violent crimes and had therefore got better cover.

## *"Keeping a lid on"*

A mother in East Docks explained the advantages of PCSOs in playing a preventive role that would be harder for standard policing methods to achieve. But she still worried that criminals found their way round the protection they offered:

> *Having a high presence of community police officers around does make a difference in terms of people being more cautious.... If you have police officers outside all of the time, it might keep a lid on, but I think you move it on to somewhere else, and you also don't address the underlying issue.... It's almost like the analogy of putting a sticky plaster on something and not actually dealing with what the problem is. So I think, yes, ... they build relationships in the community and people like to see them around. But I'm still not sure they're dealing with the underlying issues or the problems.* (Andrea, East Docks)

Another mother explained the positive way they approached the community:

> *We do have two community police, see them on foot. You can talk to them. They are nice.* (Bess, Kirkside East)

Many parents saw the presence of PCSOs in their neighbourhoods as helping relationships and therefore community well-being. Their involvement with local children and young people and their generally approachable manner were particular sources of praise:

> *The community police are really nice, because they don't go in all guns blazing. They talk to kids, treat them with humanity.* (Amanda, Kirkside East)

The following story illustrates how they could help break the grip of peer pressure. PCSOs had the flexibility to react quickly to what was happening and take unusually responsive action:

> *It's funny actually, 'cos I was going to the shops a couple of weeks ago and these two community police officers were talking to this boy but they knew him by his name. His friend was like 'Ah, you mug, how can you let 'em know your name'. And I just thought, 'look, these children, they were so young as well', and I thought 'look, these police'll become familiar at least, and they know their names', d'you know what I mean. So they must be like little tearaways for them to be recognised. And his friend was like, laughing at him, and they said to him 'Why you not at school?' He said, 'I'm going there now'. They said, 'Okay, get in the car, we'll drop you off'.* (Flowella, East Docks)

Other parents praised how they controlled behaviour:

> *[The] Community police walk about and stop and check kids hanging about, so they help.* (Tracy, Kirkside East)

They often played a positive role in restraining children's behaviour, working closely with local residents and schools:

> *We have, at the moment, lots of community support police on patrol, which I think has made a difference. Children know that they're walking round. They don't tend to hang around corners so much. I think they're a bit more involved with schools now, the police. When we've had problems or we're not happy with what the children have done, they will come in and talk to them, to that particular child. If we had a problem with a student, they will actually come in. We've got good links with the police, actually, we have good links now.* (Barbara, East Docks)

As a result of more direct links with the local schools, local children developed more positive attitudes towards authority, and police–community relations improved as a result. Parents praised the way they won trust by adopting a gentler, more understanding and accessible approach:

> *We have community support officers in the schools. That's brilliant, they walk around the school. It stops truanting. Yes. They're a good influence on the children; fighting's a lot lower, and weapons and that. The children feel safe that they're there, it's stopped bullying altogether. They've been in our school for a while but there will be one in our school full time soon.* (Sonia, East Docks)

One of the London mothers mentioned the value of street patrols and how they helped reduce crime:

> *I don't know, when we spoke last time, if I brought up the security, how they patrol around the area now … that has changed. Maybe it's because my car is too old or something! But you hardly see crime.* (Andaiye, West City)

The PCSOs appeared to be taking crucial steps to break down barriers and reduce tensions in communities. This parent was extremely positive about their approach and their accessibility, but she realised they were up against many negative attitudes towards the police:

> *We've got the community police coming in now. They come to the parents evening and they even come to the Fete, to try and get their faces known. Because one of the community police ladies, she said, 'They hate us', which is not very good, you know. So they are trying very hard to make things a little bit more friendly, which would be good. You know, a bit more trust. Strike up a relationship there that they could work on, perhaps, improve the area.* (Peggy, East Docks)

By far the biggest gain from community policing was the reassurance parents felt as they saw a stronger and more consistent police presence on the streets. This mother liked the fact that PCSOs 'belonged' within the community and referred to them as 'dedicated community people':

> *… you see the PCSOs all the time, you see them in the shopping centres, you see them in stations, you see them on the streets. So, it helps, you have to feel somehow safer. So it's dedicated community people wanting to help to reduce crime, so that's a positive thing as well.* (Oni, East Docks)

Another mother in West City described a similar reassuring impact:

> *Big improvement in the number of community police in the last*
> *a year. They walk in twos, they go up and down. Yes, there's a big*
> *increase in the number of those. I don't know about the rest of the*
> *community but I think it looks good to me, just to look out the*
> *window and see them going up and down there. I don't know how*
> *much power they have or what they can do. But I think it's good*
> *to see them in uniform anyways, going up and down the road. It's*
> *definitely been a big change that way. I honestly never saw one*
> *five years ago when you started this survey – I never saw them.*
> (Sinead, West City)

PCSOs in the East End even used the local churches to break down barriers with minority ethnic residents. The mother who related that experiment was herself black and was amazed by the positive reaction the police received in church:

> *I was at a church service last week, and they actually had a slot*
> *for the police who came and spoke to us, and the woman there,*
> *the police officer said that the fear of crime has gone down because*
> *they're on the beat, and they're there to remind people that if we*
> *don't approach them and tell them what's going on, they won't*
> *know –' we're the eyes' – it was a sort of 'promo' thing but it*
> *was actually trying to communicate that we actually all have to*
> *recognise that we're all in partnership. And I think that was quite*
> *enlightening. It was quite clever to do it in a black church as well,*
> *because there has been hostility I think, with most of the police being*
> *white, and most of the people being stopped being black. That was*
> *well supported by the church leaders, challenging the young people*
> *in the congregation to be a police officer. It actually caused a huge*
> *outburst of laughter, and then clapping – it was positive but it was*
> *actually such a shock to hear the leaders of the church suggesting*
> *it, which was quite an eye opener really.* (Erin, East Docks)

### *"Taking it into their own hands"*

One of the problems the police were up against in traditional high crime areas was the idea of 'self-help' policing. With a pervasive atmosphere of violence, at least some sections of the community had more faith in taking the law into their own hands than in the law itself.

Citizens simply took their own action when they saw too big a wrong. Obviously the police wanted to avoid this:

> *People round here, if they was robbed and they was aware of the people that robbed them, rather than phoning the police, they'd take the law into their own hands and do something – use violence themselves.* (Flowella, East Docks)

The East End 'self-help' policing was mirrored in the North, where a young mother praised her partner for leaping to the defence of a friend:

> *A friend got punched so Sam went up and grabbed the biggest lad. Then they came down with stones, throwing them at the window. So Sam went out with a baseball bat. There's been nothing since that…. If anything happens, you best sort it out yourself.* (Olivia, Kirkside East)

## Difficult tensions between community policing and law enforcement

The police trod a thin line between trying to win the confidence of the community so that they could police, and enforcing the law when it was transgressed. It was very hard for the police to be both friendly and detached, to forge closer community links and to use the full force of the law when it was necessary. They risked the alienation and mistrust of teenagers whom they had befriended when they had to take police action, and people did not automatically trust the police when they did take action:

> *I think it probably aggravated the people in the area. The teenagers, I'd say, it aggravated more 'cos I think they pull people innocently. I heard some complaints last year.* (Julie, East Docks)

Several families had direct experience of police action against their children, which was always upsetting even when it was justified, and some parents saw this. Jane knew that her sons were involved in crime and that the one already in prison had done something really serious:

> *My son's just got eight years and his brother's on the run. He'll stay on the run 'til he gets caught because he's facing a long sentence.* (Jane, The Valley)

Jane tried to help her runaway son, even though she dreaded her younger children "ending up like their brothers, into crime". Jane had lived in a semi-derelict block due for demolition which was at the very centre of shooting incidents. She seemed so hardened to crime and violence that she almost accepted the fact that things were deteriorating around her:

> *It's worse. The shootings don't bother me at night. If it started happening during the day, it would be more of a problem.* (Jane, The Valley)

Policing troubled areas was an ongoing, year in, year out task, and any gains had to be sustained through a long-term area-based policing system. Several parents thought that the positive gains of having PCSOs would be quickly undermined by a new generation of gangs growing up and following in the footsteps of the previous generation of youthful troublemakers, thereby replicating the same social and community problems in high crime areas. A long-standing resident in the large Northern estate had seen this pattern over and over again:

> *I think it has got better, especially since the community police turn up more, and the ordinary police a bit. And because the kids have grown up and gone to school and work and stuff, and the group of youngsters have therefore grown up. Now you see the next lot coming up. In five or six years they will be 13 or 14 and hanging out on corners and that is the problem.* (Peter, Kirkside East)

The same happened in East London, with waves of trouble sweeping through successive groups of teenagers:

> *We've got this pack. It isn't the same boys that used to sit round the other end. They've grown up now, so we've got a new pack.* (Cynthia, West City)

A big advantage in the way PCSOs work is the reinforcement that they could call on, what were sometimes referred to as the 'real' police:

> *In local areas, that's all the police you see, the CSOs [community support officers]. But when there's something wrong, the real police come zooming in. It does make you feel safer. In the local area where I work, the teenagers hang around and it feels a bit scary. It makes the area feel safer.* (Carmen, East Docks)

> *The more there are, the better.* (Carmen's husband, East Docks)

On the other hand, the recurring problem of engaging with young people in the community and becoming too familiar with particular groups in an attempt to foster good relations sometimes reduced the authority of the police. This mixed-race mother talked about how difficult it was for the police to handle relations with black teenagers and strike the right balance:

> *There's been loads of CSOs. But what bugs me is – we've got the Balance Boys, young black boys, 13 to 14 years old but they look like grown men – the CSOs just joke and laugh at 'em. I s'pose they have to – they moved the crowds on. It did work but now it's stopped working because they only had a certain amount of time they could do it in. They could only do it for a short time. The elderly people, they're frightened to go out.* (Zoe, West City)

Gatherings of young people on street corners, at housing entrances and around the shops, were often looking for amusement, but simultaneously striking fear in the community through their size, their exuberance and noise, their seeming lack of purpose or sense of direction, their alienation from school and learning, their bad language and aggressive manner. The lack of purposeful, easily available activity for young people, discussed in Chapter Four, spilled over constantly into crime.

## The limits of local anti-crime initiatives: "We need more visible proper police"

Wardens and PCSOs only have restricted powers to enforce and they rely on higher authority to back them in tackling problems. PCSOs have even been nicknamed 'plastic police' by some not fully enamoured of the initiative.[7] Several parents were worried that PCSOs and wardens might replace proper policing:

> *The one big problem is the drugs, but the police don't do anything about it. We have wardens who think they can do anything but they can't. The only thing that's good is they walk through the estates. We need more visible, proper police. These 'help policemen', they help but they don't take the place of real policeman.* (Trudy, West City)

Another parent believed that they were only effective with younger children:

> *They've got no power. They're only a deterrent for a certain age group.* (Rosemary, West City)

> *Where there's any aggro they're never around.* (Rosemary's husband, West City)

Some mothers wanted much more security, as they worried that community police support might not be enough to tackle violent crime:

> *I've seen wardens walking up the main road but not round here, where somebody was killed. Who's going to do anything on the main road? Since the taxi driver was killed, I've seen a couple of police – that's it. They should have CCTV behind the house because it's only garages. People deal drugs there.* (Hannah, East Docks)

## "The kids know their limited powers"

Another parent thought the fact that they weren't 'proper police' undermined their authority:

> *The PCSOs get belittled because they know they've not got as much power as the old bill. They clock off at night times when you need 'em, when there's lots of drugs on the street.* (Alexa, East Docks)

There was a inevitable conflict between community police powers being too limited to enforce on young people and their more continuous supervisory presence helping the streets feel safer:

> *PCSOs – I know a lot of youngsters know. They don't see them as having power so they don't look up to them – they're aware of their rights and they use it to their advantage. It doesn't matter if they're on the street or not. Some people could argue that it's a waste of resources. But for those vulnerable people that feel intimidated, they feel more secure, so there's pros and cons.* (Erin, East Docks)

Another mother expressed a similar worry:

> *It is mainly community police. They probably have helped to reduce crime but the only thing is, like, the kids know their limited powers basically. So, in terms of the teenagers or whatever, I don't think they're that effective because the kids, they do know their limited powers. But sort of their presence round the street is not a bad thing anyway.* (Barbara, East Docks)

Another mother felt that the presence of PCSOs prevented crime just by their presence, but did not reduce the need for 'proper' policing:

> *Where I work, there's fights, stabbings everyday, but you can't get in at groups of 16- to 18-year-olds. I'm unsure how much they can actually do and they get paid an awful lot of money for it. They're probably going to report what's going on but nothing's going to go on in front of a fluorescent jacket, telling 10-year-olds to move along. They're a positive thing to have around but there's a limit. They're just replacing what the police should do.* (Rosemary, West City)

Another London parent pointed out the valuable role they could play as ground-level informants for the police, even though they played a limited role in combating crime:

> *At the back of me, there's a gang doing things at the back – I haven't seen that for about three years. I don't know if the PCSOs help to reduce crime as they're not as powerful as real police. But the PCSOs help to inform the proper police of anything happening, so there's less sirens around.* (Shushan, West City)

## "They're just jobsworths"

Preventing crime, whether by community police or wardens, was a fairly unpredictable business, and it was easy to misjudge reactions. The display of limited authority in non-threatening situations could alienate some parents, and some expressed their frustration over the focus on minor offences when serious crime pervaded their neighbourhoods.

This mother also felt they could 'pick on' people who weren't causing problems for minor transgressions:

> *I've had a few run-ins with the community police. They keep pulling me over. My son's strapped in the back but they were shouting at me because I didn't have a booster seat. They're just 'jobsworths'. I've paid my road tax, I've passed my MOT, he's strapped in and*

> *they still stopped me. Why are they talking to me rather than*
> *stopping crimes?* (Kerry, East Docks)

Occasionally parents contrasted the neighbourhood wardens with the PCSOs. Several parents felt that PCSOs were more useful than neighbourhood wardens, precisely because the PCSOs had a direct policing role, albeit a low level one that, in the eyes of some parents, was still inadequate:

> *When the community police are walking around here, it's just nice*
> *to see, it's that reassurance that they're there. The wardens, not really.*
> *When the wardens come round it's normally in the afternoon about*
> *12, 1 o'clock and there's never really nobody much round here. The*
> *community police are more often here quicker.* (Faye, West City)

Other parents agreed that wardens did not have as strong a presence as PCSOs:

> *No, I don't think so, I really don't, 'cos you don't hardly see*
> *'em really [wardens]. I think they're quite lazy actually. We see*
> *community police officers from time to time, more than you do*
> *normal policemen. Which I think, you know, s'pose it's a good thing.*
> *I think they can help to reduce crime yeah, because they're more on*
> *the scene than what the normal police are.* (Kerry, East Docks)

The presence of PCSOs greatly expanded the visible supervision of the areas, but there were major limitations on what they could achieve. In these high crime areas community policing helped to build confidence within the local population, but the initiative wasn't a substitute for full police provision, and parents clearly felt this.

## Neighbourhood Watch

We asked about other local crime reduction measures on our fifth visit, particularly Neighbourhood Watch schemes and other local community crime prevention groups. The majority of parents in all four of the neighbourhoods had not heard about a Neighbourhood Watch scheme in their area, and over three quarters of the parents believed there were no local community groups tackling crime in their area. Most parents did not know about any local anti-crime initiatives – over 80 per cent of parents in the two Northern areas and in London nearly 70 per cent. Those parents who knew about Neighbourhood Watch did not generally have very positive views, believing that visible policing made much more of a difference to their neighbourhood. West City was the exception, with more parents thinking it helped than not. In London, parents were more positive about what could be achieved by local groups tackling crime, and the response was particularly positive in West City, where community involvement had been crucial to big reductions in violent crime. The proactive policing approach of West City, including many officers on the beat, PCSOs, wardens and a lot of community involvement, definitely paid off among families, giving them greater confidence, more cooperative relations and reduced crime.

Some mothers in Kirkside East were part of an informal Neighbourhood Watch organisation, organised by parents with the police. One mother couldn't do much herself but she acted as a link for the organisers who tried to detect and report local crimes that would otherwise go unchallenged. This parent could not actually be part of the Neighbourhood Watch 'phone tree', due to her work commitments, but she attended the meetings in the planning stages. Seeing other local people's involvement in Neighbourhood Watch made her feel that her neighbourhood was improving:

> *Quieter, got Neighbourhood Watch now: because there are a lot of unemployed people at home and at home mums and also OAPs, who do it. We said 'no' because we work. We have a phone tree with a map, so we can track anyone suspicious, We had a lot of meetings with the police and counsellors to sort it out. It has deterred people, so we notice the few.* (Chloe, Kirkside East)

Preventing and directly tackling crime were often great motivators for community involvement.[8] Other parents described what triggered their involvement in Neighbourhood Watch. A series of extreme incidents led to this mother from West City getting involved:

> *Only last week, I went to a Neighbourhood Watch meeting, as eight women and children have been held at knifepoint in the area. They issued us with personal alarms.* (Destiny, West City)

Another West City mother explained how glad she was that Neighbourhood Watch kept her in touch with her local 'beat bobby':

> *We have a Neighbourhood Watch for this area and I'm a coordinator and I have been for years. So I know our beat officer*

> *but I would say probably most people might not know him.*
> (Kathleen, West City)

Parents who got involved in crime prevention were definitely more positive about policing, but combating crime and winning the confidence of families needed to be part of a much bigger effort to strengthen communities.

## The families' views on Anti-social Behaviour Orders: *"People need support, not a label"*

Anti-social behaviour has become a big concern in communities, on high streets, in shopping centres, pubs and other social gathering places. The problem is particularly stark in disadvantaged areas.[9] In an attempt to curb this pervasive problem of rough, noisy, disruptive and threatening behaviour that affects many people and undermines their sense of security, the government introduced Anti-social Behaviour Orders, or ASBOs as most people know them, giving the police local powers to make special control orders that restrict the behaviour of the person causing nuisance. If the conditions of the Order were broken, then the police could take stronger action. Very few parents saw ASBOs as helping neighbourhood crime reduction in spite of their high profile, because they were almost exclusively placed on children and therefore did not tackle crime directly.

Parents who spoke positively about ASBOs favoured such an approach which had to reach the parents of children who got into trouble as well as the children themselves. Many of the parents blamed other parents for losing control of their children who then went on to cause anti-social behaviour problems. Clearly it sometimes made a big impression on the parents:

> *It is the ASBOs that have made the difference, the parents getting into trouble because of the kids. It works.* (Nita, The Valley)

An East London parent had seen its powerful impact directly, in this case linked to a threat of losing the tenancy of their home:

> *They're good, them anti-social behaviour things. They evict families now. 'Cos usually you go and knock on someone's door and they're like, 'What do you want me to do with them'. They don't care about the kids, once they're out the door, they don't care what they get up to as long as they don't come home again 'til 10 at night.*

> *But now they've brought that thing out, they're going up to parents saying, 'If your kid misbehaves one more time, you're out'. And it's making 'em think.* (Natalie, West City)

## "Dumped on the estate"

Some parents saw crime and anti-social behaviour as endemic, and thought that ASBOs were just another sign that problems had become concentrated in 'bad areas'. This father described the way social problems were 'dumped' in the least popular estates, leading to accumulated behaviour problems:

> *All ASBOs do is move people on so other people get problem people. Basically, they create their own monster. When the other big estate was built it was for unruly tenants, 'bad tenants', and now it is a nightmare, no-go zone. So half empty, no one will live there now. I imagine they are using the same methods with ASBOs.* (Fiona's husband, The Valley)

Fiona believed that informal community controls might work better than ASBOs:

> *I've not seen first-hand evidence of any influence. I know no one with an ASBO. Everyone complained at the new neighbours here, complained at the noise, and sorted it out within the street. No need for ASBOs.* (Fiona, The Valley)

Some parents felt uneasy about ASBOs as a method which might show short-term gains but would fail communities in the long term. Debra and Alan in West City felt very upset about the re-housing of difficult and troublesome families on their estate, but were clear that a more fundamental and more supportive approach was vital if such distressed families were to improve – simply trying to exclude people would only make things worse:

> *Living here on a day-to-day basis you're trying to build a community on our little estate of 85 homes and all we get is people moved here who the council are getting off their list, whether they're coming out of prison, or drug users, or mental health issues. They get dumped on the estate with next to no support and cause a nightmare for everybody else. You only need one crack house for everybody's lives to be a nightmare. You only need one nuisance*

*neighbour who just doesn't give a regard for anybody else, whether it's loud music at night or whatever.*

*And ASBOs ain't the solution. Again, it doesn't really tackle the problem. People need support, not a label and being banned from an area, they're just gonna be in another area. You know, it doesn't actually tackle the behaviour issues.* (Alan, West City)

Another parent believed that ASBOs were labelling children from difficult areas, without helping them:

*The ASBOs, in theory, a good idea. But say you are in an open plan office and you smash your desk, the police would come and deal with only you. It is not like that with ASBOs. They see one child and all children as the same. I got yelled at by men who saw kids throwing stones and all mine are in the house at such times and I say that it's no good. All kids on the street get ASBOs, n'all they do is criticise and condemn, no constructive help.* (Holly, Kirkside East)

The use of ASBOs seemed to offer a blunt and unsophisticated way of addressing anti-social behaviour, the roots of which were far more difficult to address. Parents' worries about 'blaming, naming and shaming' underpinned their overriding desire to see young people more constructively occupied with more to do locally. This parent summed it up:

*I think the kids need something to keep them going. They've grown big now, hanging about there, and I'm terrified of them.* (Cynthia, West City)

The connection between the problem of young people 'hanging about' and getting up to mischief reflects a chronic lack of cheap, accessible, safe and constructive places for young people to 'let off steam'.

## Does crime prevention work?

During our final visits in 2006, we asked how far anti-crime initiatives had improved conditions in the neighbourhoods, including ASBOs, and security cameras (CCTV) alongside changes in policing.

Eight years after our first visit, parents were much more positive about the active efforts to control crime in all neighbourhoods compared with the outset. Three quarters of parents in all the neighbourhoods felt that crime reduction initiatives had improved their neighbourhoods in some way. Many parents could not pinpoint precisely which anti-crime initiatives had helped their areas most, but only a minority of parents saw no difference in crime conditions. The initiative that stood out as being by far the most effective by the end of our study was the Police Community Support Officer (PCSO) initiative, and to a lesser extent, the neighbourhood wardens. Over a quarter of all parents praised these initiatives, a surprisingly positive endorsement, given the high level of continuing fear and earlier reservations among many parents. The biggest change in attitudes was in East Docks, where half the families thought community policing had made a difference – parents thought that the visible presence of community policing helped bring about a tangible reduction in crime over time.[10] An East Docks mother of African origin pointed out that her visiting relatives had also noticed the changes:

> *We don't have kids kicking doors. Our security door has lasted a year rather than two months because the community police are everywhere, on bikes. Before the off licence would get smashed. My relatives from Uganda visited four years ago and they saw a boy break into a car. Our aunties came and visited from Denmark and said how quiet it was! I said 'Are you sure?'.* (Sasha, East Docks)

Parents were able to sum up what had made most difference: a stronger police presence, increased deterrence and more direct action with children and general greater feelings of safety.

## Summary and conclusions

Crime, drugs and anti-social behaviour, much bigger problems in disadvantaged urban neighbourhoods than in more average places, have multiple negative effects on family life. They generate great fear among parents for the direct safety of their children, but also for their children's friendships, linked to the constant risk of them getting drawn into crime themselves. The parents were particularly afraid of drugs, knife and gun crime. In their conversations with us they often connected crime, violence, bad behaviour, gangs and drugs. Crime problems play out differently in different neighbourhoods, and so do the responses by public bodies. Communities also react somewhat differently, and both crime and fear can become 'infectious' and spread rapidly through community networks, causing seeming epidemics of trouble.[11]

The government over the past 10 years developed many initiatives to reduce fear in communities and to deter crime on the streets and in neighbourhoods. They showed their anxiety to be 'tough on crime and tough on the causes of crime' by the sheer range of actions they supported. Yet it was often difficult to be as tough as the interventions needed or set out to be, and the underlying problems often eluded them because they were so multi-pronged, long-lasting and pervasive. The parents' reactions to the crime prevention initiatives and their overall assessment of the crime trends in their areas showed just how difficult policing such areas is and yet how real gains can be made. Toughness on its own was certainly not the answer in the eyes of most parents.

The frequency of crime meant that a third of the parents directly experienced crime in a single year, so it is not surprising that virtually all parents registered their fear. News of crime spread far and fast and sustained itself through informal gossip. Most parents would not allow their children to play out or even go to the shops unsupervised, sometimes even up to secondary school age. In many ways family lives were unhealthily constrained by the general atmosphere of foreboding on the streets.

It was these fears, affecting large parts of the population, that drove councils and the police to re-establish a local street presence in the decade from 2000, using uniformed PCSOs and neighbourhood wardens employed by local councils and sometimes by local housing associations. Both types of local 'guardians of security' patrol the streets, maintain order, report trouble, tackle street problems on the spot and create more positive relations with the local community, particularly children and young people, building greater trust and confidence.

Over time, the anti-crime initiatives positively changed neighbourhoods in many different ways. Visible law enforcement was the most commonly mentioned change. Beyond this, the initiatives provided increasing deterrents to crime and had tried to deal positively with children who might otherwise get involved in criminal activities. But reducing the visibility of crime and possibly simply moving crime on to other parts of the area worried some parents, as it might then lead to greater problems in other neighbourhoods, as well as failing to address the underlying causes of crime. However, parents valued the overall benefits of increased enforcement, more control over children and increased deterrence more than they worried about the possible risk of displacement to other areas. In fact the overall trend of falling crime suggested better street supervision and enforcement were working.[12]

Very few parents thought crime prevention efforts were fruitless, in spite of their sometimes harsh criticism of their limitations. Crime initiatives had clearly reduced and to a large extent contained local crime while improving the neighbourhoods where they lived, in spite of some parents still feeling that too little progress had been made. The efforts had some measurable impact.

The success of these schemes depended on several factors identified by parents:

- high visibility;
- a proactive, supportive role;
- frequent patrols covering the whole area consistently in small tranches;
- familiar, known faces;
- a good rapport with the children;
- rapid, consistent back-up from the mainstream police and the council.

Winning over children and young people through a friendly approach, and direct engagement with them were both critically important. Parents endorsed these approaches and felt that over time they made a real difference. They felt that the respect and sympathy wardens and PCSOs displayed won the support of the community, although they still worried about the 'hard' kids and the dilemmas facing the PCSOs when they had to enforce the law on children they had befriended.

The schemes were particularly successful in the two London areas, which had experienced spates of violent crime. Local patrols had to be accompanied by full-scale police interventions when necessary which acted as serious deterrents, while the constant presence of lower level supervision gave reassurance as well as deterring more minor transgressions.

Parents were aware that wardens and community police did not solve all the problems, and some were critical of their limited roles, fearing they were no more than a smokescreen to cover up the lack of real policing. A much bigger worry was the sense that they could not cope with older teenagers, that they avoided confrontation and that their enforcement powers were too weak. Youth problems – disaffection, lack of purpose, surplus energy, gathering in large groups – far outpaced the scope of crime prevention projects; full-scale youth initiatives were the most common need highlighted by parents. Nonetheless it was clear that a recognisable but familiar presence representing higher authority on the streets helped to reduce trouble, solve problems and build confidence. It made families feel more secure about where they lived.[13]

There was a more mixed reaction to ASBOs. They curtailed some bad behaviour and influenced the parents of children receiving ASBOs, leading them to exercise more control over their children and use more authority to curb their behaviour, but some parents and children seemed beyond the point of reason and needed special, intensive help.[14] In the eyes of many parents, they were only just able to 'keep the lid on'.

Most parents had little knowledge or experience of local community groups set up to fight crime and seemed to feel that crime was too big a problem to be tackled by local people, although the parents who were directly involved in crime fighting groups were very positive.[15] They most of all wanted reliable, regular street policing and enforcement in ways that would lead to underlying changes in general patterns of criminal behaviour, building stronger communities. Pervasive social problems, particularly community instability, family insecurity and lack of organised activity for children and young people, all undermined and weakened progress. But over the years of our visits, over three quarters of parents believed that the level of crime had fallen, that the police were doing better, that there was less to fear. This was an area where real progress was found and where parents recognised and supported it.

**Notes**

[1] Annual Home Office Statistical Bulletins on Crime in England and Wales, including HOSB 07/02, HOSB 07/03, HOSB 10/04, HOSB 11/05, HOSB 12/06, HOSB 11/07, HOSB07/08, HOSB 11/09, HOSB12/10 (http://rds. homeoffice.gov.uk/rds/bcs-publications.html); Department for Communities and Local Government (CLG) (2009) *Survey of English Housing preliminary report: 2007–08*, London: CLG.

[2] Home Office (2010) Crime Statistics, available from http://rds.homeoffice. gov.uk/rds/soti.html; Centre for Longitudinal Studies (CLS) *Millennium Cohort Study*, London: CLS.

[3] http://rds.homeoffice.gov.uk/rds/soti.html

[4] Social Exclusion Unit (SEU) (2000) *National strategy for neighbourhood renewal: A framework for consultation document*, London: Cabinet Office; SEU (2001) *National strategy for neighbourhood renewal: Action plan*, London: Cabinet Office.

[5] Office of the Deputy Prime Minister (ODPM) (2004) *Neighbourhood wardens scheme evaluation*, Research Report 8, London: ODPM.

[6] www.met.police.uk/dcf/c_focus_work.htm

[7] Paskell, C. (2007) '"Plastic police" or "community support"? The role of police community support officers within low-income neighbourhoods', *European Urban and Regional Studies*, vol 14, no 4, pp 349-61.

[8] National Communities Resource Centre (2010) *Community crime fighters: Report to the Home Office*, Chester: Trafford Hall.

[9] Power, A. and Tunstall, R. (1997) *Dangerous disorder: Riots and violent disturbances in thirteen areas of Britain, 1991–92*, York: Joseph Rowntree Foundation.

[10] http://rds.homeoffice.gov.uk/rds/soti.html

[11] James, O. (1995) *Juvenile violence in a winner–loser culture: Socio-economic and familial origins of the rise in violence against the person*, London: Free Association Books.

[12] http://rds.homeoffice.gov.uk

[13] Casey, L. (2008) *Engaging communities in fighting crime*, London: Cabinet Office.

[14] Lane, L., Power, A. and Serle, N. (2008) *Report to Incommunities on the About Turn Project*, CASEreport 5, London: LSE.

[15] National Communities Resource Centre (2010) *Community crime fighters: Report to the Home Office*, Chester: Trafford Hall; Casey, L. (2008) *Engaging communities in fighting crime*, London: Cabinet Office.

# SIX

# Family health and neighbourhood conditions

*The smell of that thing they burn at night time, that's terrible. The dust that comes from it is terrible. I have never suffered so badly from coughing since I've come here. I have to dust my house all the time now. I get that on the house, I get that on the car, I go outside sometime, it's thick and I'm thinking 'where is this thing coming from?'. And since I move here I find my hay fever and the coughing is really bad. At night times sometime I don't sleep 'cos I cough so much.* (Gabrielle, East Docks)

## Introduction

The previous chapters highlighted the connections between crime, anti-social behaviour and poor conditions. We showed how young people's positive development was hampered by the lack of safe, useable outdoor space to exercise, play and do sport in. Area conditions shape family development, create social pressures and in seriously deprived areas, can damage health.[1] This chapter explores the health of the 200 families, and investigates their experiences of local health services. It examines the links between the families' health and area conditions, particularly the impact of wider problems on mental health. It explores some of the common health problems affecting families across income boundaries as well as highlighting problems that are made worse by poor conditions and lack of resources.

We do not fully understand how environment influences our personal health, but we do know that life expectancy is lower in poorer areas and that the incidence of many serious conditions is higher.[2] Poor environments also affect our sense of well-being and make it harder to live a healthy lifestyle. Exercise, green space and fresh food are commonly harder to find in poorer than in richer areas.[3] Children need outdoor space, unpolluted environments, good diets and a sense of security, but parents' mental health suffers particularly when they see their families surrounded by poor social and environmental conditions. Many studies have shown that neglected, decayed environments have a serious impact on family health and well-being.[4]

When we are ill, our spirits become low and other problems and external pressures affect us more. The converse is also true, so a healthier environment helps families. The inter-play between cared-for places, better social conditions, a sense of control, physical and mental health are subtle but strong.[5] Among the families we visited, mental ill health, depression and anxiety were far more common than in the population as a whole, and the families frequently referred to area problems as depressing and affecting their health.[6]

## Ill health and local services

Parents during our visits talked very little about the big organisational changes in the health services over the decade from 2000, and far more about their struggles with their families' health problems and their reliance on the health service. Two thirds of the families were fit and well, except in West City, where nearly half were, one third dealing with serious health problems in their children, partners and themselves. One fifth had long-standing illnesses or disabilities that limited their ability to function (see Figure 6.1).

**Figure 6.1:** Health status of the family, 2006

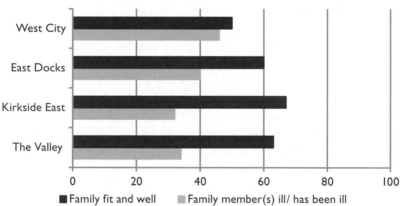

The families depended a lot on their local general practitioner (GP) for their children's and their own health. We did not probe people's lifestyles, diet and exercise more closely than they wanted to share with us, but some parents shared intimate experiences of personal health problems, largely as a result of our regular visits and a build-up of trust and rapport. Many talked about their smoking habits, being overweight and their lack of fitness. They often recognised the links between behaviour, alcohol and drug abuse and mental health:

> *I've noticed that a lot of these people that are on these sorts of drugs have got mental illnesses as well. I don't know if they had the mental illness and then taken drugs, or it's the drugs that caused the mental illness.* (Julie, East Docks)

Nearly half of the families had directly experienced health problems. By far the biggest gap in health services was in the outer East End, where the health services had a generally poor reputation. This was partly due to crowded waiting rooms, long delays in appointments, the pressures of emergency cases and the general ill health overload on East London surgeries, but East Docks was served by a hospital that many parents rated very badly.

Parents relied heavily on their GPs and their local hospital. A few parents found help via work, walk-in clinics, counselling or their children's schools. Around one fifth used several services to secure treatment. In the Northern neighbourhoods more families relied on hospitals than doctors. In East London it was the other way round. There were big variations in the help on offer. Under half in East Docks, Kirkside East and The Valley received direct help, while another fifth received indirect help, for example through Sure Start, from their GPs or schools or family. In West City parents did much better and 70 per cent received help.

We asked parents how satisfied they were with their GP and the hospital they were under. Most parents praised their GPs, but London health services were under much greater strain and pressure, so much so that sometimes they refused to take on extra patients, as this mother explained:

> *The GP did not want to register us permanently. We were only temporarily registered, so they didn't want to see my son when he was ill. One night my son was very ill, but they said they couldn't register him, so they didn't treat him. We had to take him to the hospital. At least they saw us.* (Luiza, East Docks)

Some London parents were strongly critical of their local health services. Both the standard of treatment offered and the local organisation of medical services appeared inadequate to the task in East London. Some parents coping with family health problems felt at a loss over the confusing and inadequate medical support they received:

> *My daughter's been suffering pretty badly from asthma. It has been pretty bad. At one point she was going every week to hospital, for*

> *three or four days....We had to wait two days for a pump.You can't wait two days for a pump.When we've got letters coming from the hospital, the GP's not aware she's been hospitalised.We've now got referred out to an asthma doctor in a neighbouring area. It's worrying, you know.* (Oni, East Docks)

Parents with severe health problems sometimes felt they were having to take too much responsibility. Megan illustrates this:

> *He's been fitting since he was a baby and they said it was convulsions but they said 'children have fits and grow out of it'. I asked for a brain scan – you've got to ask for everything. I'm not happy with the doctor.The doctor doesn't want to help you.When I found out my son was epileptic, the doctor gave me print-outs to 'get on with it'. I had to ask about medication.* (Megan,West City)

Other mothers found queuing at the surgery, even where there was an appointment system, very frustrating. One mother thought it helped to explain the pressure on local hospitals:

> *I have a huge gripe with the system.To get a doctors appointment you have to be here queuing by 8.15am. By 8.30 I was behind 35 people. It does help me to understand why people go straight to A & E. I went with my daughter when she had a chest infection. It's not good, it's very disempowering.When I queued at 8.30, the appointment they gave was at 12.10 so I had to come back again.* (Erin, East Docks)

London families who relied on the local hospital tended to be much more dissatisfied. In West City, three quarters of the parents with health problems were under their local hospital for treatment, and a third were dissatisfied with the service they were receiving. In East Docks, nearly 85 per cent of the parents with health problems were under their local hospital for treatment, but of these, nearly two thirds were dissatisfied, mostly very dissatisfied.This poorly rated hospital stood out as offering a very bad service. In contrast, in the two Northern neighbourhoods, half the parents were under their local hospital either for their own, or their children's treatment, and the overwhelming majority were satisfied with them.

## "The hospital was a joke"

One East Docks parent described the poor hygiene in her local hospital, particularly in the maternity ward:

> *The hospital was a joke. I'm currently under the local hospital – I'm sure you've probably heard all the horror stories. It's rundown, it needs a lot of money put into it, it's disgusting. The last time I had to go in for my treatment, they messed up anyway. I had to go in for a few days when I had my daughter.... They said the baby's head was engaged, it could come early, so they had me up in the delivery suite and it was filthy. It was so bad I didn't want to hover over the toilet ... and I thought, 'This is a health place, this is a hospital. I've bought my bits and pieces to go to the hospital, and I've literally had to go out and buy Flash wipes and scrub and things because there's no way I am going to give birth to a baby in that room, it is filthy. There's just no way!'. And I think to myself, 'If I have a caesarean I'm going to have to stay in here for five days, in this filth – I'm not going to be able to handle it!'.* (Flowella, East Docks)

Another mother confirmed the bad conditions:

> *When I was in for my minor operation I was begging my husband to take me home. The registrar had to sign me out and they said that they'd sign me out at six. I just did not want to stay, it was horrible, really horrible. If I did fall pregnant I'd have to go and see and check it out and ask before I felt comfortable enough to make a decision. I wouldn't just say 'Yes, I would go there'.* (Tamara, East Docks)

East Docks is among the three most deprived areas in the country,[7] where health needs combined with poor performance in the local hospital to create a vicious circle of inadequate and over-stretched services. Healthcare services were better in West City, and far better in the North, in the eyes of parents.

## Do neighbourhoods affect health?

We asked parents whether they felt their health problems were linked to other aspects of their family lives such as area conditions. Only around one in ten Northern parents with health problems made this connection; the rest made no connection at all. But where they did, family and work problems, crime and general pressures were the main causes of health problems. Sometimes a chain of events, starting with earlier injury or illness, made living in an inner-city area difficult. Others blamed their health problems directly on problems such as noise and traffic. Parents in Kirkside East occasionally made a direct connection between poor health and poor conditions. In The Valley, a few parents thought there was a 'postcode lottery', with primary care trusts (PCTs) offering poorer treatment in poorer places.

London families far more often connected their health problems with other pressures in their lives, such as schooling or other area problems. In all, nearly half of East London parents attributed their health problems to area-related stress-inducing aspects of their lives, and only a minority saw no connection. It was clear that the overcrowding, the shortage of open space, traffic congestion, air pollution and the general 'high pitch' atmosphere of the London neighbourhoods had much harsher impacts on family lives, as we show later.

We asked families about illness in their families early on our visits. Over a fifth of the parents had a longstanding illness themselves, and such illnesses were also common among partners and children. There was a higher level of serious ill health among the families than the national average, rising to a quarter in East London. Nationally, 16 per cent of working-age adults have a long-term health problem serious enough to limit their activity.[8]

In three neighbourhoods around one fifth of parents took medicine regularly, but in Kirkside East about one third of the parents did. This may have reflected more relaxed medical attitudes to prescriptions, but we found evidence of more unhealthy lifestyles in this large estate, for example, much higher levels of smoking.

## Health and lifestyle: *"Really abusive"*

We know that smoking has a strongly adverse effect on people's health, often affecting parents' health problems, or their families'. Levels of smoking among parents in the four neighbourhoods and among partners were extremely high in all areas. Around a third of parents smoked across all the areas, but this rose to almost half (48 per cent) in Kirkside East, over a third (36 per cent) in The Valley and in East Docks (34 per cent). It was just over a quarter (28 per cent) in West City. Kirkside East had the worst health problems, almost certainly linked to smoking, with its strong, traditional working-class culture that may have influenced behaviour. Fewer male partners smoked than the mothers themselves. The health implications for children were compounded by the cramped indoor spaces that families occupied and the limited outdoor spaces they could compensate with. The children of smokers often lived in smoke-filled homes. Regular smoking in low-income families reduced parents' available cash for healthy food and other essential items. The smoking rates were far higher than the national average of 22 per cent and higher than the average for low-income groups (30 per cent).[9]

We did not ask parents directly about their own habits in relation to drugs and alcohol; they explained how serious the problems were. They saw drugs as an all-pervasive threat. Many parents described the drug and alcohol abuse that children in the neighbourhoods were exposed to. Only occasionally did they directly relate these problems to health, but they often related them to risky and reckless behaviour, to violence, and to people 'not knowing what they were doing'; they witnessed the impact of substance abuse on mental states and conditions. Flowella, in East Docks, whose former husband was an alcoholic, referred to this chain effect:

> We found out he'd got a crack addiction.... Of late he's become really abusive. He drinks a lot.... I felt traumatised by that 'cos I thought 'My child's been exposed to this', and I wasn't even aware of it.... We just found out last week he's in prison. (Flowella, East Docks)

Several parents referred to teenage drinking as a problem. Such social problems had big implications for public health. One parent talked about her teenage daughter drinking:

> She has been truanting but she got excluded for taking alcohol into the school. She shocked herself, her dad and her teachers. Alcohol is around and it's what they do. (Judith, The Valley)

Another parent was suffering the health aftermath of drug and alcohol abuse and other health problems, compounded by living in a high-rise block that brought on other problems:

> Although I've conquered my addictions, I've been left with the panic attacks.... Living on the tenth floor is a particular problem as I'm asthmatic. On Thursday and Friday of last week both lifts were broken so I had to wheeze up the stairs with bags of shopping. An elderly man also needed help but I couldn't do anything because

*of my condition. Having to walk up 10 flights of stairs, not very
good.* (Beth, West City)

Sola, in West City, referred to the terrible effect drugs had on her
teenage son's behaviour and his mental state:

> *My son was on crack. He's changed now, but while it was happening
> he was robbing from the house. My son told me one time that he
> wanted to die. If you lose them to drugs and crime it's hopeless.
> There's a lot of suicide, drugs, crime.* (Sola, West City)

Some mothers talked about health problems that they thought arose
from other social problems. Obesity was a common problem we picked
up. It could actually become very serious. This mother's husband had
chronic diabetes which followed from his time in prison and the
amount of weight he put on while 'inside':

> *All okay apart from my husband, ongoing diabetes, for life…. He
> is under the hospital, they are brilliant. He is going for his feet
> tomorrow as they are going manky because of the diabetes and
> circulation. He was skinny when I met him. He is clinically obese
> now…. He went into prison and put loads of weight on and never
> lost it.* (Laverne, Kirkside East)

Several mothers referred to their children being overweight as a result
of lack of exercise and this compounded other problems, both physical
and mental, as stressed in Chapter Four.

## Chronic illness: *"More medication"*

At our last visit parents talked freely about the many forms of chronic
and longstanding illnesses, some semi-permanent health conditions
that their families suffered, including asthma, eczema, osteo-arthritis,
rheumatoid arthritis, multiple sclerosis (MS), cerebral palsy, diabetes,
obesity, back problems and depression. Many mothers also mentioned
pre-menstrual tension (PMT). It was far harder for parents with very
limited resources and with many external constraints to cope with these
problems than it would be with more resources and less constraints.
Some parents described their own serious health problems, which,
coupled with looking after children and struggling with poor area
conditions, made life very difficult, as this mother explained:

*My health's not so good, I'm back on the steroid tablets at the moment. My chest is really bad with angina. Asthma – steroid pump. I got the all clear with my breast lump. They said if anything appeared after that, just to call in.* (Nora, East Docks)

Another mother had such serious back and mobility problems that she ended up disabled by them:

*I'm permanently on sickness now because there is a lot I cannot do, for example, bending down, I am unfit for work, because of the slipped disc, which happened not long after my last interview, and inflammation of the tailbone and lack of feeling in my right leg as a result which may not come back fully, I'm not sure.... I'm under the hospital for my disc and leg and tailbone problems.* (Cara, Kirkside East)

Some parents proactively explored alternative medicine when conventional medicine failed. The Kirkside East Sure Start Centre offered some alternative treatments, both to mothers and to their children, that Louise, with a disabled baby, talked about:

*I take the baby to complementary health. It's free to parents. He's had five sessions of massage and he sleeps right through now. It's nice to be able to offer things we couldn't afford otherwise.* (Louise, Kirkside East)

Another mother wanted to escape the side-effects of heavy doses of mainstream medicine:

*I'm still suffering with rheumatoid arthritis. I'm fed up of different medicines giving bad side-effects. So I'm looking into homeopathic ones.... I am under my GP for my rheumatoid arthritis but I am looking into homeopathic treatment. Some are coming up at my GPs so I will look there too.* (Cynthia, The Valley)

Another mother was very worried about her son's worsening epilepsy and the heavy medication that it involved without seeming to prevent the fits:

*My son's on epilepsy medicine. It's keeping him okay. He's on more medication than in the other house, because he had another scan and he was fitting during the scan. I wasn't too happy with them highering the medication. He's a bit shouting, things like that, headaches, but he's just getting used to it. I thought he was gonna come off his medicine but when he got his scan I was shocked because they said it's not good.* (Megan, West City)

Some health problems were made more acute through poor diet and being overweight. Others seemed more closely linked to air quality and pollution such as breathing difficulties. This mother explained just how serious asthma, which her daughter suffered from, could be:

*My husband's been suffering high blood pressure and cholesterol, probably to do with age as well, and diet. My daughter's asthmatic, though it hasn't been so bad this year. We went through the whole of last summer taking her to hospital, and the stays was getting longer and longer. But this year it hasn't been as bad. She still under the asthma clinic and they've made it more manageable.* (Barbara, East Docks)

Another mother was pleased that treatments were in train but had very little confidence that her child's acute eczema and asthma would get better:

*Fine, no problems, except my son [age 18 months] has very bad eczema and asthma and had to have his adenoids out for his breathing.... He is under a consultant at the hospital. Every month he goes for eczema, and for asthma every two months.* (Jessica, The Valley)

## "He will be a child forever"

Some of the parents had a child with a severe disability. This imposed a very heavy load on the parents, even though these parents invariably praised the health services for the help they gave. Louise, in Kirkside East, was an extreme example of this. Her child had a heart condition but her youngest son was the most severely disabled:

*My son [age 3] has autistic spectrum disorder as well as cerebral palsy. We work with an educational psychologist but he says he has done all he can. It won't get any better. He hurt my arm, it is in a sling. He didn't know he'd done it. He has no idea and it will get worse. He will get to the age when his brain stops developing, staying as a child, so he will be a child forever.* (Louise, Kirkside East)

The parents we spoke to who had a child with disabilities identified strongly with their children's health problems and participated to the full in their care. This seemed to help them carry the load, but it also weighed on them. One parent was very worried about her daughter's hormone deficiency:

> *My daughter is – she has delayed developmentally – she's on this hormone replacement. She gets treated at the Endocrine Unit at the hospital. But she's fed up of injections and has stopped the treatment for a while. The biggest blow is she might not be able to have children, it's something she was born with. We had our emotional moments, we cried and cried. We live in a society where childbearing is so important.* (Natalie, West City)

Poor health could be a major drag on opportunity since longstanding and chronic conditions invariably had a major impact on family lives. Some parents with continuous health problems managed to work, but often they were unable to. Parents with children suffering from serious health problems or disabilities carried a burden of care that limited their opportunities to earn. Health problems could make it impossible for them to work in spite of the government's efforts to encourage families into work as a route out of poverty. There were even families where a partner gave up work in order to care for a seriously ill parent or where both parents were needed at home to cope with multiple health problems among their children. Angela, in Kirkside East, suffered from severe depression. She and her partner had five boys, and Angela had never worked as she had started having children early. Her partner was extremely supportive:

> *He gave up his job when I was ill last year. Now he can't work, so he can help and be there for me.* (Angela, Kirkside East)

Louise's boyfriend, father of all three children, moved in when the third baby was born severely disabled and Louise was only 23:

> *Their dad lives here now and looks after the baby and gets a carer's allowance. It's hard, specially three children with two years between them. Last year he gave up work to be full-time carer.* (Louise, Kirkside East)

## Stress, anxiety and depression

The Office for National Statistics (ONS) suggests that overall one in six adults at any time suffer from 'significant' mental health problems.[10] Anxiety and depression are the most common forms of mental distress, experienced by at least one in ten adults in Britain, and clinical depression afflicts one in 30 people.[11]

On our last two visits, we asked parents about the families' experiences of mental ill health, depression and anxiety. We wanted to know what help parents had received. A quarter of parents said that they or a member of their family had experienced depression, significantly higher than the national average. In two of the neighbourhoods, depression was particularly common among mothers, 31 per cent in Kirkside East in the North and 26 per cent in East Docks in London, three times the national average. In all four neighbourhoods, mothers experienced far higher levels of depression than partners, reflecting a wider pattern.[12] Given the stigma surrounding mental illness, there is the possibility that this problem may be even more pervasive. Among the 24 detailed family studies in *City survivors*, drawing on families in all four areas, two thirds suffered from depression. Figure 6.2 shows the proportion of families affected by depression.

In all the neighbourhoods, depression, anxiety and stress were the most common health problems. There seemed to have been a decline in mental health problems in the two Northern neighbourhoods by our last visit, but in East London we saw the opposite trend, with an increase in mental health problems. One possible explanation was the rise in gun and knife crime in the areas, particularly West City. The intense fear it generated in parents and children had abated, but it may have had a more lasting impact on levels of anxiety, as shown in Chapter Five.

One striking impression across all four areas was the burden that mothers bore as a result of mental health problems. Where there were very serious health problems, other family members played a much smaller role, although partners were sometimes very supportive, as the case of Louise showed.

**Figure 6.2:** Household members experiencing depression, 2004–05

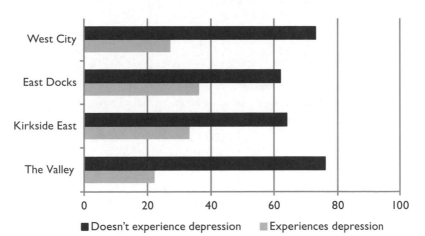

■ Doesn't experience depression    ■ Experiences depression

## "I couldn't cope"

The parents' descriptions of the impact of depression, including treatments and help received, offered great insights into how they coped and what helped. For some parents, the health services offered positive support as well as actual treatments. Several mothers talked about the relief they felt at being able to talk to their doctor. For example, one parent explained:

> *I see my GP monthly for a prescription of anti-depressants and a natter, she always ends up having me laughing.* (Angie, Kirkside East)

Other parents did not have a smooth journey with anti-depressants. One parent explained that it took more than one prescription for her doctor to find the right one for her. Another explained that the anti-depressants she had been prescribed worsened an already serious condition. This was heightened by traumatic circumstances when the father of her children was shot in a local gun battle.

> *I received a packet of tablets from the GP, I didn't go for help to be honest. When the kids' dad was shot I couldn't cope, they blamed me, I got sent to the GP, I stopped taking the pills, they made me worse. It affected the family. I had to cope though.* (Anita, Kirkside East)

### *"You know how to handle them"*

Some parents took the decision themselves to abandon medical treatment for depression:

> *I had post-natal depression after I had my daughter. I went to the doctors and said I kept getting headaches and he sussed it was post-natal depression because of my moods and I got tablets and then different ones which worked, I took them for six months, then another six months, I weaned myself off them.* (Heather, Kirkside East)

Another mother received counselling advice that gave her new confidence to handle problems:

> *Yes, seeing the psychologist. I can now handle anything that's thrown at me. She said to me, when you have your arguments, you know where you've gone wrong, you know how to handle them.* (Zoe, West City)

A London mother was very positive about the help she received, with counselling alongside medication:

> *I'm on anti-depressants. They're fairly good through the hospital. The doctor's been good. I was offered counselling.* (Rachel, East Docks)

One parent talked positively about the group therapy her husband had been involved in for several years:

> *My husband's on tablets for depression. He did go to group therapy for a couple of years, it was quite a long time ago. He doesn't go anymore, his group just finished and that was it. I think it was helpful.* (Kathleen, West City)

One mother, who suffered from severe and prolonged depression, described the support she had received but the limits of external help:

> *I see a community psychiatric nurse and art therapist and GP and psychiatrist for depression. The services are all very good. They don't have any answers though. I'm not cured, they help me manage*

*it. I went through a very hard patch in the summer. I had to get anti-depressants.* (Fiona, The Valley)

A husband of one parent we interviewed found support from many different sources, including counselling through the local Sure Start. He rejected medical or therapeutic treatment in favour of relying on social networks and more supportive counselling. He didn't want just to keep taking pills and luckily could rely on a strong and supportive wife:

> *I have reactive depression, it comes and goes, I never get rid of it, I had depression three years ago.... I go to the GP when I need it, I get a lot of support from work friends actually, and Sure Start counselling. All the GP will do is offer me tablets and I don't want them again, I have anxiety attacks. My wife supports me 100 per cent.* (Lisa's husband, Kirkside East)

In the case of Hannah in East London, her physical and mental health had deteriorated as a result of anxiety and poverty. Hannah had such severe problems coping that at one point she told us that while she was depressed, she completely ran out of money for food, and was forced to 'beg for surplus food' from a local restaurant. In this situation her faith and her far-reaching social supports helped her:

> *I have back and neck problems. Twisted ankle. I also sank into a depression. Sometimes I wished I was dead. Friends and family rang from all around the world and prayed for me, saying it will pass.* (Hannah, East Docks)

Another mother talked about the direct impact on her children suffering with depression. She eventually resorted to her GP because she did not want her children to be neglected:

> *I've suffered from depression, still do. I just see my doctor and I'm on medication but I'll be coming off soon as I am a lot better. At one point, when I first decided to go to the doctor, I was very weepy and low, and my oldest one will have noticed, and that was why I went to the doctor. Things have changed since the children were younger, things are easier.* (Liz, The Valley)

Phoebe, a lone isolated mother in The Valley, often suffered from anxiety and depression. She used to go regularly to her GP to talk through things that troubled her. She summed it up this way:

> *There's always things troubling me.* (Phoebe, The Valley)

## Neighbourhood conditions and health problems: "I need to get away from this noisy place"

On our last visit, we looked at a possible connection between depression, families' stress, anxiety and the deep social and environmental problems that surround the families. Two connections stood out clearly: parents' mental health problems as a result of neighbourhood or housing problems; and mental health problems resulting from family pressures, including the sheer struggle of raising a family in such difficult and restricted circumstances.

Parents sometimes made an explicit link between housing conditions and health problems, both physical and mental. High-rise tower blocks were often linked in parents' minds with ill health:

> *I had post-natal depression after I had my daughter, now age nine. I think it was because we lived in a ninth floor flat, I hated it.* (Olivia, Kirkside East)

Overcrowding was a big problem provoking depression in some families, including Hannah, whose problems have already been described. With better housing her health improved:

> *When we moved from that place to this place, everything died away, the depression stopped. We were overcrowded but since we moved here and the two older ones have moved out, it's much better.* (Hannah, East Docks)

Joyce from East Docks simply said "I love it", after she moved back to the North.

On the other hand, Phoebe, who suffered continual depression, was forced to move because of demolition plans, and did not settle into the much better estate she moved to:

> *I hate this area. I'm neither in the city nor out of it. I'm forced to be an island.* (Phoebe, The Valley)

Unfortunately, some families were trapped in accommodation with little hope of improvement, and this affected their personal relationships as well as their health. One mother in West City, in a small flat, found it very hard to cope with her father's moods, because they all lived together in such cramped conditions:

> *Just my dad. He sometimes can't stay in the house. We've been living here 13 years now, he sometimes gets stressed and walks out.* (Karli, West City)

Another mother suffered from MS and was badly affected by the stairs and by noise:

> *I need a bungalow as I cannot manage the stairs when I have an attack and I need to get away from this noisy place.* (Amreen, The Valley)

In some cases, damp could be so severe it affected health, yet it was often not given priority by landlords:

> *I've been up to the council three times to complain about the damp in the bedroom. I had to throw away the mattress. Both boys have runny noses and chesty coughs. The council don't want to know. I've begged them to move me.* (Kerry, East Docks)

Another mother explained how her housing and the neighbourhood made her feel unhappy and depressed. She pinpointed the main problem as she answered our questions – she hated being in a flat because it made her feel isolated, a prisoner in her own home. She was depressed and hated the area anyway, so she had no incentive to go outside, and the flat just reinforced her depression:

> *I'm unhappy in the area. It's the area, the flat, the whole area, as well as caring for my mother and husband. Being in a flat is the main concern, I don't like the area, but being in the flat is more troublesome as I feel trapped. Being trapped in the flat is really bad, particularly for doing the shopping. When the lifts are not working, I have to carry the shopping up three floors and I have a problem with my arm. The only time I go out is when I really need to.* (Yonca, West City)

Mothers sometimes found the social atmosphere of the area very depressing and this compounded their own feelings. By the same token, positive experiences reinforced parents' ability to cope, so parents with depression often felt they were on a rollercoaster. One mother admitted that her own depression might make the area seem bleak, whereas meeting positive people, doing some constructive activity, actually cheered her up:

> *Probably me suffering from depression, off and on. It's not so bad now, but I think I've got nothing here. Even though I go to this course and there's some lovely people on these courses, they're different to like, the area people, does that make sense? They're like different – you see the people in this area, on their drugs and just, and then you see these type of people on the course. Even the parents, it's just like, on a different wavelength. These people, I s'pose, have given me some hope. I think of the area, there's nothing around you anymore. A lot of people round here don't give a damn, they don't give a damn, on the drugs or drink or, just wondering how they're going to get money to do whatever. The lady upstairs, she wants to move out, she's only lived there two years. Her daughter's hanging around with bad children and she's not doing her homework, know what I mean? Same sort of thing I s'pose.* (Julie, East Docks)

Moving sometimes made parents realise the impact their neighbourhoods were having on their health. Other mothers explained how much better they felt once they had moved, including feeling unsafe in such a bad area. Some of the parents who moved during our visits described how previous living conditions had taken a toll on the family's health:

> *My breathing problems have gone. I haven't had them back since I've moved here. Before moving everyone had something – tummy bugs, chest infections.* (Linda, West City)

> *It's only moving away from the area that I realise how edgy and stressed I was – 'Where's that noise?' et cetera.* (Tracy, West City)

> *Not since I moved from there [laughs]. I felt panicky and anxious et cetera on my own with kids in Kirkside East whilst my husband was away working a lot.* (Sadie, Kirkside East)

## *"My husband had counselling over it"*

For some parents, there was a vicious circle at play between their own anxiety and area problems; one problem fed another. Parents needed more resilience to handle harsher problems:

> *I can't say if I'd be different somewhere else, obviously. For example, I think because you have anxiety anyway, you are not at your strongest, so when something kicks off here, aggression wise, it is hard, it is not in your nature.* (Holly, Kirkside East)

Some parents suffered acute anxiety because of real fears for their children, particularly when they became teenagers and gained a little freedom, but there were also some direct links to health. This mother described the level of stress and fear that she and her husband felt for their son's safety because of local conditions:

> *Yes. Drugs, crime, anything like that. Street robbery, things like that. My husband's had counselling over it, it did help. I mean I worry but I don't get into a panic. One night when my son went out, he didn't come home till quarter past one. He didn't have his mobile phone on him and he said he'd be in by half past 10, and I was frantic. Frantic I was, out on the streets, I was out looking for him in the car.* (Destiny, West City)

A common thread running through parents' accounts of the link between area troubles and their own mental health was a sense of 'threat'. One parent attributed health problems to a traumatic mugging of her son in the area and its direct impact on the mother's ability to cope. Nora remained traumatised by this incident and could not allay her anxieties through any measures:

> *For two weeks after the mugging I was really like I just couldn't function properly. I kept looking over my shoulder, and, so probably yeah, I mean it made me feel sick to think that they can do something like that to another human being. His personal space was violated, just like that, in a second. It just happened so quickly, they just jumped on him. Literally 20 seconds and it's over, and he was just stood there, like, you know, hold on a minute. But it was the ferocity of it as well, you know, they could've hurt him. They could've backed off of him and he could've been on the floor dead. It was that quick, they could've killed him.* (Nora, East Docks)

Sometimes the fear and anxiety generated by these experiences lasted for several years:

> *I don't feel threatened here although a pizza delivery man had his arm almost chopped off, stabbed in the arm. After that incident, when we get in the lifts I'm scared. Sometimes I come home late at night, and downstairs can be very threatening. I come home sometimes at 10 o'clock.* (Cynthia, West City)

We had recorded this incident earlier, and Cynthia spontaneously confirmed the huge impact it still had on her feelings and anxieties three years later.

Health problems and area problems fed each other through social disorder. This included irresponsible and disruptive neighbours. One West City mother who suffered from depression explained how she had intervened to help a troubled neighbour's children but when the police got involved, her problems became even worse and she found it hard to shake off the effects:

> *I went through a bad patch with the neighbour upstairs. I went to the police as she was threatening me and everything. All the neighbours are nice but she is one of the women who goes out and does anything. She smokes ice and crack, does everything and has children. She went missing for three days to a flat in another local area and I had to look after her children. She leaves her baby with an 11-year-old. What sort of mother leaves an 11-year-old with a three-month baby? She attacked me, pushed her way into my home because I called the police. She was calling me names along the street, cussing my son. She verbally abused me so I wrote a letter to the Housing Office so they have it on record if it happens again.* (Zoe, West City)

There were many other examples like this where the anxiety level of the mother was driven up by an encounter with extreme behaviour.

## "Coughing since I've come home"

A particular connection was made between air pollution in East London and health problems. Many parents in this area live near a dual carriageway, a major airport and an incinerator. Parents were acutely aware of the impact this had. East Docks was particularly hard hit by environmental problems, which were set to get worse as the main road was widened and city airport expanded:

> *There's noise from the planes, and the smell of the factories is very bad. It's … busy because of all the traffic going through not because of lots going on.… You can't keep the windows open when you're going to sleep. The whole house shakes when lorries go past.* (Nadia, East Docks)

> *I can't taste nothing, always got a bunged up nose. That's why I've got that nasal spray thing. It ain't a bug. It's in the environment I think. Ain't a bug, you don't have a bug for a year. Motorways, factories with big bleeding, them big chimney pot things.* (Kayla, East Docks)

> *Yeah actually, my doctor says in the last five years he's given out so many of them nasal sprays. My sister has one now. And you're forever dusting. You dust your television, next day's its all back there again. And I don't even live near a main road anymore, know what I mean.* (Hailey, East Docks)

Often it was the children who were affected by the air pollution:

> *Certainly with my daughter's asthma, it's pollution, because if she goes up near the A13, that's when it hits her very, very bad. It certainly is pollution.* (Barbara, East Docks)

## "Better be ill here than elsewhere"

There were some parents who took comfort in their surroundings, although they tended to be in the minority. This mother was sure there was no connection between her depression and the area:

> *No, not at all. The opposite. Happy here, so better to be ill here than elsewhere. I am under my GP for depression, he's good. I walk in, burst into tears and he says 'I always have that effect on you!'.* (Carol, Kirkside East)

Many parents adopted a 'better the devil you know' approach, suggesting that 'you get these problems wherever you are':

> *You get used to an area. It's like the devil you know. At least I
> know what to expect in this area. If I was put in a different area,
> I would be worried about what I didn't know.* (Ellie, West City)

One health problem affecting families was the health of grandparents and
the caring responsibilities of the parents we visited in relation to them.
Over half the families had close relatives nearby, mostly grandparents,
and most had frequent contact with them. Grandparents and siblings
often helped where there were health problems with children or
parents, but this was reciprocated, and many parents wanted to be near
their own parents to help them when their health deteriorated. Several
mothers referred to sick parents and their responsibility to help them.
This form of family support in relation to health is easy to overlook
or under-value, but among the case studies in *City survivors* it showed
up in over half the families. It made living near older parents very
important. For example, Joyce moved back up North to help:

> *My mum and dad've had bad health problems recently, and I
> don't think they would move here. So I'll move up there.* (Joyce,
> East Docks)

Others helped out because the strain was too big on one person:

> *Their father's lost the use of his legs.* (Peter, Kirkside East)

## Family pressures and mental health

We explored the link between mental health and family pressures.
Parents always find it hard work raising a family, particularly on a low
income, as a lone parent, in a poor environment. One mother went
through a bout of depression until her son was diagnosed as autistic.
The relief of knowing what was wrong and the help she then received
made her much more able to cope. Many times behavioural problems in
children were simply recognised as ADHD. Several parents mentioned
that knowing made it easier to share the anxiety. This mother described
her feelings once her son was on the way to having his problems
recognised:

> *My son is very close to an ADHD diagnosis. I have known since
> he could walk there was something. They just need to say it now. It
> is on paper.... I suffered from depression. I felt no one listened to*

*me about my son, but he is very close to a diagnosis now.* (Deidre, The Valley)

## "I can't do anything"

Family relationships in low-income areas sometimes became more fragile because of financial and social pressures. When relationships broke down, as the frequency of lone parents in these areas underlines, there could be serious consequences for the parents and children.[13] It was hard to judge how much mental instability and depression were a cause or effect of personal and family problems. The children were sometimes torn, making parents unhappy, unsettled and mentally unwell. Parents often struggled to cope in this situation. Sola, in West City, explained some of her boy's behaviour and addiction problems this way:

> *Breaking up with my husband affected my son. I've had nothing but problems with him. It's making me ill.* (Sola, West City)

Many mothers had to rely on relatives to help. One mother became severely depressed and her mother basically took on responsibility for her grandchildren. Then Sophie, the mother, felt very inadequate and her depression intensified:

> *My depression comes with my children who are not with me. My mother phones, saying they want this and that and I can't do anything for them, then I become so low. I've missed a lot of stages after all those years, I keep playing back all those years. It hurts so much I wasn't there.* (Sophie, East Docks)

With some mothers, earlier mental health problems could be reignited by the emotional demands of having children and caring for them with too little support. Sometimes in the aftermath of a relationship breakdown, the parent has to try and share the caring responsibility, but that can be traumatic too:

> *I am always stressed and depressed. But not on medication for it. It is not severe.... It is a lot to do with my kids, being split up from them, not being a proper family anymore. I had a really bad breakdown six years ago and it is a lot to do with that, the fallout from that.* (Becky, Kirkside East)

Low-skilled male manual workers are far more likely to be out of work than average because of the disappearance of manual work, and they can easily become troubled, absent fathers.[14] Several mothers mentioned problems with their children's fathers as contributing to their mental distress:

> *I feel anxious, stressed, et cetera, at the moment, because of my son's dad.* (Amy, Kirkside East)

In another case, the mother mentioned problems with the father, alongside her own problems, as causes of her intense anxiety and depression:

> *I had post-natal depression when I had my daughter, I was having problems with her father. I didn't want to go on. Every little thing triggers it. I can't even go to the second floor, I get panicky.* (Selda, East Docks)

One mother, having split up from the father of her children, wanted to buy out his half of the house in order to gain a sense of control, but she could not afford to do so. She became anxious because of all the pressure she was under:

> *I've had a lot of stress, particularly dealing with my ex, their dad, with the house.... But since Christmas it has got a lot better. He still tries to throw a spanner in the works now and then. And I get stressed with two children and a job.* (Rosemary, The Valley)

Another mother explained a very different problem – the demands that her wider family placed on her, intensifying her depression:

> *My family lives close by. I think it's probably to do with my family. I think when I was low and I needed help, I think they didn't, not really, help. If anything, they made me feel ten times worse. 'Cos when I was feeling low, going through everything with my son, they were screaming at me, 'Where have you been? Why ain't you been round?'. And I think they made me feel even lower, so I ended up distancing myself.* (Julie, East Docks)

## *"I feel I've let you down"*

A sense of failure was a very common companion of depression and of relationship troubles. Parents with severe depression who received good support explained the impact their condition had on their role as a parent, revealing the internal family pressures depression could cause and the acute worry these parents felt about letting their children down. One mother talked in front of her young son about it:

> *I just don't feel – I have bad days when I feel I'm not good enough to be his mummy. [Says to son] I feel I've let you down.*
>
> Son: *How have you let me down?*
>
> *I just feel it. When you get older you'll see what I mean.* (Zoe, West City)

Another mother described her feelings of letting her children down, explaining how she couldn't pretend in front of them. She linked her depression to her loneliness and no longer having her mother nearby:

> *I was in the hospital with health problems. I can't put a 'face' on. You feel you've let your children down. More financially, it's a big thing. Not having an adult to chat to in the evening. I've missed not having me mum so near. It all happened at the same time.* (Rachel, East Docks)

For other mothers, as the stresses of childrearing reduced, depression shrank too. This mother had received the kind of help that made it possible for her to climb out of her severe depression:

> *I'm probably the best I've been for a while – a combination of being a bit better and less physically exhausted as the boys are older and I take less work. I still see the psychiatrist each three months for severe and prolonged depression, and the doctor every 2–3 weeks.* (Fiona, The Valley)

Based on the parents' own accounts, it seems clear that mental ill health has severe consequences for the family and the children. This link helps explain some of the behaviour problems that parents described in earlier chapters among young people. Depressed mothers often have poor control over their children, causing more aggression, particularly among boys.[15] It affects daughters too, making depression more likely as they grow up.

Overall we concluded from the parents' repeated accounts of stress, anxiety and depression that both external environmental factors and internal family pressures contributed to their mental health problems. Parents' own vulnerabilities, coupled with other pressures, made depression and anxiety seem almost inevitable in many cases.

## Summary and conclusions

This chapter is as much an account of the cumulative burdens of personal and social responsibility low-income parents carry, sometimes on their own, as it is an account of family health problems in low-income areas. But it seems much harder to cope with serious health problems that many families faced when financial resources are extremely limited and when parents face constant neighbourhood and environmental problems. The pressures brought on by local conditions and poor health of itself interact with each other, helping to explain the stubborn gap in health outcomes between low-income areas and the average, in spite of a big increase in health spending.[16] The parents' accounts of their health problems underline their severity and persistence of this interaction.

Most parents with health problems managed to secure support from their local health services for their children, and themselves. Sometimes schools and pre-school services like Sure Start, or social services, got involved, but mostly they relied on doctors and hospitals. Parents saw limitations in the health services, with problems such as the over-ready prescription of anti-depressants and the bad record of one East London hospital. Generally parents praised their doctors and valued their support, however. Several parents in the North highlighted the supportive and advisory nature of their relationship with their doctor, although this was far less common in East London.

Striking accounts of how parents reacted to extreme health problems, provoked by violent incidents and personal upheaval, showed how close families sometimes came, at least temporarily, to losing their 'mental grip' or sense of control over their lives. Some mothers ended up bowed down by problems but most somehow 'got by', as they put it. Often other family members and close friends played a part in this ability to cope, a critical element of neighbourhoods and communities that is easily underestimated.

Parents often referred to the presence of children as a positive influence in forcing them to keep going and in helping them to maintain a sense of normality. At the same time, mothers often linked depression to the extreme pressures they were under through their family responsibilities, including sometimes their children's ill health or disabilities. They simply had to learn to 'manage' their depression – an outcome of low income, low status, poor environments, a weak sense of control over their surroundings, frequent stresses and shocks, multiple responsibilities and anxieties associated with parenting, all more intense in disadvantaged areas.[17]

Families in low-income areas struggle with health-related problems. Often the time needed to talk through their problems and to develop techniques for managing them is in short supply. The support lines that mothers rely on to cope with multiple health problems in their children, partners and themselves are often too fragile. But only rarely is support missing altogether. A few parents in the North recounted such positive support from their doctor, from Sure Start, and in a few cases from social workers. Throughout our visits London parents seemed to find pressure on health services greater.

Doctors and hospitals carry expensive overheads, with a high investment in training to diagnose and treat medical conditions. Alongside the clinical help, medical problems require more community-oriented supports to meet what many families need. Some health services recognise this, for example with parenting advice, child support groups and special sessions with a nurse for elderly people.[18]

The levels of ill health, of long-term limiting illness and disability, of mental stress, anxiety and depression, were extraordinarily high in the four areas. Yet this is not surprising given the levels of worklessness (over 40 per cent), of lone parents (nearly half) and of minority ethnic groups (nearly half). These three groups are particularly concentrated in disadvantaged areas, have disproportionately low incomes and have much worse health outcomes than average.[19] Meanwhile, health services find it difficult to attract GPs into problematic areas. East London neighbourhoods are under particular pressure.[20]

Many health reforms developed during the course of our study, giving patients more say in standards and more control over what happened to them as patients. Yet parents did not talk about these reforms and conveyed little sense of control over what happened to them when they were 'under the doctor' due to family illness. They did not generally complain about this since they didn't expect to control serious health problems in that way. One decision several parents made was to stop taking drugs that didn't seem to work. Although parents were upset about the pressure on health services in East London, in general, they drew comfort from the way doctors treated them, with few complaints.

Little preventative healthcare was available, given the high concentrations of problems. There was little mention of health visitors or health campaigns, except through the vehicle of Sure Start, which in one area offered counselling services and alternative health, and recruited local parents to train as outreach support to parents with chronically sick children. Fitness and healthy eating programmes were more likely to reach parents through Sure Start, schools and local college courses than through health services.

The problems of obesity and smoking came up in discussion with parents, but we did not glean evidence of diet-related health advice, or local anti-smoking clinics, or more direct medical interventions to help people stop smoking, drinking or over-eating. Parents occasionally referred to health problems resulting from poor diets, smoking, drinking or drugs. Occasionally parents referred to weight problems or to spending too much on cigarettes, but these were not issues they focused on, possibly because a sense of guilt attached to self-inflicted abuse. Ill health, particularly related to social causes, presents a major challenge for public health and social welfare, with big increases in long-term conditions such as diet-related diabetes, obesity and more widespread mental ill health.

One public health risk parents seemed universally aware of was the risk of their children being tempted into drugs, and connected violence and crime. They understood at first hand the effect of drugs on people's functioning and the real risk of addiction. They also absorbed alarming publicity from schools, television programmes and local papers. If parents in these areas received more support through public health interventions, the risks might be reduced and fears abated.

Our conclusion has to be that public health efforts to tackle socially embedded, class-related health problems do not carry the sense of urgency that immediate physical illness carries. Medical services in these areas are stretched to their limit with little spare capacity to adopt a more preventive, less reactive, approach towards more generalised problems that do not immediately display acute symptoms.

Parents found it hard to prioritise their own health when their children's needs seemed more pressing. Lack of adequate health education meant that parents often did not recognise family health as affected by regular healthy meals, regular bedtimes and regular exercise. More often parents saw health as connected with illness that doctors could cure. Parents had little sense of agency over their general health; rather the opposite – many parents seemed unclear what to do in order to prevent health problems arising. It was the parents' lack of comments about these preventive health measures that led us to feel that health education could play a much bigger role.

The external pressures on parents that they felt affected their health, such as housing or caring for parents, made them turn to doctors for much wider help. Area conditions were a large influence, including overcrowding and damp homes, but most important influences were crime, bad behaviour and fear of trouble. These external factors often triggered depression, so that family life became more enclosed to a point where of itself it could intensify depression, pointing again to low-income parents' urgent need for organised activities outside the home. This was a most urgent priority for health reasons as much as for young people's social and physical development. It might make more difference to the health of children and families than almost any other move, as parents often juxtaposed the problem of depression with the benefits of social activity. They talked of a Sure Start equivalent for older children and families.

Mothers with medically diagnosed depression had greatly reduced capacity to cope. They found it hard to deal with tasks like leaving the house, getting the children to school on time and organising meals. In their own words, their ability to do more with their children, to put in the extra time on cooking, cleaning, organising, to take on or hold on to jobs, was restricted by their debilitating depression, compounded by their depressing circumstances. In most cases there seemed to be some connection between socially and environmentally driven conditions and actual depression.

A change in approach, that emphasised healthy lifestyles, educating parents about the dangers of poor diet and lack of exercise as well as smoking, drinking and drugs, could help disadvantaged areas.[21] It could counter two other related problems that affect family health – the shortage of money and the isolation of lone parents. It would create local, low level jobs, and it would provide low- and no-cost shared spaces for families.

Many potential solutions emerged. A more preventative approach to health is yet to flourish in the areas where it is most needed. Health problems are deeply entrenched within people's personal lives, within cultural patterns of social behaviour and within the much more pervasive social inequalities that the family lives reveal.[22] It requires multi-stranded actions on the environment, play and social spaces, community supports and meeting points to close the persistent and troubling health gap.

## Notes

[1] Power, A. et al (2009) *Strategic review of health inequalities in England post-2010 (Marmot Review): Task Group 4: The built environment and health inequalities*, London: The Marmot Review.

[2] The Marmot Review (2010) *Fair society, healthy lives: Post-2010 strategic review of health inequalities*, London: The Marmot Review.

[3] Sustainable Development Commission (SDC) (2010) *Sustainable development is key to tackling health inequalities and climate change*, London: SDC.

[4] Sustainable Development Commission (SDC) (2010) *Sustainable development: The key to tackling health inequalities*, London: SDC; Perpetuity Research (2008) *One more broken window: The impact of the physical environment on schools*, Birmingham: NASUWT (The Teachers' Union); James, O. (1995) *Juvenile violence in a winner–loser culture: Socio-economic and familial origins of the rise of violence against the person*, London: Free Association Books; The Marmot Review (2010) *Fair society, healthy lives: Post-2010 strategic review of health inequalities*, London: The Marmot Review.

[5] Foresight Mental Capital and Wellbeing Project (2008) *Final project report*, London: Government Office for Science.

[6] Power, A. (2007) *City survivors: Bringing up children in disadvantaged neighbourhoods*, Bristol: The Policy Press.

[7] Hills, J., Sefton, T. and Stewart, K. (eds) (2009) *Towards a more equal society? Poverty, inequality and policy since 1997*, Bristol: The Policy Press.

[8] Salway, S., Platt, L., Chowbey, P., Harriss, K. and Bayliss, E. (2007) *Long-term ill-health, poverty and ethnicity*, Bristol: The Policy Press.

[9] Office for National Statistics (ONS) (2009) *Smoking-related behaviour and attitudes, 2008/09*, Opinions Survey Report No 40, London: Office of Public Sector Information.

[10] Office for National Statistics (ONS) (2000) *Psychiatric morbidity among adults living in private households*, London: The Stationery Office; Foresight Mental Capital and Wellbeing Project (2008) *Final project report*, London: Government Office for Science.

[11] Foresight Mental Capital and Wellbeing Project (2008) *Final project report*, London: Government Office for Science.

[12] James, O. (1995) *Juvenile violence in a winner–loser culture: Socio-economic and familial origins of the rise of violence against the person*, London: Free Association Books.

[13] Kiernan, K.E. and Mensah, F.K. (2010) 'Unmarried parenthood, family trajectories, parent and child well-being', in K. Hansen, H. Joshi and S. Dex (eds) *Children of the 21st century: The first five years*, Bristol: The Policy Press, pp 77-94.

[14] Gregg, P., Propper, C. and Washbrook, E. (2007) *Understanding the relationship between parental income and multiple child outcomes: A decomposition analysis*, CASEpaper 129, London: LSE.

[15] James, O. (1995) *Juvenile violence in a winner–loser culture: Socio-economic and familial origins of the rise of violence against the person*, London: Free Association Books.

[16] Sassi, F. (2009) 'Health inequalities: a persistent problem', in J. Hills, T. Sefton and K. Stewart (eds) *Towards a more equal society? Poverty, inequality and policy since 1997*, Bristol: The Policy Press, pp 135-54 ; The Marmot Review (2010) *Fair society, healthy lives: Post-2010 strategic review of health inequalities*, London: The Marmot Review.

[17] James, O. (1995) *Juvenile violence in a winner–loser culture: Socio-economic and familial origins of the rise of violence against the person*, London: Free Association Books.

[18] The Laurels Healthy Living Centre; Broadwater Farm Community Health Centre; Bromley By Bow Centre.

[19] Power, A. (2007) *City survivors: Bringing up children in disadvantaged neighbourhoods*, Bristol: The Policy Press; Power, A. et al (2009) *Strategic review of health inequalities in England post-2010 (Marmot Review): Task Group 4: The built environment and health inequalities*, London: The Marmot Review.

[20] The Laurels Healthy Living Centre; Broadwater Farm Community Health Centre; Bromley By Bow Centre.

[21] Dyson, A. et al (2009) *Strategic review of health inequalities in England post-2010 (Marmot Review): Task Group 1: Childhood development, education and health inequalities*, London: The Marmot Review.

[22] Wilkinson. R. and Pickett, K. (2009) *The spirit level: Why more equal societies almost always do better*, London: Allen Lane.

# SEVEN

# Families move into work: skills, training and tax credits

*I like the job. It's just a cleaning job. I've got a lovely day ward. It's so clean and nice and everybody is nice. But personally I think I'm capable of doing more. I feel a bit frustrated and they can tell that because I keep applying for jobs here and there. They're saying, 'oh don't worry, something'll break through soon'. I think I'm capable of doing something better. I tried – I wanted to do an Access test – I always pass and get admission, but I don't have the money to go.* (Cynthia, West City)

## Introduction

Work invariably brought benefits to all family members, particularly when coupled with training opportunities, even when the work itself was relatively low paid and low skilled. It expanded family incomes and broadened horizons; it generated social contact and gave children positive role models. In this chapter we summarise the evidence from the 200 families about their work experience, the evolution of jobs in their families over the course of our visits and the links between parents' work ambitions and training opportunities. We then explore the parents' direct accounts of work, studying and training, using parents' own words to convey their experiences, including the work history and prospects of 'work-poor' families. The work background of the families clearly influences why some parents do not work, including inter-generational worklessness. The impact of working tax credits, childcare worries, knock-on effects on benefits and associated problems in relation to jobs, suggest what might help.

Parents who did work were generally positive about the experience even though it created extra pressures in their lives. Work was an ambition that many parents had within themselves, as well as a strong goal of government to get more parents into work. As children got older, this allowed mothers more scope to work, and over the course of our visits there was also an expansion in jobs and training, the introduction of tax credits, offering new incentives for part-time, low-paid but vital service jobs. These jobs in public services particularly benefited mothers, and this chapter draws mainly on evidence from mothers.

Not all parents were able to work, some through ill health or caring responsibilities (discussed in Chapter Six), some through tenuous work histories and lack of experience or confidence, some through a fear of losing the safety-net of benefits without a guarantee of continuing reliable work, the well-known poverty trap.[1] Many lone parents felt too burdened by the responsibility of childrearing alone to be able to work. To understand why up to half the parents don't work while half or more do, we start by looking at the work histories of the families.

## Where families started from

At the onset, we asked the parents about their work experience and qualifications before having children, and their current employment status. We also asked about their partners' work experience. The work patterns and experiences of working parents fell into six broad categories:

- *Career progression:* about a quarter of the parents were gradually working their way up the career ladder, from basic jobs such as attendants in swimming pools or sports centres to jobs with some training requirement such as sports instructor or assistant.
- *Consistent career:* one fifth of parents moved from one reasonably steady job to another, often involving some basic training and qualifications such as practice nursing.
- *Steady mixed jobs:* about one sixth of parents did jobs carrying some responsibility, involving some training and skills, but unspecialised and changeable tasks such as section manager in a shop.
- *Unsteady mixed jobs:* another fifth did short-term, casual jobs, including some caring jobs with low status and low pay such as childcare, housekeeping and other essential services.
- *Mixed low-paid jobs:* a tenth of parents had done a variety of low skill but fairly steady jobs.
- *Unsteady career:* a small group of parents had higher level qualifications but moved in and out of jobs on a casual basis, working through agencies in nursing or other social care fields.

Among the mothers we spoke to, three quarters were not working in 1998 at our first visit. The great majority of these had children under 10 and over a third had pre-school children. A majority of the non-working mothers had a much weaker work history, often within the last three categories of work patterns. Already by our second visit, a majority of mothers were in work. By our last visit in 2006 around two thirds of mothers were in work, and the proportion not working had fallen dramatically. In London where jobs were easier to access and parents were generally more experienced, more were working and more were employed full time. There was something of a virtuous circle, where the stronger London economy created more opportunities and generated more skills and attracted more mothers into work (see Figure 7.1(a) and (b)).

**Figure 7.1:** Work status of mothers* at end of study, 2006

(a) Mothers in work

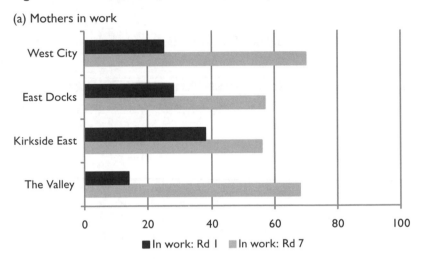

(b) Status of those in work

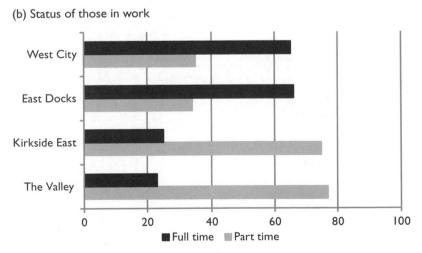

* Parents we interviewed who were in work were, with only one exception, mothers.

By our last visit many more parents in all areas were in work, although the gaps between full-time and part-time work, North and South, remained stark. Overall far fewer parents were not working, partly as a simple result of their children growing up and going to school (see Figure 7.2).

**Figure 7.2:** Mothers not working, 2006

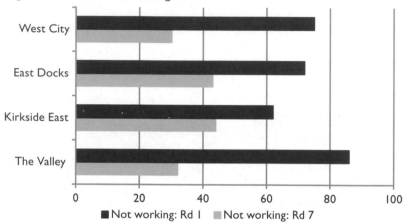

■ Not working: Rd 1   ▩ Not working: Rd 7

We collected information on partners working in 2005–06. They were far more likely to work than mothers, and many more of them worked full time. Family conditions and relations were greatly helped by having a full-time working partner, affecting about half the families. Figure 7.3 sets out partners' work status.

**Figure 7.3:** Work status of partner, 2006

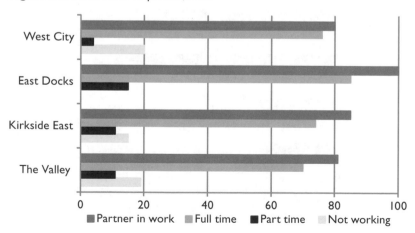

■ Partner in work   ▩ Full time   ■ Part time   ▢ Not working

There was a big gap between the work experience of non-working and working parents. Working parents had a much stronger employment background and work history, giving them more confidence and know-how in approaching the job market. A minority had done responsible jobs in shops, offices, health or public services such as libraries, nurseries or schools, either as assistants to someone senior or as section managers responsible for a particular counter or section in a shop. Parents who had only done casual or short-term jobs had far more difficulty getting work, let alone rising up the job ladder or accessing work-related training without help. Three out of ten parents we spoke to had never worked at any time in their adult lives.

Parents in East London had more recognised skills and more work experience than parents in the North. This was particularly true among the more numerous London families of international origin who had come from Africa, Latin America and other less developed countries with the hope and ambition of progressing their own training and careers and their children's education. Throughout our visits, most mothers from all areas showed a great interest in and keenness for training. By the end a high proportion of working mothers were training while working, believing that training would enhance their job prospects, as Figures 7.4(a) and 7.4(b) show.

Over half of the families were on very low incomes (less than half the national average income) in the four neighbourhoods when the study began. Over the period of our visits from 1998, tax credits were introduced, providing parents with an incentive to work and an income supplement for low-paid and part-time work. Figures 7.5(a) and 7.5(b) show the high proportion finding themselves better off as a result.

**Figure: 7.4(a)** Mothers studying for qualifications while working, 2006

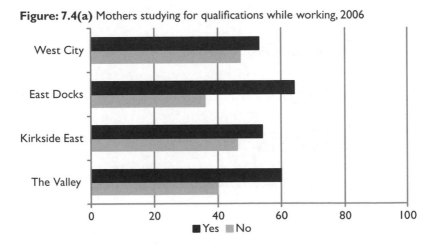

**Figure 7.4(b):** Training has enhanced job prospects, 2006

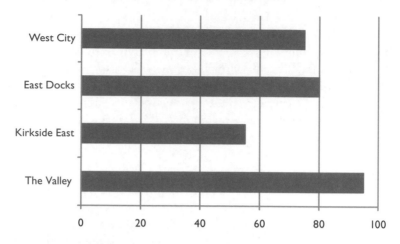

**Figure 7.5(a):** Families receiving tax credits, 2006

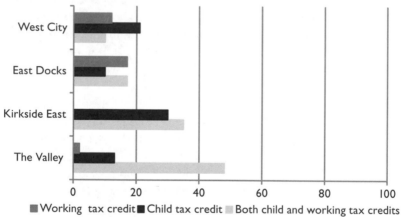

■ Working tax credit ■ Child tax credit ■ Both child and working tax credits

**Figure: 7.5(b):** Families finding themselves better off with tax credits, 2006

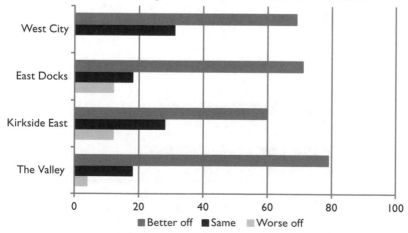

■ Better off   ■ Same   ■ Worse off

## Low-paid jobs and parenting

Low pay and low skills were recurring issues, making some parents question the value of working:

> *The sort of money I could earn in a shop job wouldn't make it worthwhile to pay someone to look after the children.* (Jenny, The Valley)

> *The majority of those who work in the area as dinner ladies and cleaners struggle financially. I would like to work in a job I could afford to work in.* (Jacqui, Kirkside East)

At the beginning of the our visits, in 1999 the problem of 'work poverty', where no one in the household was employed, studying or in training, affected nearly half the families in the Northern neighbourhoods: 45 per cent of adults in the households in Kirkside East and 51 per cent in The Valley were not working, studying or training; among the families in the two East London neighbourhoods, 33 per cent of the adults of working age in East Docks and 42 per cent in West City were not working, studying or training. These proportions were far higher than the national average of 25 per cent, almost double the national rate in the North and over 50 per cent higher in East London. It was hard to make ends meet with the work-related costs and the levels of pay:

> *I tried to go back to work but the child minder for him is £75 a week and with the other three I can't afford. I want a job that I can take them and pick them up from school.* (Belinda, East Docks)

Most parents described the basic, low-paid, service-related jobs they had done and when they worked, still generally did:

> *I'm fairly satisfied with my job, because I have time to take the kids. I have to drop my son at school and pick him up. To get someone to pick up my older son for me has been really hectic – picking up and dropping from one child minder to the next. The money's low but I love the clients I work with.* (Frances, East Docks)

Beyond these groups there was a large band of parents with very limited and only casual, informal work experience who did not work. This parent was open about the dilemmas:

> *I love fiddle work and I can get it, but you get caught. If it's official
> I have to pay full rent and council tax. I went to the lone parents'
> adviser and even she said it wouldn't be worth my while. (Jane,
> The Valley)*

A London mother explained how her only choice was low-paid work:

> *That's my life history. There was 15 of us, I'm the oldest, so I
> didn't have any choice. My son thinks I'm joking – who'd work
> for £4.50 a week? But it was a lot of money back then. (Niamh,
> West City)*

Childcare, particularly for pre-school children, but also for school holidays and after school, was particularly difficult. Many parents relied on relatives where they could. This problem was compounded by a poor work history, lack of skills or formal training, coupled with the responsibilities and cost of childcare itself, and prevented many mothers from considering an early return to work. This was particularly true of lone parents.

> *She's at the childminders at the moment, but it's so difficult. For the
> prices that people are paying for childminding – they're registered
> but the environment is poor – I wish my company could do more
> for parents, like offering us crèches – even if it meant docking our
> monthly wages. A lot of people have to take special leave because
> of children and employers aren't that sympathetic. (Sushan, West
> City)*

Government efforts to improve the quality of childcare through the National Childcare Strategy sometimes works against parents in low-paid jobs because formal childcare must be used and this pushes up costs. Often they try to find relatives or neighbours who will help informally – three quarters of families get some kind of help, particularly with children, from relatives who live nearby.[2]

## How work changed over the course of our visits

Over the period of our visits, parents, their partners and adult children progressively moved into paid employment. The increases were much bigger in the two inner-city neighbourhoods, West City where work increased by 54 per cent, and The Valley where it increased by 53 per cent. In these areas access to the centre was easier, and more local services existed, as the areas were more dense, more mixed and more established. The outer two areas were both more cut off from city centres and dominated by large council estates. They still had significant increases in work, 29 per cent in East Docks and 18 per cent in Kirkside East.

By our last visit, a sizeable majority of all households had someone in work and the levels of 'work poverty' within the households, meaning no one in work at all, had dropped significantly everywhere. Forty per cent of parents in the outer areas still had no work because access to jobs was harder as most families lived in social housing estates that were more cut off from job connections.[3] Also the proportion of lone parents was higher, making working more difficult. In the more mixed inner London area, only 21 per cent of parents were without any household member in work by 2006, and in the inner-city Northern area, 30 per cent. Not only was access easier, but also job connections were more direct as a result of small local businesses and the need for low-paid service workers.

The big shift into work was driven by six major changes. First, as children got older, it became easier for mothers to work. Second, the economy grew significantly between 1998 and 2006, so job opportunities expanded, attracting many previously unemployed people back into work. Third, the introduction of working tax credits, a direct subsidy through the benefit system for those taking on low-paid and part-time jobs, boosted the interest of mothers in jobs that previously would have seemed too marginal. It also made it possible for parents, particularly mothers, to work part time while gaining a substantial boost in their income. Fourth, and significantly for many of our families, the new emphasis on training, skills and IT had percolated through to the families and areas, with new adult education colleges in two of the areas. Fifth, many new job openings were in local services, such as teaching assistants and health assistants, warden services and so on. These local jobs were often family-friendly and helped drive mothers' aspirations for training and work, while allowing them to give time to their children. Sixth, the introduction of the Childcare Tax Credit to meet up to 80 per cent of formal childcare costs and the expansion of free part-time nursery provision for all three- to four-year-olds particularly helped mothers into work.[4]

The big rise in local, part-time jobs related to local supervision, childcare and retail, new assistant roles in schools, health and social care, fostering and special needs assistance, all favoured local parents, particularly mothers, although there was some worry about the low status of the most basic service jobs:

> *I just want to do something better than cleaning and catering....*
> *When they grow up, my children will ask, 'Mummy, where did you*
> *work?'. You understand – doing a cleaning.* (Sade, East Docks)

Alongside this movement into jobs and training by mothers many more
male partners were working by our last visit. Of the families that had
two parents (just over half), over 90 per cent of male partners were in
work. Work helped couples to maintain a stable relationship, and it was
easier for at least one partner to work:

> *It works out better if there's two of you – a man and a woman.*
> (Jackie, Kirkside East)

The increase in paid employment showed up in the income of working
households by our last visit. In Kirkside East, the large, poor Northern
council estate, three quarters of households received some income
from employment, and in-work benefits to supplement low pay. In
The Valley 85 per cent of families did the same. In the East London
areas almost two thirds of families had incomes made up of wages and
in-work benefits, 64 per cent in West City and 60 per cent in East
Docks. Wages were still generally low, and many jobs were part time,
so many families received in-work benefits and tax credits but these
acted as a positive incentive in most cases, encouraging people to work,
and significantly raising their in-work income. Even so, low pay and
struggling with the extra time pressures and costs of working made
for a constant struggle:

> *The hours got too much, my husband was having to do the dinners.*
> *It was always World War Three when I came home!* (Marilyn,
> West City)

The recession has now hit jobs hard, but the group most severely
affected is young people, particularly school leavers, and young workers
in precarious, casual jobs. We do not cover young people's access to
work in detail here, but parents worried about it. The back-up service
jobs that many parents took on, in security, health, education, childcare
and environmental services, survived the early stages of the recession,
but they may well suffer over the next period of public spending cuts:[5]

> *At the moment I'm dissatisfied with the youth service because I*
> *don't know what's happening. They're rearranging everyone's work*

*and not telling them. I don't know if I'm going to go into work and not have a job.* (Becky, Kirkside East)

## Training and studying

*I want to have something to myself – something that is my achievement. Also if beforehand I can learn the language I will be able to help my children with their homework.* (Hulya, West City)

One important influence on parents' increasing access to work was the growing availability of local training. Many parents, partners and grown-up children began studying during our visits. This was far more common in East London, where a third of families in East Docks and 40 per cent of families in West City had someone who started studying between 1999 and 2006. In Kirkside East, it was 12 per cent and in The Valley, 16 per cent. The higher figure for London reflected both the motivation of parents and their partners, and the stronger job market, generating more work potential and therefore stronger rationale and motivation for training. Families of foreign origin were often highly ambitious for themselves and their children, as they had often come here partly to benefit from education:

*I'm ready for it. It'll be very fulfilling for me after all these studies to put it into practice. The kids are older now. I always believed in looking after them, but now it's to satisfy myself.* (Aminia, East Docks)

*They had some people come down from Oxford University. They're trying to get kids from this area into places like Oxford. There's 15 kids out of the whole borough, and she was third. They said if her grades carry on as they are now, she definitely going to get a place in Oxford.* (Kayla, East Docks)

On our last visit, we asked parents about on-the-job training, and whether it enhanced their job prospects. Over half of working parents in Northern areas had done basic college courses while working – often in IT, childcare or health. Most had chosen to do this, rather than being required to do it. More than half of the Northern parents felt that their training had enhanced their job prospects. About half the Northern parents thought that studying would influence job prospects:

> *I've got a Millennium Award so I've been doing the training I've got £2,000 for.* (Adam, The Valley)

Most parents enjoyed training and felt it brought them into contact with new forms of support and greater ambition:

> *I'm going to do this dyslexia course because I want to help my son more. I know that's going to turn into a full-time job. I may end up doing two or three hours in a morning with dyslexic children but I'm not intending to. I'm doing the courses for my sake, to have a better feeling for how to help my son. But there's no harm in a few extra hours.* (Sinead, West City)

## How families' lives changed through training and jobs: "*They've improved job prospects*"

Parents explained in detail how studying, training and work affected them and their families. For some parents courses and training had developed their skills and performance in the job that they were already doing. Patsy was doing a very responsible but under-qualified caring job and she clearly gained knowledge and competence through the work-based training her employers sent her on, to help her with her current job:

> *I have done City and Guilds Adult Learning Support levels 1 and 2, in work time, through work. It wasn't part of the job, just an opportunity I could take. It didn't change my job prospects or enhance them. It showed me how to be more structured with the adults with learning disabilities I work with, and how to take notes on the work.* (Patsy, Kirkside East)

In the large Northern estate a parent praised the longer-term investment brought by a large supermarket that recruited locally and trained local people for the new jobs. She was sceptical about how well it would work with people who had been out of work for a long time, seeing a big gap in motivation and ambition that would require more serious efforts to close:

> *The most significant thing is the Tesco Centre and local learning centre. Those are the two major things that improved things for the neighbourhood.... They have improved job prospects, provided lots of jobs. People need to use these things though. A lot were forced*

*to go to the local learning centre and were long-term unemployed and had no interest in a job. That is no good. Good if people want to go and use the services. But they are few and far between.* (Margaret, Kirkside East)

For some parents, the new skills they acquired helped them to progress within their current roles, as Yetunda explained:

*… I've done an NVQ level 4 in customer service which is very useful, now they want me to do the receptionist side of it as well. They're good at training you, they allow you to progress. It enhanced my job a lot. I could move on to another side of the practice, managerial or whatever.* (Yetunda, West City)

Low-paid female service workers were sometimes able to progress through training, as this Northern mother explained:

*I have done courses through work when I worked as a support worker at Northern General Hospital. Two weeks each. Resuscitation and a health and hygiene one. They changed my job prospects and what I could apply for, in that I could work independently as a support worker, so they helped my job at the time.* (Meg, The Valley)

## "I know I want to work in special needs"

For some parents, new courses and training opened up the prospect of moving into a new area of work altogether. Sometimes this was an active career decision. One parent took a two-year-long medical secretary course. Others strategically pieced together different courses to help them move into a chosen area of work. This proactive, step-by-step approach to studying and training demonstrated a detailed knowledge of the areas of work they were aiming for, as the following mothers show, making a direct connection between the courses they took and the ambition to work in a particular field:

*I just finished a Cache Level 3 Teaching Assistant course to work with special needs kids. And I did a 28-week course on managing health and social care institutions. And I am doing a 60 credit project management course at university. I know I want to work in special needs and these extra topics are a good extra.* (Louise, Kirkside East)

> *I've done an Open College Network (OCN) Counselling course
> and recently a Reading Matters for Life OCN course. I hope
> they've enhanced my job prospects... I wouldn't look at counselling
> as a career, too long to train, I couldn't do it, but it is a useful
> thing to have done if I want to work in a school. And the Reading
> Matters course proves that I can establish a rapport with secondary
> school kids. So the two together should make it easier to get a job.*
> (Francesca, The Valley)

For another mother, her course helped her in her current post and
would help her when applying for new jobs. Her motive for doing
extra training was mainly to help her care for her son with special
needs, but she felt this training could also help with new job prospects:

> *I've done various internal courses at work, like PC training. I
> plan to do a university course, a postgraduate certificate in autism,
> an evening class. The courses at work just feed into the job I do,
> but the new skills never hurt when applying for new jobs. And
> the autism course will be for home, because my son age four has
> been diagnosed with autism, but it could open new work doors.*
> (Gillian, The Valley)

Many parents talked about their studies and training as giving them a
sense of personal achievement and increased confidence:

> *As well as GCSEs in English and Maths I've been doing art
> workshops with the kids and I do stuff at church, but that's just
> for my own time. I did autism workshops at the school because
> there is a child that I work with, he is autistic. And I've done a
> sign language workshop via the school. You are encouraged to do a
> course once a year, one course a year. It has changed my job prospects
> a lot. It has done me the world of good because I have got more
> confidence to go out there and try other things, whereas before I
> would not, I wouldn't do that.* (Faye, West City)

Training opportunities frequently helped parents to build their general
skills, helping them to cope with family problems and to contribute to
community well-being. This mother who fostered needy local children
explained how she had built up her knowledge and confidence and
was now taking the initiative in using what she had learned to help in
schools, so far without pay:

*I have been thinking quite a bit lately about whether to go back to work. It's just, all the enquiries I have made have made me think, 'Oh, it's too hard'. But I have also applied for a grant, because of speaking at these fostering meetings. It has built my confidence, so that I'm starting this thing to go into schools to talk to teenagers about the dangers of alcoholism because that's what the child I am fostering has, foetal alcohol syndrome, and what some of the foster babies that I looked after had, you know. I've managed to get a grant for a laptop and a PowerPoint thing to go into classes in local schools to talk about that. And that's a direct result of having done the training and discovered that I'm braver than I thought I was. But it's still not paid employment, so, you know....* (Trudy, West City)

## Barriers to training: *"I was frustrated"*

Parents had to overcome many problems when they tried to study or do training. One parent found that studying was not enough and her lack of experience counted against her in trying to secure more highly paid jobs. She realised that direct work experience and 'soft skills' in presentation mattered a lot:

*I have studied continuously. I have to do it at Sure Start. Like a First Aid course, Food Hygiene, Breastfeeding Peer Support.... Sure Start is not something permanent but a health position will come by, so yes, my upcoming degree will enhance my job prospects.... Well, I applied for higher jobs, lots more money, but I had no management experience. I did well other than that. So I need that training and I talked to my boss. You need the knack of talking.* (Nita, The Valley)

Another mother had too little work experience to be able to apply what she learned. She thought work experience should be built into training, although by our final visit, she had secured full-time employment:

*... you go to college to better yourself and they don't send you on work experience for a year, do they. I done 12 weeks work experience when I done the NVQ in IT and administration, 12 weeks ain't nothing on a CV, you know, so, it didn't mean a hoot. It annoyed me though. I was frustrated. I thought, I worked hard to get these qualifications, and they have done me no good.* (Natalie, West City)

One ambitious, creative, but hard-pressed mother in the North had a special interest in the environment and sacrificed a lot to do an Environmental Studies degree while her children were young. It did not lead to a job so she opted for teaching fine art, but she was not eligible for a grant and therefore was unsure. As her plans changed she needed support to continue beyond her current access course:

> *I am currently studying for an Adult Access in Art and Design. And I hope to go on to do something in fine art. I had thought of teaching Design and Technology, but my real dream would be to be a fine artist, do a degree in that. No grants for it though, so I could apply for bursaries, I've got another year to sort it out. I've used up my grant entitlement from when I became a student before in Environmental Studies. I would need a massive student loan. It would double my outgoings. And the banks would not do it. I shall try very hard to get bursaries. It would be useful to get a teaching qualification at the end of it. That would be the day job. I would be a professional artist by evening!* (Phoebe, The Valley)

## "It's very stressful, it's very rewarding"

Parents often relied on a contribution of informal and formal childcare, and it was common for parents to find expensive and unreliable childcare a barrier to work. Combining children, paid work and study could be very difficult for parents, particularly mothers. This came through clearly in what some mothers told us. Several accepted straightforwardly that they could not work because of children. Mothers on their own with little support often felt that they had no choice but to stay at home. These women avoided difficult decisions, related to work and childcare, because they saw no other option realistically open to them other than becoming a full-time, home-based mother. Fatima in The Valley was on her own so she felt she had no choice but to sacrifice her ambitions:

> *When I had no kids I worked and studied, years ago. 'A' levels at college – Art and Urdu – and I worked as a nursery nurse in a nursery. Before I had my third child I did a returning to work course in administration and IT, aiming to get a job, but I fell pregnant with my third.* (Fatima, The Valley)

Other mothers provided long accounts of the difficulties they had in juggling paid work and childcare, often a very complicated balancing act. One mother who worked in a school explained her tight timetables, a precision act of 'high-wire juggling'. She realised that with her third baby, she actually needed more time at home:

> *When I had my other two, I only worked part time, three-and-a-half hours a day, it was quite alright. I didn't go to work till 10.00 and was home by 1.30, which wasn't too bad. But now, school, you go out about half eight and you get home at quarter to four at night, it's nearly all the day gone. Especially when they're this age. I think you do things always to improve yourself. But my whole idea of going back to work after the new baby comes now is out the window. I'd like to do something different, I don't know what I'd like to do, because working with children I find, especially with special needs children, it's very stressful, very hard work. It's very rewarding but I've now got a baby and I'm going to have another baby, it's very demanding at home anyway. So if you've both had a very stressful day at work and then have to come home and look after two children yourself it's too demanding. If I hadn't had my son, I think I might've gone on to do teacher training, 'cos they'd been asking me to do that, for the last year. But once I'd had him, I was like 'no way, I'm not doing more hours', I want to cut down my hours if anything. I'd like to see my child grow up.* (Alice, West City)

Alice's words captured the feelings of many mothers; they did not want to sacrifice the time they could give their children, particularly while they were small. Annie, in East Docks, explained how she had had to abandon her degree as she could not reconcile it with her family, even though she was already working and doing well as a teaching assistant:

> *I was washing up one evening, trying to think of the next line of an essay and realised Chantelle was just sitting on the bed doing nothing – that was it. They depend on you.* (Annie, East Docks)

It was sometimes unclear whether the courses parents were doing constituted full degrees or enjoyed full recognition. Often parents referred to local further education colleges as 'university'. Also many of the local colleges were now affiliated in some way with a university, so parents often referred to training courses as degrees, and colleges as universities.

One mother talked about the 'ceiling' facing mothers in low-paid but vital service jobs like childcare in spite of her studies. Training courses were sometimes over-sold as offering more than in practice was true, particularly as they were more theoretical. Hands-on training seemed to work best:

> *The NVQ in Nursery Nursing has enhanced my job prospects more than what my degree did. The degree just gets your foot in the door, especially as everyone is looking for childcare. But there is always a ceiling with these careers, I cannot go any further.* (Rosemary, West City)

Some parents could not contemplate further self-advancement due to rigid work structures. This mother worked for the prison service. Her workplace seemed unsympathetic and unsupportive, leading to her training needs being overlooked. Hannah felt she was being discriminated against. She felt that priority went to staff who were lesbian in the women's prison:

> *I've been moved to Operations since May, but I've not even had one day of training. Some colleagues have been picked out for training. It's all self-taught, whatever I'm doing, observing other officers, asking them questions, to do my job. If you complain you'll be moved to the worst place until you get frustrated and leave the job. If you're not a lesbian or gay, you're not one of them. The minority who are not of that sexual orientation – you are an outsider.* (Hannah, East Docks)

Cynthia explained the conflict between care of her children and earning money to pay debts. This stopped her being able to train and qualify in nursing:

> *With the NVQ and the job I have no time to study. I have a mentor for the course but even this doesn't help much because of the kids. I do extra work to make up the money. I go to college at 1.30pm and come home at 9pm. Sometimes I do agency nursing as well. I'm worried about Suzie's homework.... I should be coming home at 5 o'clock to help with homework. I want to give up my evening job and involve myself more with my children's work.* (Cynthia, West City)

Parents knew just how important it was for their children to get a job, and that meant training:

> *I want them all to get a trade. There's always cause for a plumber
> or brick builder. I've always said, if he goes for an apprenticeship,
> out there and just get a job, he can get on his own little merry way.*
> (Lesley, East Docks)

Angela was desperate for her children to do better than she had:

> *Not that I had a bad life, but I've never had a job and I want
> them to have one. I don't want them to be around here. I just want
> them all to have jobs when they grown up, do well for themselves.*
> (Angela, Kirkside East)

## Introduction of tax credits: *"I have got to pay them back"*

New Labour believed that making it more worthwhile financially
for people to take low-paid jobs would reduce the level of benefit
dependency and improve people's work motivation. Tax credits were
introduced to supplement low wages, sometimes more than doubling
family income for mothers on their own taking on part-time jobs.
Working tax credits clearly offered a big incentive for some parents
on benefits to work. The childcare assistance for working mothers also
helped to cover the cost of expensive childcare. Overall, by the end
of the study over half of all the families were receiving both. About
60 per cent of the parents in the North were receiving Child Tax
Credit, Working Tax Credit, or both, by our last visit. In London, this
figure was lower, affecting 43 per cent of families in both areas mainly
because more parents were working full time. Across all four areas,
three quarters of the families receiving tax credits thought they were
better off as a result. Parents not claiming tax credits generally thought
they were not eligible. A significant minority of families thought that
the tax credit system had not helped or was no better than Income
Support – between a fifth and a quarter of the parents.

In the two Northern neighbourhoods, about half the families
receiving tax credits said that the credit system had influenced their
decision to take a job with the extra cash underpinning their work
income. In particular, tax credits subsidised low-paid, part-time work,
particularly helping mothers. In London, fewer families felt that tax
credits had influenced their decision to work, partly because many
more parents in London worked full time. A large majority of parents
in the London neighbourhoods said that they would work regardless
of the tax credits. Greater labour shortages, stronger work histories and

greater pressure to work full time because of the high costs of working such as transport, helped shape their decisions.

## Confusion in the system: *"They've got it all wrong"*

During our last two visits, many parents brought to light the defects in the tax credit system. The dominant problem, highlighted again and again, was the risk of 'being messed about', having to rely on a badly organised system that created confusion and uncertainty:

> *I was told I should be able to claim, my husband works for himself, but it has taken two-and-a-half years to sort it out. They messed us about, I think.* (Poonam, Kirkside East)

Miscalculations, unpredictability and uncertainty deterred many families:

> *The tax credits have been confusing because they've got it all wrong. My son and daughter-in-law are one of the few people that they got it all wrong with. First they got it back, then they got it taken away, so I don't really know. And now it's all took off again, 'cos they're earning. It was horrendous.* (Peggy, East Docks)

Occasionally, a parent managed to put a positive spin on the experience of overpayment:

> *The repayments make a little bit of difference now, about £40 a month. So not much. We owe about £1,000 so it will take forever to pay it off. It is like we had a £1,000 interest free loan from the Inland Revenue!* (Laura, The Valley)

Some parents lost out because of the bureaucratic difficulties of the system:

> *Child Tax Credit, I started getting it in May this year [2004] for the first time. I did apply for it last year but they lost the form, well, they said they had never heard of me and they will only back date it three months. I could not find a copy of the letter I sent. If I had, they would have backdated it fully.* (Shirley, Kirkside East)

One parent had heard such bad things that she just gave up:

*I'm sick and tired of them. I saw about it on Watchdog. Even if
I'm entitled I don't want the hassle, I just put the form in the bin.*
(Hannah, East Docks)

The unpredictability that stemmed from people earning variable
amounts could cause serious problems.[6] Inevitably the system is geared
to offering parents a standardised entitlement based on earnings. When
pay changes, tax credits often take a while to catch up, as this case shows:

*Our income has not significantly changed, so no, we did not get
much at the start and they took it back and now we will end up
being owed, because we earned more before, now we earn less, not
much. I think we are better off with it, but as I said, it has been a
bit of a farce, how they did it.* (Heather, Kirkside East)

One parent did not think officials were calculating the sums correctly.
Another needed independent help to get her payments sorted out. Yet
another had to cope with the upset of having to pay the money she had
received back. Other parents were disillusioned with the complexity
of the system. The following quotes illustrate these problems:

*We don't understand, sometimes they are paying. They say, they
give too much or too little. It changes all the time. What they
want, we just send to them. They don't know as well. Always
the same, our money's the same. I don't understand, it's not clear.*
(Ece, West City)

*I had them not pay it for ages and tell me I had been over paid.
And I had to go to the CAB [Citizens Advice Bureau] to get it
sorted out. Running smoothly now.* (Gillian, The Valley)

*Worse off, because they are crap. They cannot manage the work
load. They say all on Income Support will go over to tax credits
and when that happens their system will go to pot because they are
useless now. I got over paid. I have got to pay them back.* (Carrie,
Kirkside East)

*It doesn't make a difference. It's all very complicated, they don't
know what they're doing.* (Marilyn, West City)

### "I'm worried I'll be in a worse situation"

A mother who didn't work was worried about the impact on her benefits of working and believed that the system would be beyond her and was therefore too risky:

> *I'm not quite sure what would happen when I'm out of work. I want to work but I don't know how the benefits system works. If I work over 15 hours, they would cut my income support. Before they award Working Families Tax Credit, you have to deal with accountants, it's really confusing. I want to work but I'm worried I'll be in a worse situation.* (Hulya, West City)

Another mother did not want to tamper with her benefits because it worried her too much:

> *... I find the system and benefits office too stressful.* (Ellie, West City)

The fear of losing benefits was by far the most common reason given by parents for not working; tax credits simply seemed too precarious to help.

Because so many families were operating at the very margin of viability, they found the additional childcare costs hard to cope with. In spite of the tax credit system helping with part of this cost, childcare costs could be so significant as to undermine parents' ability to work, as this two-earner family found:

> *My husband has a lot of debt and we get a small bit towards childcare but we could do with more because of the debt. Only £60 a month and if you pay for childcare yourself at the nursery you pay one third retainer if you're away on holiday or something. Even if you get Child Tax Credit, you have to pay the same amount still. You cannot ever rely on it. And my husband never gets around to sorting out the right amount and he hadn't done the tax return last time I saw you but he has now, and got a big rebate which I got most of. They tried to tell us they were taking a lot back. It's been a mess.* (Ellen, The Valley)

The uncertainties built into the system sent a very negative signal to parents and increased 'the benefit trap', reinforcing parents' desire to stay with the security of low income and benefits, rather than risk the exposure to financial risk and uncertainty.

## The stress of overpayments and loss of tax credits: *"Spend it before they could take it back"*

One or two families receiving tax credits actually realised that they were being overpaid and quietly hoped the mistake would go unnoticed. This strategy did not usually work for long. Families who were not aware of the penalties could hit real problems:

> *They messed up recently. Said we owe £2,500 from over a year ago, because they overpaid us. They will take it back weekly. At first they said I would get nothing, then they said I will have to get something so they will take £7 a week. It will take forever. They said his [my partner's] wages had gone up, but he is in sales so it changes a lot, and they base it on last year's earnings, you see, and it changes.* (Rosie, Kirkside East)

Another mother who was training to be a lawyer had managed to appeal successfully against an overpayment decision. Her legal background probably helped her follow the correct procedure:

> *I need to phone up as I've had a slight increase in salary. But they said I owed them thousands. Then they apologised as they owed me money! I wrote a very strong letter to complain. It helped significantly. This was when I was a trainee solicitor, when my daughter was three years old.* (Oni, East Docks)

Another mother was in the process of appealing but in the meanwhile relied on family support to help her out while she had no tax credits coming in:

> *They say that they have overpaid me about £400, I have appealed and they have acknowledged it and I am waiting now. I had no income for nine weeks except for £154 a month Child Benefit, I had family so I was fine, but what if I had no family? My friend has no family and you can only get a crisis loan if you're already on Income Support. When a job ends and you have got no benefits sorted out that's when you need it!* (Holly, Kirkside East)

Once overpayment had been detected, families immediately lost a portion of income that they had grown used to. It requires great self-assurance and confidence to argue a case against an official decision by a complex bureaucracy, and most parents did not have support to rectify mistakes, whoever was to blame. The examples of mistakes we have highlighted show that it was often inadequate understanding by parents and an expectation associated with traditional benefits that once entitled to a benefit you would remain entitled to it that led to confusion and bad decisions. Many of the families where mistakes occurred did not tell us whether the overpayment resulted from under-reporting, a time lag in the calculation, a miscalculation by Inland Revenue or a mistake by the parents.

## "Worth having"

The tax credits were much more volatile than benefits because people's wages were variable month by month.[7] A particular problem, apart from the fluctuating incomes of families, arose from the fact that the tax credit assessment was based on the previous year and therefore could be out of line with actual current income. One mother illustrated this point by describing her mixed feelings about the tax credit system – it was a great help in supplementing her income, but the loss of income following a mistake in assessment put impossible strain on her already over-stretched budget:

> *They are worth having, definitely. Especially when my hours at work were reduced. It was so noticeable when they took it away, because they overpaid me. I really noticed it and had to move back in with my parents.* (Patsy, Kirkside East)

Relationship breakdown could sometimes lead to a loss of tax credits, greatly intensifying an already stressful situation. This most commonly happened when the working partner left and that share of the family income disappeared. Sometimes a relationship breakdown could lead to a mother having to stop work to care for the family and cope with the upheaval of loss of income while carrying the extra load on her own over an anxious period of sorting out her new situation:

> *I got Working Families Tax Credit but that's now stopped. Everything's on hold.* (Charlotte, West City)

There were some parents in all the neighbourhoods who no longer received tax credits, following overpayment, although such overpayments and reclaims were fortunately rare. For example, four families in East Docks faced this problem. The consequences could be disastrous when Inland Revenue claimed back large amounts of overpaid already spent money.

## A mixed blessing, but on balance tax credits helped: *"It's good to work though"*

Most parents found that they were better off under the tax credit system, even though it took some adjusting to. A few parents felt that tax credits simply organised the same benefits money differently, leaving families in much the same position. This parent only calculated the money she directly received from the government which stayed the same, rather than her total income, including what she earned, which was clearly higher than benefits alone:

> *They just split the funding pots and you get the same money.... The position I am in at the moment, I'm the same. They have split the one benefit I had before into two.* (Holly, Kirkside East)

In reality, tax credits provide a form of benefit that is in addition to, rather than a substitute for, earned income, making working parents on tax credits clearly better off, because tax credits were a supplement, not an alternative. Parents who received tax credits were able to do very low-paid, part-time, flexible jobs that helped them as parents, as Sharon, who works in a school, explains:

> *The pay's crap, but I don't know what other job would pay as much for fairly sociable hours. I'm home by 5 and I get school holidays.* (Sharon, The Valley)

Many parents, used to depending on benefits and living on limited incomes, found it hard to adjust to having to pay more of their own direct costs because of earning more, such as school dinners, after-school clubs, and so on. Parents with this experience were still on the whole better off, even if it was harder to control additional expenditure. And parents receiving tax credits were still eligible for some forms of help. One parent with a severely disabled child talked about the benefits of receiving tax credits. As the family's overall income had risen, she

missed the security of some specific cash benefits, which had come
directly to her:

> *Well, I don't think it really makes any difference to us now. Like,*
> *we get tax credits but did not get milk vouchers for him, my*
> *13-month-old son, and then when he got to one, they put the*
> *money [tax credits] down and we still needed milk tokens. So no*
> *better off with it. And we get no uniform allowance for my daughter*
> *[age nine].* (Olivia, Kirkside East)

Other parents were keen to escape benefit dependency and were willing
to put up with the extra costs they had to meet just to be in work.
Sometimes, they got a psychological and morale boost simply because
the new system made their work more worthwhile:

> *I love it. I'll be there until I retire unless I don't have to be at work*
> *for some reason. I'll get a good pensions.* (Audrey, Kirkside East)

## "You're not sort of sponging"

There were particular problems with Housing Benefit and Council Tax
Benefit because they were organised and run through local councils, not
the Inland Revenue. Rent and Council Tax were big weekly outgoing
and parents were scared by the sudden steep cut-off they might face.
In practice most parents who were working and receiving tax credits
were eligible for Housing Benefit. This parent had her rent covered but
had to meet some associated housing costs herself, which she found
difficult. On the other hand, she was determined to work:

> *I did claim tax credits before, when I was working, but then I*
> *used to rent private and my rent used to be £200 a week, so it's*
> *a different ball game. It helped but what you had in one hand*
> *went out in the other. I paid me own water rates and all. What*
> *the government gives you in one hand, it seems to get swallowed*
> *up with things like that. It's good to work though. Stopping you*
> *getting brain dead, keeping you active. You feel like, even though*
> *you're a one-parent family, you're still doing something. You're not*
> *sort a' like sponging.* (Elaine, East Docks)

Many parents receiving benefits or tax credits found housing costs very
worrying. They often relied on hearsay from family and friends to work
out their entitlements. This was not always reassuring or accurate and it

undermined many parents' confidence in the system. This mother had picked up various unclear messages, not knowing how entitlements were calculated:

> *Just the thought of rent really, having to afford rent and poll tax on your own because you don't get much rent rebate.... I knew about tax credits when my mum was at work, 'cos she had my brother. They brought what they call Family Credit in then. It wasn't a lot, about £22 a week. My niece, she's got two little 'uns on her own, she says 'I'm not better off, but I'm not worse off'. She just got a big bill for poll tax, this, that and the other.* (Natalie, West City)

The families' perceptions and misconceptions about tax credits could get muddled up with parents' previous experience of benefits and work. For one mother, her own experience proved that the government was failing to follow through on its declared intention of helping mothers into work, leaving a clear poverty trap in place:

> *I did filing and photocopying for 12½ hours and lost my Income Support. I did it for four months but had less money, they gave me benefit of one pound. I went back to 7½ hours and Income Support. They want mothers to go back to work but they're not helping them at all.* (Megan, West City)

A precondition of claiming childcare support through working tax credits is using a registered childminder. Even if parents could arrange this, and they weren't always available, it invariably increased their costs, because the childcare support vouchers only covered part of the full cost, which was often over £250 a week in East London:

> *If I wasn't using a registered childminder it would save me £200. It's a catch-22, as I have to pay extra. I'm still thinking about it – getting someone who's not registered. I'm looking to get my daughter into a nursery setting.* (Delilah, West City)

Other mothers had a very different perspective on the childcare subsidy, believing that the extra cash it gave them made the difference between being able and not able to work:

> *I would prefer to work part time and I can because of Child Tax Credit. I could not afford to work and pay childcare fees without them.* (Gillian, The Valley)

Another Northern mother thought that both the tax credits themselves supplementing her low wages and the financial help with childcare were what made the difference:

> *They have helped me be able to work part time, I couldn't otherwise, and they help with childcare.* (Rosemary, The Valley)

## "I would lose credits"

There was a perverse incentive within the tax credit system that the government was increasingly aware of. Tax credits deterred parents from doing longer hours or overtime, even when incomes would rise with longer hours. The fear that tax credits might fall if incomes rose often influenced parents' decisions about how much to work:

> *If I doubled my hours to 22 a week I would lose my tax credits. We are £1 a week better off than a one-parent family. I did get two job interviews ... but the hours were too long, I would lose credits, so I said no to both.* (Sara, Kirkside East)

Another parent and her partner both restricted what they did because of this belief:

> *It does limit my hours, and both me and my husband do not do overtime because we get the tax credits instead.* (Liza, Kirkside East)

Liza's husband explains his worries about losing tax credit money because extra hours in the current year would affect his assessment for the following year, when there might no longer be a chance to put in the extra time:

> *It puts you off because you cannot earn much overtime. I do not work on a Sunday, I could earn a fortune, probably more than the tax credits, but I don't, because why lose it next year, the tax credits? And if there is no overtime in winter we'd be stuck....* (Liza's husband, Kirkside East)

Although some parents limited their hours in order to qualify for tax credits, the opposite could also occur. One parent had in fact increased her hours in order to maximise her in-work benefits:

> *They have influenced how I work, like, I job share with a neighbour,*
> *two-and-a-half days a week. I would have done two days but I*
> *needed to do 16 hours plus to be eligible for Working Tax Credit.*
> (Louise, The Valley)

A completely different approach was adopted by parents who would
have liked to work, but wanted to keep the security of benefits. These
mothers opted out of official working altogether but did odd jobs on
the side, like Zoe in West City, who picked up children after school,
so she could "get my son trainers". Some of the parents found it hard
to make the leap from seemingly secure benefits to seemingly insecure
tax credits, despite the open, friendly tone of the public campaigns
promoting tax credits. It seemed easier to 'make a little on the side' while
claiming benefits than to work and receive tax credits, which would
expand family incomes and offer parents greater opportunities. Lack
of confidence, based on fragile, broken, sometimes almost non-existent
work histories, often persuaded mothers that working couldn't pay.

Tax credits failed to lift parents clear of reliance on the benefits system.
Even where they helped, which on balance a large majority of those
who received them confirmed, they still left parents worried, creating
a desire to keep a foot in both camps – work and benefits. The rise in
joblessness over the period of the recession will in any case push many
families back into dependency, making parents feel vulnerable again.

## Helping parents work: *"I can't survive without them"*

In spite of many different problems, the core advantage of the tax
credit system is that it supplements the income of poorly paid, in-work
families. The criticisms of the tax credit system were counterbalanced by
positive comments from parents. For those parents who had navigated
the system successfully and were avoiding or overcoming the pitfalls,
tax credits were potentially life-transforming. One mother could attach
a cash value to it. Another mother was quick to acknowledge that she
got help with costs she would have to pay without them:

> *I have seen improvement from Family Tax Credit. It's really helped*
> *me.* (Sasha, East Docks)

> *Better off. Definitely. If I didn't have it, I'd be £450 a month*
> *worse off. It buys all my shopping!* (Cath, Kirkside East)

> *Yes, I can't survive without it, the tax credits. It helps with the dentist and eye tests.* (Rose, East Docks)

> *I could not do this job if not for the tax credits. Managing on my part-time wages would not be possible without them.* (Jenny, The Valley)

Tax credits made parents realise that low-paid jobs could be worthwhile compared with benefit security, since low-paid work was boosted by the tax credits. This mother realised that prior to the tax credit system, she would have gained very little by working:

> *We'd be just working to pay the rent. I've been on job interviews and people'd honestly said to me, 'I'm not being funny, it's not worth your while to work here 'cos the money ain't high enough'. I had to be on, like, £250 and up, 'cos otherwise it just wasn't worth it by the time you get taxed and all that. I don't think I'd have gone to work without tax credits. I think it did, you know, help....* (Natalie, West City)

Some parents valued the way tax credits allowed them work-limited hours to qualify. Parents in part-time work did not earn as much with tax credits as full-time work would have brought in, but it helped parents, particularly mothers, to combine work with spending more time at home with their children. This mother had three children, aged 7, 9 and 11:

> *I suppose I don't have to work full time because of them. I mean, it doesn't make up a full wage but I can be at home with the kids.* (Tina, Kirkside East)

Tax credits had also occasionally encouraged fathers to work fewer hours as the tax credits almost made up for the reduced earnings:

> *It has been great to have that bit of extra, almost worth my partner's working four days a week, as we get the same money and he gets an extra day off.* (Adele, The Valley)

## "That crucial bit of extra money"

The way tax credits played out in practice showed that, as planned by the government, tax credits brought more cash to families in low-paid and part-time work. Their families gained as a result and work could offer the promise of wider benefits – a greater sense of contributing to society, a better role model for children and a sense of self-worth.

The overriding benefit of tax credits was work itself. One recipient gave real insight into the positive effects of tax credits as opposed to the serious strain of trying to make a go of things in low-paid work without tax credits:

> *Working is something I'd want to do anyway. I must say, it is great to get money back though, from the government. It really, really is welcome. And it does make you think, well, it adds up, it's one of the reasons for returning; or at least to keep you in work. I mean, if you're working very long hours and you go back and the children are tired and you got a childminder who's whingeing about money and all that, just thinking, well, when you sit down and calculate how much you're taking home, it's just that crucial bit of extra money which tips the balance in favour of you working.* (Jasmine, West City)

## Parents need a clearer and more generous system: *"It's targeting the most vulnerable of society"*

Clearly tax credits had permeated many of the families, but many harboured worries. This parent explained the difficult crossover between out-of-work and in-work benefits, showing how the system could alienate the very people the government wanted most to help and who most deserved it:

> *All this blarney about parents simply going back to work is just rubbish because it's built on flimsy foundations. It's hard enough giving your time to your children, then studying and working and applying for funding. Then you're relying on someone else in a similar situation to help you care for your kids. I'm sure the people who make the policies have no idea what life's like.* (Phoebe, The Valley)

The urgency of simplifying and targeting the system is particularly clear, because the most vulnerable families are not able to deal with it. The complications of keeping the Inland Revenue informed and keeping abreast of quite sophisticated calculations of entitlements simply escape those who most need it. Debbie and Alan, the East London community activists, worried about the elusive nature of the system. They favoured a more targeted system with all its problems and disincentive. At least they felt it would be clearer:

> *I think it's a positive policy but I think the whole scheme is a total nightmare and so confusing. It's got so much negative publicity now.... I think the reality is the paperwork is complicated and the onus is on you as an individual and when it's targeting the most vulnerable members of our society perhaps they're not best placed to have that responsibility. It's just kind of very hard. The onus is on you to report all those changes. For a lot of people who are in receipt, that's the sort of stuff they're not very good at doing.... I agree with the sentiment, but I'm not sure that tax credits are the best way of delivering additional money into pockets of people who need it. Whether it's means testing child benefit ... redistribute child benefit to those who need rather than if you're a millionaire, you still get child benefit. It just seems a bit odd, especially as they use that as direct income as well and if you're on Income Support or any of those other benefits, they just take your Child Tax Credit off. It just seems mad.* (Alan, West City)

Hannah, meanwhile, believed that the only way out for her was to work long enough hours to get clear of benefits all together. They simply posed too many problems and encouraged the wrong attitude in recipients:

> *They sent me a form for tax credits but I never heard back from them. But I've made up my mind: I'm not going to rely on state benefit.... The government's not helping those of us who decide to work. If you don't work, you get everything; if you do, you lose everything. It's hard to work in this country if you have children. I think this benefit system has spoiled so many people. I always advise people to find a job.... The children know what I'm going through. I tell them when I'm upset after work. Charity begins at home. I had every right to be on benefit with four kids but I went out to work. Being on benefit makes you so dependent.... Even though the kids are young, I sit them down and explain my finances. I show my daughter my payslip – the payments, insurance etc – so they understand a new mobile phone is not a necessity.* (Hannah, East Docks)

Other mothers echoed these sentiments, particularly the view that "if you don't work and are a lone parent, everything is paid for, whereas a working parent has to pay for everything from her hard-won wages". In the eyes of another London mother, this imbalance was simply not fair. In spite of this, she decided to work, partly because she realised she would be better off in work anyway, but partly because she wanted to progress:

> *If you're on Income Support, it's free, and I think, 'There we go again'. What's the point of working when you can't have nothing free? I'm not saying it should be free; but if you're on Income Support it is clearer and more secure.* (Cynthia, West City)

Cynthia's strong feelings about the 'costs' of work and the 'benefits' of not working were belied by her own decision to work and train.

The biggest cost barriers for parents were: good quality inexpensive childcare, rent payments and associated housing costs and more stable incomes while in work. It became clear through our visits that a simpler, more predictable, more transparent way of delivering tax credits to parents wanting to work and contribute to society would overcome many outstanding barriers to work.

This East London mother felt that much stronger signals were needed:

> *What this government has got to do, is simplify the tax credit system for people that want to go out to work and need childcare. They have got to simplify it, and they've got to make more childcare places available, to get especially single parents off benefits and out of poverty. It's still got a lot of work to do on that. A tremendous amount of work to do on it. A child that I look after, her mum is a single parent, alright, she gets her childcare tax credits, she is better off, but not a lot better off. She still has to seriously juggle her finances. 'Cos you know, she has rent, council tax, and things like that to pay. I personally think they still need a lot, lot more help. There's still a lot of work to be done on it.* (Destiny, West City)

## Summary and conclusions

This chapter draws almost entirely on mothers' experience of work, training and incentives. Most mothers wanted to get on and believed that work offered a positive example to their children. A majority of them worked part time although this was less common in London; for many, juggling home, childcare and work would be impossible full time. They took for granted low pay and restricted hours, but generally seemed to feel that they were making a valuable, often caring and responsible, contribution. Many of them worked in public or social services, particularly schools, health-related and environmental services. Many saw the benefits of working to their pride, their skills and learning, even their mental health. Most working mothers also believed that their children gained from the motivation, the extra cash and the link to wider experiences, in spite of the increased pressure on their time.

Most of the jobs that parents did were relatively low-skilled or semi-skilled, but working parents were often on an upward trajectory, progressing through the courses they completed, the experience they gained and the confidence they developed. They did not generally climb out of their low-paid, low-status jobs, but many hoped that they were building up towards more rewarding, more responsible and more secure work through training. Practice nurses, teaching assistants, play assistants, dinner ladies, support workers, sports assistants and childcare workers were some of the roles they filled. Retail was another area of expansion in this period, although fewer mothers were involved in this because fewer jobs were local and hours would be less suited. 'Low level' career progression helped these parents more than the more obvious standard professional career paths that inevitably seemed hard to reach.

The new service jobs that arose over the last decade to supplement professional jobs are called 'para-professional' in that they require a basic knowledge of the field of work, some basic training in the social and professional skills required and experience and aptitude in the service area,[8] coupled with an ability to take responsibility for particular tasks, albeit limited ones. Para-professional jobs and workers are not generally recognised in spite of the important role they have come to play in core services, particularly education, health, play, supervision and security.

Training opportunities and the development of new skills helped parents in many ways – boosting their confidence, widening their horizons, offering more job satisfaction as well as directly helping their careers. Qualifications generated great pride, while basic training for people doing the most menial jobs raised the status of those jobs and offered recognition to people who otherwise enjoyed only very low status. Parents pushed themselves to advance as much as possible through training. They enjoyed learning and generally felt that they benefited as a result both in their workplace and at home with their families, often applying what they learned through work to helping their children with homework and as role models.

A big lever into work, during the period of our visits, was the expanding economy, growth in training and cash incentives for low-income households. Tax credits encouraged people to work who otherwise might not have considered it. In spite of serious teething problems, they made a real difference to people's incomes and actually made work worthwhile. However, jobs that depend on public subsidy, including publicly funded 'para-professional' jobs and some private sector service jobs, are vulnerable to public spending cuts. Many short-term initiatives that generated local jobs particularly in regeneration and neighbourhood renewal have already run out of money, and funding for further education has been cut. Meanwhile public services are generally being severely cut back and although the government has guaranteed to protect the front line, it is quite hard to see how they will protect lower-skill 'para-professional' jobs, which for mothers offered the best opportunities.

Around half the mothers had poor work histories, often bringing up children on their own, and sometimes suffering ill health or depression; they often did not believe it was possible to work and bring up children. Childcare was a constant worry, even where it was readily available and heavily subsidised. Timetables, travel, children of different ages and unsociable hours often made it difficult for vulnerable parents with very young children to work. They were afraid of losing the 'security' of benefits and could not cope with the worry of expensive childcare problems and rents, so they opted to stay at home with their children, occasionally doing simple casual jobs for cash in hand, as they had in the past. This group of parents needed better basic skills and more support in building up work experience before they could enter the job market. Similar work histories often applied to their partners, although they were often lone parents.

The big gap between the ambitions of high-aspiring parents and the demoralisation and apathy of low-aspiring parents was very noticeable, even though it is often assumed that all low-income, poorly qualified parents have similar problems and attitudes. The lower-aspiring group was commonly resigned to being on benefits as the safer option, although even non-working parents sometimes took short courses and usually contributed in some way to their community. They did not generally cut themselves off into a life of inactivity – their children made this impossible.

Overall, moving into work was an ambition held by most parents and the rewards of doing so, although small compared to the population as a whole, made a big difference to family morale, family ambitions and family capacity. Two factors were important, in addition to simply getting out of the home and feeling useful to society: first, the great boost that elementary training gave to people's work ambitions had spin-offs within the family and for children; and second, even if tax credits only added an extra £50 to weekly family income, that could boost low incomes by as much as 30 per cent.

Families hardly ever made reference to 'crap jobs', often used by more professional people to express their distaste for what less skilled people actually do to keep the system working. Retail was considered by these professionals the most conspicuous 'crap job', yet some mothers we spoke to enjoyed the work, became section or floor manager and did training which they enjoyed. All forms of cleaning, such as office contracts, hospital and school cleaning, dinner ladies and security were also in this 'crap' category. Parents did not talk or think about the jobs they did in these terms.[9] One clear step forward would be to devise more ways of offering recognition for these often 'caring' jobs, including better pay and more training.

Many of the problems in getting more families into work would fade if:

- a higher priority was given to low-cost childcare;
- the problem of school hours, ending at 3.15pm, was compensated with after-school activities;
- the transition between benefits and tax credits was smoother and less threatening;
- the 'poverty trap' or 'marginal tax rate' was less harsh;
- low level service jobs were more recognised and rewarded;
- and a living wage was the absolute base line.[10]

There is an acute need for job mentoring and advice, for hand-holding people into work and for creating easy transitions from voluntary to paid work, from no training to basic to advanced training. With a clearer progression, more parents would not only make the transition into work, but would move more easily further up the ladder of opportunity. The services on which society depends would disintegrate without these jobs and this workforce.[11]

## Notes

[1] Mumford, K. and Power, A. (2003) *East Enders: Family and community in East London*, Bristol: The Policy Press; Power, A. (2007) *City survivors: Bringing up children in disadvantaged neighbourhoods*, Bristol: The Policy Press.

[2] Department for Education and Employment (1998) *National Childcare Strategy*.

[3] Hills, J. (2007) *Ends and means: The future roles of social housing in England*, CASEreport 34, London: LSE; Labour Force Survey statistics at www.statistics. gov.uk; Department for Communities and Local Government (2008) *The English Indices of Deprivation 2007* (www.communities.gov.uk).

[4] Hills, J., Sefton, T. and Stewart, K. (eds) (2009) *Towards a more equal society? Poverty, inequality and policy since 1997*, Bristol: The Policy Press.

[5] Power, A. (2007) *City survivors: Bringing up children in disadvantaged neighbourhoods*, Bristol: The Policy Press.

[6] Hills, J. (2010) *An anatomy of economic inequality in the UK report of the National Equality Panel*, CASEreport 60, London: LSE.

[7] Hills, J., McKnight, A. and Smithies, R. (2006) *Tracking income: How working families' incomes vary through the year*, CASEreport 3, London: LSE.

[8] Tim Brighouse, Evidence to Birmingham Housing Commission, 2001.

[9] Toynbee, P. (2003) *Hard work: Life in low-pay Britain*, London: Bloomsbury Publishing PLC.

[10] www.citizensuk.org/campaigns/living-wage-campaign

[11] Power, A. (2007) *City survivors: Bringing up children in disadvantaged neighbourhoods*, Bristol: The Policy Press; Power, A. and Houghton, J. (2007) *Jigsaw cities: Big places, small spaces*, Bristol: The Policy Press; Reich, R. (1991) *The work of nations: Preparing ourselves for 21st century capitalism*, London: Simon & Schuster; Jacobs, J. (1970) *The economy of cities*, New York: Random House.

# EIGHT

# Housing and regeneration

*I'm sure there's some connection between all the changes that are happening, all the building and development, and people not being listened to, and people feeling insecure and threatened in lots of ways, and not feeling part of what's going on.* (Andrea, East Docks)

## Introduction

Housing marks out and shapes disadvantaged areas, creating the physical conditions that help or hinder family futures. It is a dominant issue in the lives of families because it links with so many aspects of local life including neighbours, schools, the local environment and income. When housing conditions are poor, environments deteriorate, people with little choice get trapped and social problems become magnified. So housing underlines the wider problems families face. Housing is far more than a box on the ground that shelters people in their private lives; it is shaped by its owners, its age, its occupants and by the wider local environment. In this chapter we look at basic housing conditions, investment in housing upgrading, the social and management problems attached to social renting and the regeneration programmes the areas underwent during our visits. The 200 families, from many different backgrounds, live in these areas mainly because they cannot pay their full housing costs. So social landlords play a dominant role in their lives as housing and regeneration agencies.

Resident owner-occupiers are in a minority in all the disadvantaged areas we explored, and most bought their homes from the council under the Right to Buy, tying their housing investment into the social make-up of the areas.[1] This pattern is common in low-income areas across the country.[2] The small number of older terraced properties in the two inner-city areas are a little different, as they have increasingly been bought and done up by incoming 'gentrifiers', and were traditionally owned by low-income families or private landlords or local housing associations; a handful of the families lived in these terraces.[3] There are new blocks of flats being built for higher-income, younger households in the two London areas. The families did not regard these new flats as housing they could possibly aspire to. First, we look at the way housing is owned, then at who occupies it, and then at wider repercussions of these patterns.

## Council landlords and other tenures

Councils and housing associations, the dominant 'social' landlords in the four areas, are able, with government subsidies, to rent properties at roughly half the rate for equivalent private homes. Housing associations were relatively small landlords in the areas compared with councils, but they housed similar groups of people to the councils and faced similar neighbourhood problems, resulting from the dominance of large council estates. As social landlords alongside councils, they had a similar share of needy households, albeit more often in smaller developments. Social landlords are obliged to rent to people on low incomes, in housing need or facing special difficulties.[4] Most of the families were tenants and a large majority lived in council estates. The families were more heavily concentrated in social housing than the overall population of the four areas. Figure 8.1 shows the make-up of housing in the areas among the families.

**Figure 8.1;** Tenure of the 200 families at outset, 1999–2000

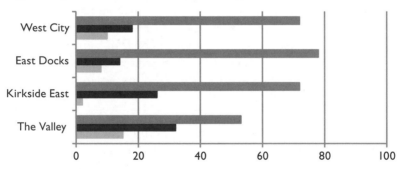

■ Social rented: Local authority / Housing Association / Registered Social Landlord

■ Owner occupied

▨ Private rented

Although needy families have become more concentrated over the last 20 years, deprivation in the low-income areas has built up over many decades, since most council estates in cities were built as part of big slum clearance programmes, housing eligible families from the poorest areas and the worst housing conditions into the new council estates:[5]

*They're creating ghettos by putting people all together of one kind.*
(Tina, West City)

Across the UK, including these areas, large-scale public building programmes delivered over-sized, mono-tenure estates owned by councils in distinctive, highly conspicuous styles over the pre-war and postwar periods. Management and repair were neglected in the rush to keep up with the pace of building, and disillusionment quickly set in.

The initial problems of unsettled new communities were compounded in the 1980s and 1990s by the sharp loss of industrial manual jobs in all four areas. Over the 1980s council estates became much less stable communities as those with choice and in work tried to leave, and were increasingly replaced by vulnerable newcomers. The two London areas, and the inner-city Northern area, The Valley, experienced a rapid change in the ethnic composition of their communities as many more minority families from poor, often seriously overcrowded, conditions became eligible for social renting.[6] Vulnerable households with complex problems, because of their special needs, received high priority for re-housing by councils or other social landlords. This made the areas harder to manage, requiring more housing-related social support. The rapid change in population helps explain the community tensions that arose:

*When we moved here first, it was majority white. Now it's multi-cultural and the white community are not ready to accept the change.*
(Louise, East Docks)

Figure 8.2 shows the ethnic make-up of the families.

**Figure 8.2** Ethnic make-up of the 200 interviewees at outset, 1999–2000

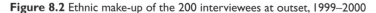
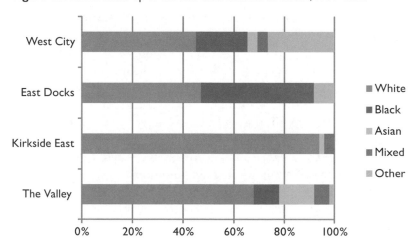

As wider support for social housing declined due to its problems, a new government housing policy emerged early in the 2000s to replace large, unpopular, mono-tenure council estates with 'mixed communities'. As a result, major regeneration programmes were under way in three of the four areas during our visit. The fourth area, the large Northern council estate, was also subject to radical proposals which were slow to materialise in concrete form.

## Owning or renting a home

The owner-occupier families we visited, whether on low incomes having bought under the Right to Buy, or the very small number of gentrifiers, all faced similar neighbourhood conditions to tenants but enjoyed a far greater sense of control over their homes, and they generally felt more secure because of the fact of owning. However, the threat of demolition of large estates or blocks through regeneration plans could unsettle communities:

> *They're moving lots of people out, pulling buildings down and replacing them.* (Diane, East Docks)

Owner families compared with tenants were more often married, or in long-term couples, more often worked and therefore tended to have higher incomes.[7] They invested more in their homes, and were committed to the areas in ways that some tenants found more difficult. To some extent they acted as 'guardians' over conditions in ways that older long-term tenants also did.[8] Peter, who is a Right to Buy owner on the estate he has lived on all his life, put it this way:

> *It often lifts people up, because when they own it, they look after it more.* (Peter, Kirkside East)

Most of the owner-occupier families lived in former council housing and the London families invariably lived in flats, as leaseholders from the council rather than as outright owners; therefore they discussed housing and area conditions without making the fact of owning or renting an issue. The absence of a sharp division between owning and renting within the areas, according to parents, resulted from families having a shared interest in improving conditions, regardless of tenure. Private renting could result from the Right to Buy, as former tenants bought, then rented out, their property so that they could move out, using their rent income to secure a mortgage. Neighbourhood renewal and regeneration activity, often instigated because of social problems, affected tenants and owners alike, and generally provoked positive reactions:

> *So much has happened, the renovations around the place. Flats and parks redesigned, transport has really improved.... Think about the children and the people who work now, you feel so happy, attracting so many people.* (Sasha, East Docks)

## Housing conditions

When we first visited the areas in 1998, problems with housing were common. The overall shortage of low-cost renting and family-sized social housing were major problems, far more so in London:

> *There's not enough accommodation out there.* (Kate, East Docks)

> *I've been told I've no chance of being re-housed.* (Hannah, East Docks)

> *The council doesn't have many three-bedrooms, they've sold off all the three-bedrooms years ago.* (Jess, West City)

Repair, maintenance and modernisation of homes were big concerns for tenants in all of the neighbourhoods and a lot of activity was starting up. Run-down and empty properties in blocks of flats or houses made families feel insecure. In the two Northern neighbourhoods, some pockets of housing were losing their viability through low demand. Negative signals about area problems emanating from boarded-up property were quickly picked up by the families living nearby, as a Northern mother explained:

> *I don't know why empty houses should bother me, but it doesn't make it look attractive to the people coming onto the estate.* (Becky, Kirkside East)

Parents felt that boarded-up houses and half-empty blocks made parts of their neighbourhood look abandoned, increasing tenants' fears for the future. In The Valley, many parents felt insecure about the rapid deterioration of properties in the area. They were unsure whether refurbishment or demolition was on the cards, whether re-housing to somewhere better was an option. Parents talked about the impact of conditions on their ability to cope:

> *The block didn't have security doors. I wouldn't go back there. It was a sink place. I was being sunk as a single parent and pregnant again. I was homeless before that and in bed and breakfast.* (Phoebe, The Valley)

Many parents wanted to move because of local conditions; more in the North than in London wanted to stay within the areas, moving only nearby if they moved at all, simply to escape the poor state of their property. It was much easier in the Northern areas to move because of lower housing demand, and in these unpopular areas there was usually spare capacity, as Becky explained when she was re-housed.

> *I knew I'd get a house here because other people see it as a dumping ground.* (Becky, Kirkside East)

In East London, many more wanted to move away from the area altogether. Pressure on space led to most families living in flats, and families talked about the difficulties of bringing up children in flats, with no outside space. This mother talked about the impact on communal areas of children not having enough space to 'let off steam' constructively:

> *The children don't respect the improvements … any facilities are constantly vandalised by local youth.* (Flowella, East Docks)

Living in a flat with poorly supervised communal areas and inadequate outdoor play space or activities penalised families with small children. On one estate the council had removed swings because they were vandalised and a magnet for trouble with local teenagers.

> *They've pulled all the swings down. The kids have nowhere to play.* (Zoe, West City)

As our visits progressed, major repairs and upgrading work got under way on homes in the four neighbourhoods. On our fifth visit we asked parents about their housing conditions and whether they wanted to move. Over two thirds said they were satisfied with their housing in all the areas, even though the difference in housing conditions between North and South was stark. Thanks largely to the improvements under way, only a quarter of the parents in the two Northern neighbourhoods wanted to move out of their homes. However, in the two London neighbourhoods, over half the parents wanted to leave (66 per cent in West City and 59 per cent in East Docks) even though most were satisfied with their housing. In these areas, the poor neighbourhood conditions, the lack of outdoor space and the lack of prospects for transferring within the areas made them want to leave. One London father described the enormous housing pressures in the inner city. He ascribed much of the inter-ethnic tension and even violence to the shortage of affordable homes:

> *The danger is the pace of change. Unless the housing situation is solved, resentment is going to rise. Someone was nearly kicked to death here last month.* (Alan, West City)

The contrast between North and South was there throughout our visits, although fewer parents wanted to move as time went on, thanks to far-reaching improvements. By the end of the study, none of the parents in Kirkside East planned to move home and only 6 per cent wanted to in The Valley, whereas in East London 20 per cent of families in West City and in East Docks a third did. Far fewer parents wanted to move from either area than had at the beginning. Chapter Nine examines this change more closely.

In 2006 in the Northern neighbourhoods, over four fifths of parents were satisfied with their housing in spite of some outstanding problems, compared with just over half in East London where it was virtually impossible to secure a transfer, even when the family was seriously overcrowded or they needed to move closer to family support. Delilah explained this problem. She lived with her husband and five girls including a baby in a small two-bedroom flat:

> *I can't wait to move. I've done everything I can to move. They've told me I've got all girls so I won't move from here even though the rooms are not enough.* (Delilah, West City)

Housing problems often dominated other family problems. Overcrowding and disrepair particularly pre-occupied East London families.

Over the period of visits investment in the stock from special major repair funds to tackle problems made parents more satisfied and less keen to move house or area in spite of remaining problems. Nearly one third in East London said they had no problems at all and in the North two thirds said this. Although a quarter of families were still waiting for modernisation under the Decent Homes programme on our last visit in East London, the process was far advanced and generally tenants were pleased. Figures 8.3(a) and 8.3(b) set out the outstanding housing problems, and the number of parents experiencing no problems at all.

**Figure 8.3(a):** Housing problems experienced by parents at the last visit, 2006

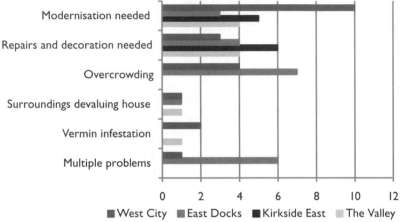

**Figure 8.3(b):** Parents experiencing no housing problems at the last visit, 2006

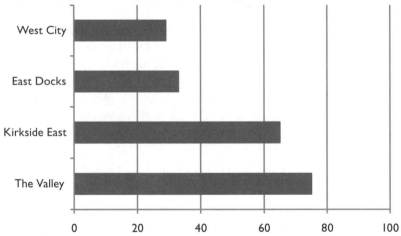

## Upgrading social housing – the Decent Homes programme: *"You need a decent home"*

In 2001, the government announced a comprehensive reinvestment programme for social housing, offering around £10,000 per home to bring all social rented homes up to a decent minimal standard of repair, making them weatherproof and warm, with basic modern amenities, generally including modern kitchens, bathrooms, windows and central heating. Council estates had built up a backlog of repair and modernisation problems. The Decent Homes standard was very basic, too basic in the eyes of many landlords, housing professionals and tenants.[9] It ignored important elements of maintenance such as the external areas surrounding rented homes, local estate environments and energy saving. Nonetheless, the Decent Homes programme was highly visible, improved the parts of homes that most affected tenants, and pushed up basic standards. For these reasons it was popular among tenants. It also had an uplifting effect because it made estates look more cared for, and councils often diverted some extra funds into upgrading environments:[10]

> *Regenerating the estate, new doors and windows and kitchens and rewiring, upgrades, updating what you've got, not leaving it. It makes a difference to you wanting to stay and raise your kids there. If things improve you feel confident to stay.* (Louise, Kirkside East)

One family's experience illustrates the very substantial improvements that her home underwent, including double glazing, which was not on offer in many areas:

> *They've started doing work on council houses, we've had central heating and an alarm and are getting all new windows, got one downstairs but it is single glazed, getting all new double glazed windows. Had new front and back doors. You need a decent home. It affects people daily, a good home, and it affects bills.* (Jackie, Kirkside East)

Modernisation and repair work always caused some difficulties, however. One common complaint was the wait and uncertainty involved. Some parents felt that other estates were getting a better deal; others felt that other streets within their estate were being given priority:

> *The Decent Homes initiative. I've seen it in other areas, people saying 'I've got new windows' or 'a new kitchen'. It really perks the older people up, which is nice.... I wouldn't compare myself to other people but I would compare the area where I live.... When you see other estates, how they're always getting things done,*

> *we've been waiting so long and still not getting the work done.* (Yetunda, West City)

A Northern parent experienced similar delays but allowed for the fact that it took time, and not everywhere could be treated simultaneously:

> *I've got a big problem with the kitchen window, a big crack and when it rains hard, it pours in. The council are in the boarded-up house on this Close daily since my neighbour moved out. They haven't done my window. They are doing all the houses but in sections, so I can't have it yet. All got to be done by 2010.* (Cara, Kirkside East)

Sometimes parents weren't prepared for continuing problems after modernisation. For example, new plastering cracked as it dried:

> *We had a lot of problems but they're trying to renovate them one by one. They've changed the kitchen and bathroom which were really bad, although the walls in the kitchen are starting to crack already.* (Josephine, East Docks)

## "I can't have improvements"

Parents who had exercised their Right to Buy and become owners faced having to pay for modernisation on their leasehold council flats because as Right to Buy owners, they had responsibility for repair; they also had to contribute their share to the cost of any collective work to their block such as the roof or lift, since they would gain directly from any improvements, both in their homes and in the area. One parent thought her leasehold service charge was a form of rent that should entitle her to repairs and improvements:

> *The condition of houses, supposed to be modernising them all. They're not. We've been told we can't have new doors. They need re-wiring. Some get central heating. They make you pay for it, four to five years, added to rent, they shouldn't. Rent is enough. That's why I can't have improvements. It should be the landlord, the council, paying, if houses have to be a standard.* (Carol, Kirkside East)

Some houses had faulty design and structural problems that blocked tenants exercising the Right to Buy, and also held up basic improvements. At our last visit, Lisa was still in limbo waiting for central heating:

*I'd prefer it if the council would update it. Like central heating.
They keep promising it. We were going to buy it, then were told
we would never be able to sell it, because it's a steel frame house.
So we didn't spend the money on it. The council say it is not on
the list for this year.* (Lisa, Kirkside East)

## "Water comes through the children's window"

In spite of the urgent need for basic housing repairs, the Decent
Homes programme was slow since it covered several million homes
and individual problems had to wait until the programme reached the
area in spite of very poor conditions:

*The windows, water comes through. The radiators have to be open
all day to be warm. When the heating is switched on, it makes a
sound. I think it might be dangerous but I don't know. A year
ago, someone came and looked at the boiler and said it had to be
changed but I had to wait. Nothing has happened. The kitchen and
bathroom are really bad. The bathroom has dampness. I repainted
it, but three months later the paint fell off. Water comes in through
the children's window. It causes smells and dampness. I have to put
cloths down and wipe the windows every day.* (Hulya, West City)

A major defect in the Decent Homes programme was that it did
not tackle the need for insulation. Damp and condensation were big
problems in some flats, particularly in concrete slab blocks. Yet low-
income families were having to use their more efficient central heating
system to warm flats to a point where damp evaporated. It is a short-
term approach that government is planning to rectify.[11] One parent
had been advised to apply for a heating allowance for her cold flat
because she couldn't afford the energy bills to keep it warm and dry:

*In the winter it's freezing, it's absolutely freezing. I mean, the
heating is full on right now and it's not that cold outside – so
imagine when it gets really cold. You have to have extra heating
and it's expensive. We had electric fan heaters last year and it cost
so much money. But I was told – I'm not sure, I'm going to look
into it – that I might qualify for a heating allowance since I have
asthma and I don't have a choice. I'm going to check into that. It's
quite harsh. I end up sleeping in sweat pants and a sweat shirt.
My asthma has been much worse since I came back to London*

*anyway, I just think it's because of the climate, it's just so different.*
(Beth, West City)

Another mother explained that she had taken the council to court after 12 years of no repairs being done:

*With the house, I've been taking the council to court for years. The windows are streaming wet. We're always getting sick – head colds and chesty coughs. I've been on the list to move for seven years.*
(Sophie, West City)

A minority of London tenants still hadn't seen any progress in upgrading by our last visit. Unclear information frequently undermined parents' confidence, following fears of neglect:

*My kitchen's fallen to bits and the bathroom's not good. And the council would never come and fix anything. I'm not sure if I'm on the list to be refurbished because it's hard to get to the people doing it, I'm just finding out who they're doing it for, 'cos so few people have had it done. I just found out Friday that we could design our own kitchen 'cos I didn't know that!* (Rose, East Docks)

### "It'll be a nice area"

Parents were enthusiastic about the prospect of upgrading. Families were attached to their community and the prospect of upgrading could change their views about moving, as Sola in West City explained:

*It looks like eventually it'll be a nice area.... I just hope it improves. It if does improve, I might be changing my mind about moving because you do get settled in an area.* (Sola, West City)

Some parents commented that their council was trying hard to bring the properties up to modern standards:

*Apparently, I believe starting either the end of this month or next month, our building's getting done. So we're going to get double glazing and then eventually central heating and kitchens. We do have a brand new lift, I don't know if you noticed. It's part of the Decent Homes by 2010. My friend lives across the street, and hers has totally been redone and it's lovely, it's so nice. I like my flat already, you know, size and location and everything, so once it's all modernised it'll be great.* (Beth, West City)

When parents could see the improvements already in place, they were full of praise. This London mother was thrilled that her father's flat had been done:

*What they're doing to the properties – what they've done for me dad is out of this world. They've put in a brand new kitchen, he's got more cupboard space, a new bathroom, double glazing – that's really good.* (Sonia, East Docks)

The acute problems of disrepair, neglected, unmodernised conditions and the long delays in carrying out improvements sometimes drove parents to near despair. However, the Decent Homes programme, which offered modest but conspicuous improvements to all council homes, area by area, over several years, definitely worked to boost family morale, improve area reputations and standards without dislocating or disturbing too much the stability of the community.

## Local environment: *"The areas we all share"*

The funding for home improvements did not allow for the immediate surroundings of the homes. Some parents were upset that so much money could go into home upgrading without tackling the public spaces in between. Debra and Alan, the East London couple who worked tirelessly for their community, believed that consultation with residents might have changed priorities. After many objections, around 5 per cent of the total sums allocated were allowed for local environmental improvements. They were upset that the common areas of estates, that everyone could see and had to use but no individual could control, were ignored:

*They're appalling. They're in the middle of their Decent Homes programme which is the most mad standard going. 'Decent Homes' is the fabric of your home, it doesn't deal with common areas, doesn't deal with the environment, the space, that's not what they're spending any money on whatsoever. How you can just isolate individual flats without spending money on the areas that we all share? It's just such a short-sighted government policy, but it's just about cash isn't it. If they actually included the environmental work, security and everything else that people want, then the cost of that would just be phenomenal so they've gone for the smallest, and lowest common denominator. They never asked us who live in the estates, what we think and what we want.* (Alan, West City)

The real problem of common areas was the need for ongoing supervision and maintenance, a recurring problem for parents and social landlords. In two regeneration areas local community attempts to upgrade a park were thwarted by lack of revenue for maintenance:

*The reason they didn't spend £1.4 million on the local park was the council wouldn't agree to maintain it. And we won't put in capital money unless there's maintenance agreements.* (Alan, West City)

As the programme progressed, attempts to tackle environmental problems bore some fruit including improved maintenance:

*The environment looks cleaner. They've improved the local environment a lot.* (Cynthia, West City)

But some parents worried that the modernisation and renovation work would not last, or be sustainable. This mother was critical of the way residents themselves failed to live up to the improved conditions:

*The flats have been done up to look nice, then they hang out their washing: I think, why bother? They've made some lovely improvements along the canal side but it'll deteriorate in the next three or four years.* (Tracy, West City)

## Facelift scheme to upgrade street facades: *"Improved a lot"*

The Valley, the Northern inner-city area, had an unusual improvement scheme, doing up the facades and front wall of the attractive but run-down terraced streets in the area:

*It's so visible, the Facelift scheme, you see it as soon as you come into the area and people don't have enough money to do up their houses and gardens, so it's really good.* (Fatima, The Valley)

The Facelift scheme ran alongside and complemented the Decent Homes programme. It was partly European Union (EU) funded through the Objective One anti-poverty programme. Many of the old run-down street properties were owner-occupied, quite poorly maintained, and presented a very negative image of the area. One mother explained the benefits and problems of this approach:

> *The neighbourhood has been improved a lot. Via the Facelift scheme. But I am annoyed about that. It is the main roads that been done, the main bus routes, but we got nothing. We did get £500 for windows but had to jump through hoops to get it.* (Judith, The Valley)

A few parents were critical of the standardisation that came with doing up the outside of the houses, including the low stone walls separating the fronts from the pavement. Many of these had broken down or been replaced with cheap fencing or brick, instead of the traditional stone. An active father fought to restore the original stone front walls, and he did notice the increased investment in maintaining the area:

> *It is cleaner. Been some bad planning decisions made though, like the Facelift scheme, a very narrow view architecturally. Victorian terraces, they force anything through as anything is seen as an improvement. The environment has improved. It was neglected. Now they do their job. They deal with empty houses too now. But we had to fight to not have the Facelift scheme make our house look like everyone else's. We fought via the council.* (Adam, The Valley)

Another mother praised the Facelift scheme for improving the looks of the area, recognising that this had in some ways an even stronger impact than Decent Homes themselves; she too felt it made the area a bit too tidy and homogenised, however:

> *I think it's environmental improvements that are the most significant neighbourhood changes, like the Facelift scheme made the main roads a lot tidier. It looks a bit sterile though, cut out a lot of the green.* (Louise, The Valley)

One problem the Facelift scheme was designed to overcome was the general sense of insecurity in the area. People were increasingly 'barricading' their homes, and the improvements aimed to remove the need for this:

> *I'm not happy that there's stuff next door, grills on the windows and front door, with no planning permission, that makes the area look oppressive.* (Paulo, The Valley)

A low-income, unemployed owner-occupier, who had been worried about falling property values, valued the greater social mix the Facelift scheme would attract:

> *Image-wise, the Facelift scheme has changed the area; new homeowners, a mixture of young families and professionals and social workers and council employees. There's a mix of people coming to use the shop. It feels more comfortable, it's good … it avoids being a ghetto.* (Kamal, The Valley)

## Social problems and housing: *"They should get their priorities right"*

Parents explained that upgrading and home modernisation on their own were not enough to overcome the management problems that continued after the physical improvement. Zoe's block was improved but the extreme problems of anti-social behaviour overshadowed the upgrading in her eyes:

> *The properties: new doors, windows, intercoms. They put new lifts in but you wouldn't know it, the state of it. The lady on the fifth floor, I saw her squatting in the Close. The intercom hasn't made a difference. Someone will put something at the door and all the druggies come in. I saw a couple having sex on the stairwell. A man decided to come all the way from Clapham to jump off the building in the early hours. The body was still there at 9am. I had to stop my son coming to the window.* (Zoe, West City)

The physical reinvestment left outstanding the acute social problems concentrated in these areas. One mother in East Docks, waiting to be re-housed, argued that too much emphasis was laid on the physical structure of dwellings and far too little on social conditions.

> *It is more important to instil something positive into them [young people] so they can get jobs and make themselves better people? Or is it more important to re-modernise a bloody house? I mean, come on now, they should get their priorities right.* (Flowella, East Docks)

It was hard to separate home upgrading, facelifts and environmental care from more socially derived local problems. Sometimes real improvements were undermined by social problems that no one seemed able to solve:

> *I think it is generally good, the neighbourhood, but there are pockets of neglect and deprivation, like the drug dealing house that got raided. It is boarded up now, a shame, and it was part of the Facelift scheme too, a shame.* (Kerry, The Valley)

A mother, who lived in newly built housing in a regeneration area, felt that it was reserved only for very needy families, stigmatising it in her eyes:

> *People at the bottom of the pile have been dumped here; it used to be so much better.* (Nadia, East Docks)

Some social problems related directly to shortage of money and the cost of housing. Paying rent and other regular major bills such as Council Tax and electricity was something that worried low-income families, which is why some parents preferred to stay on Housing Benefit rather than working, as shown in Chapter Seven. Several families highlighted the problem of rent arrears. The following illustrate the feeling of helplessness that arrears induced:

> *Housing, umm, yes, I am happy. But it is a struggle to go to work and pay rent and raise teenagers. I feel I am paralysed. I am in rent arrears and the housing man only cares about rent arrears. I'm going to go to social services and see if they can help.* (Adele, Kirkside East)

Another mother in West City had borrowed money from a loan shark to try and stay out of arrears and avoid eviction. But she was then on a treadmill of working 'all hours' to try and pay if off. She couldn't move or take up the course she had been offered because of it:

> *I've got two jobs because of the debts.... I will just have to go on paying my arrears.* (Cynthia, West City)

Several parents could not move because they were in arrears and one family was actually evicted for this reason. This mother had been caught working and claiming and was in very poor condition as a result of having to pay back over £1,000. She recognised that she had brought the problem on herself:

> *It's a bit cramped at the moment because I've got arrears and they won't re-house me. He's diabetic and obese and we haven't got a toilet inside, it's in the outhouse. It's my own fault really....*
> *We're not refusing to pay it but they won't re-house us till we do.*
> (Laverne, Kirkside East)

## Access to housing

One extremely contentious housing problem was the allocation of available subsidised rented homes. Unlike private renting, people could not simply apply for an available home, prove that they could pay, show a clean rent record, then sign up. A long and elaborate process of awarding points for different categories of deprivation, such as overcrowding, prioritised the most 'needy', most 'deserving' and most 'housing-poor' households. This is a much bigger problem in London where nearly half a million households are on council waiting lists.[12] A lack of transparency and sometimes a deep sense of unfairness resulted from the intense competition for subsidised housing. This often translated into racial prejudice:

> *There's more black people coming in. They get everything they want, but we don't. It's housing, we've been waiting 11 years.*
> (Theresa, West City)

A new 'bidding system' for people registered on the waiting list and wanting a home, known as 'choice-based lettings', was operating in the hope of giving people a greater sense of control over options, but it was confusing and frustrating to families, because only the most acute cases with the highest number of points qualified under the bidding system for family homes. It did not seem to increase the stock of homes nor the transparency of the system.

### "I need to move"

The 'choice-based lettings' system advertises vacant properties, and eligible applicants register on the waiting list, then 'bid' for the property, that is, put in a request for it. The person with the most points and the right household size would normally get the property:

*If I go to the council, they'll tell me I've got a roof over my head and there are so many people on the waiting list that don't have a place to stay.* (Aziz, West City)

*The council just say they haven't got anything suitable.* (Linda, West City)

One mother who had lost her tenancy as a result of arrears caused by overpayment of tax credits, highlighted in Chapter Seven, was having a particularly hard time trying to get re-housed using the bidding system. She almost despaired at the complexity and inaccessibility of the new lettings system. She had to bid, in competition with all other eligible applicants, for a place to live and in practice was always overtaken. It is possible that her arrears disqualified her. She explained:

*I live with my parents due to tax credit problems. But the new council houses system is a nightmare. I need a two-bedroom house. It is a bidding system and you have points, priorities, et cetera. And I've had no luck. I've been putting in for houses, two-bed, in this neighbourhood only, since I last saw you over a year ago, all the time.* (Cheryl, Kirkside East)

This mother lived in a relatively low demand area, as a result of which some demolition had already been carried out and more was planned, perversely creating a housing shortage in an area of surplus housing. Yet this mother could not get somewhere to live and no one had explained to her why.

Another family wanted to downsize, freeing up a much needed larger property, but they faced similar problems in trying to transfer from one council home to another. In this case there was a much simpler, more self-organising alternative that could help – finding someone who wanted to swap homes, often called a 'mutual exchange'. This innovation gave people much greater control over their lives, offering a way out under their own steam at no cost to the council:

*I'd like a smaller house, I've two daughters, and a five-bed house now. My oldest daughter is 18 so she'll be off soon. I need to move to a smaller house. The bidding system is awful. I can do a swap still. That is better. The Housing Manager checks them. I can do that.* (Anita, Kirkside East)

### "It attracted trouble"

Sometimes problems arose from too easy access to unpopular areas. There were initiatives to overcome the problems surrounding allocating council homes to the most needy single young people. Homeless, out-of-work teenagers could sometimes qualify for re-housing, but if they were housed together in an unpopular council block with too few supports, conditions could quickly spiral out of control. The closure and demolition of a particularly troublesome block helped solve that particular problem in one area. But the council also changed its approach, restricting flats to older people:

> *The reduced trouble from the flats being demolished. They had a lot of young kids kicked out of school and home in them, and there were lots of drugs and fights there. It attracted trouble. I think there is a ruling now, need to be over a certain age to get a high-rise flat now. For example, some are designated for older people.* (Denise, Kirkside East)

An all-pervasive problem in the three multi-racial areas was the displacement of the traditional white working-class community and the rapid change in ethnic composition. Black and Asian parents were acutely aware of this process and worried about it:

> *There's more African people in the area and there are more white people going away. I feel bad because it's like we're chasing them and they don't want to live with us. Maybe they're scared of our attitude, they're not sure what to expect.* (Josephine, East Docks)

The biggest problem was meeting legal obligations to prioritise acute need. Inevitably, councils used the least popular areas to house the most difficult cases. This was a major cause of unease for parents.

> *When it comes to crime, they concentrate a lot of people of the same type in one area....You feel you should be entitled to a decent place to live in, not just the rejects, because it makes you feel you're not worth anything.* (Sola, West City)

Other parents echoed this sentiment:

> *All the burglars are placed in this building. This area's never been good....Yet we're obliged to live here.* (Yonca, West City)

Many parents felt that the priority lettings system concentrated need in difficult areas where property became available. It also made transfers, or any movement within social housing, extremely difficult. It created particularly intense problems in London because it often prevented family members being housed near each other for mutual support:

> *They should share it more equal.* (Ellie, West City)

Maybe the biggest problem was that it made families feel worthless, undeserving, as Safia said:

> *There's no choice. We have no choice, but we're not animals.* (Safia, The Valley)

## Paedophiles: "One moved to a high-rise block here"

Social services had warned us at the outset about the problem of paedophiles being re-housed in East London estates and a number of parents were very worried about this. Parents of young children living on council estates were particularly upset by their communities being used to solve the problem of re-housing discharged sex offenders, and during our visits we came across a number of families with local knowledge about re-housed paedophiles.[13] Following custodial sentences, re-housing in unpopular council estates satisfies the requirement to house 'priority need' cases. Understandably, parents do not allow children outside, out of sight, or away from home if they think this is happening. The media play an alarmist and exaggerated role in fuelling these fears.

One mother explained her fears:

> *Cars and honestly paedophiles. One moved to a high-rise block here and told my sister why – because they are safer, because they can't have their windows put through or have their homes torched. Two years ago a man was beaten senseless outside my house, because he had interfered with children, told them how much he enjoyed doing it, so they hit him. I rang the police, they came quickly but they'd gone.* (Jacqui, Kirkside East)

A mother and her neighbour in East Docks, where social services had informed us about the presence of paedophiles, talked openly about the problem:

> *I mean there's three paedophiles living in this one road, convicted paedophiles. My neighbour but one's an ex-policeman, he told me. He said to me one day, 'They're all disappearing off up the road and they know they're not allowed'. I'm only telling you, not to scare ya. One of them's just done a six-year prison sentence.* (Kayla, East Docks)

> Friend: *And right next to a school, which is absolutely terrifying.* (Hailey, East Docks)

These worries went beyond generic parental concerns over 'stranger danger', to the need for safe, supervised children's activities, particularly if parents work:

> *Not great, paedophiles live in the area, and they have approached children at after-school club. There's lots of latch-key kids.* (Angie, The Valley)

When we asked what would make the area better, one mother did not hesitate:

> *Have the paedophiles leaving. More controlled, safer places to go. A playground nearby.* (Rose, East Docks)

One of the biggest and most problematic legacies of council housing is the idea of solving the most difficult social problems through housing policy, thereby concentrating the very problems council housing is supposed to address in the most vulnerable areas. This approach seems bound to fail:

> *The area's getting worse. When people move out, they put problem families in and there's more trouble.* (Megan, West City)

Yet the alternatives for hard-to-house groups are scarce and require intensive support through specialist provision which is expensive. The fact that so many intractable problems were dumped into social housing, out of the way, reinforced the sense of powerlessness and low value that beset council housing:

*Most people that move here had no choice, because the council said, if they didn't take it, they would be in the streets.* (Sola, West City)

*Outsiders think it's rough and they're right.* (Ellie, West City)

## Regeneration and the impact of demolition: "More far reaching than you think"

Neighbourhood regeneration has the aim of making areas more liveable, more attractive and more viable in the long run by literally 'bringing back to life and stimulating new growth'. But demolition plans unsettled many of the affected families, causing big problems in The Valley and East Docks:

> *Houses are being knocked down. They say it isn't going to happen for another five years but its already started! I'd like to know I can call someone in confidence about it and they wouldn't slag me off.* (Joyce, East Docks)

Another parent who knew her flat was due for demolition supported the idea because of the promise of re-housing, although in practice she remained stuck in an increasingly blighted area for the eight years we visited her. But she felt sorry for the older people who don't want to move, particularly as the traditional community would be replaced by much wealthier people:

> *I don't think demolition really affects me as I don't mind moving away.... I don't really want to keep my daughter round here ... but my next door neighbour is quite elderly and has to move out of the area she's lived in for years and years ... it's going to be a very rich, expensive area.* (Flowella, East Docks)

In the short run, regeneration often has a very damaging impact, particularly when it involves the demolition of whole blocks or streets, as these have to be emptied first, causing uncertainty and physical blight over large neighbouring areas, lasting several years:

> *There's been a lot of disruption, it's very unsettling for people. A lot of the changes they see happening, local people don't think they'll benefit from them. The general feeling from the community is that they're not really being considered. Things that are happening are out of their power.* (Andrea, East Docks)

Parents talked about problems that arose from regeneration, with homes awaiting demolition, current demolition sites awaiting new uses, and neighbourhood services, particularly schools and shops, becoming unviable. Generally regeneration areas suffered long delays to programmes, making information inadequate. Neighbourhood regeneration led to gradual withdrawal of care, attracting children on the lookout for fun, and generally 'unsettling' the local community. Some parts of all four areas suffered badly, as parents in The Valley explained:

> *It is a real mess, because they are tearing down rows of houses here and lots of people are still here, vandals get in, kids, fire brigade comes here nightly.* (Gloria, The Valley)

Flowella, who saw demolition as a way out for her, also saw the decay and lack of supervision that accompanies area decline, affecting young people very badly:

> *They know they can swear and smash things and no one's going to take a blind bit of notice.* (Flowella, East Docks)

A Northern father who was very involved in a big regeneration scheme put it bluntly:

> *Community regeneration's first aim is to break up communities.* (Adam, The Valley)

There was another argument against demolition of sound homes that it involved wasting precious resources:

> *It gets me down seeing so many derelict buildings and uncared for things.... The blocks getting emptier and crying out to be vandalised.* (Phoebe, Kirkside East)

The environmental damage caused by demolition actually harmed the long-term prospects for regeneration areas:

> *The area will only improve if people stay and improve it. There's a drain because people feel disheartened and more aware.... I think demolition's a big mistake because it feels like the council's throwing away a resource.* (Phoebe, Kirkside East)

A Northern parent was deeply upset by the whole process. The family lived in the large Northern estate where there was talk of major 'regeneration', meaning clearance and rebuilding a 'mixed community'. That plan was very uncertain but parents were very worried:

> *Definitely this house business! All are out of their heads. I'm so worried, it's a nightmare, especially the last 12 months. The worry is, where will the council put us all? And how will the council give people like us £3,800 to move and £80,000 for the house? We need to buy a replacement because we bought it. How the hell will we get sorted? Re-housed? This is the most significant thing in the last five years. We are all in a real worried state about it in these houses. One friend is very worried…. She is terrified of being put in a high-rise flat. We bought land next to the house too for my husband's job, so it is big loss for us.* (Enid, Kirkside East)

## "They've moved away"

In East Docks a private finance initiative (PFI) to fund the regeneration of the area took several years to agree, eventually triggering demolition, but along the way unsettling the community:

> *I was told that all the houses that are empty are for the people that are gonna be moved from the area first. And then when they've built their new places, they get the option of staying where they moved to or going back. Then I went to another meeting three months after that, and was told 'No, all the empty properties in the area are being let to a housing association for five years', and we had four empties in this block, and they have been let, and we've got people moved in them.* (Gillian, East Docks)

The regeneration would not benefit many of the families during their children's childhood and the costs of a decade of disruption were extremely high. Not only was it eroding the sense of community that was a mainstay for families with young children, but they knew that they were unlikely to stay in the area after regeneration, so their motivation for helping or being involved was minimal. Although area conditions would eventually improve, the families we visited would not be the direct beneficiaries. Some families didn't know whether they'd be forced to move or not.

> *We used to have lots of families with children, but they've moved away. Maybe the regeneration programme is why the families have moved.... Ten years ago transport was a problem – now it's not.... But I don't see the area getting better yet. There's still drugs and youth crime.... I've seen a lot of changes over the last 10 years. People coming in and going out. In general things are improving but I'm worried about regeneration plans, if they might move us.* (Josephine, East Docks)

Another parent was fairly philosophical about the process:

> *This part is looking a bit run-down because the properties are meant to be coming down. Some that are to be knocked down have been left empty. It's going to take a few years for things to take shape. It does look run-down but then we know what's going on, why it looks like that....* (Barbara, East Docks)

Re-housing options and the timing of moving created uncertainty, even when re-housing was guaranteed:

> *Really looking forward to moving. They told me about a year ago [that I could move]. It is dragging. I've packed most my stuff up. They've just given us Priority Extra, so I think it will be before Christmas.* (Rosie, Kirkside East)

Another mother described how the demolition plans had 'put her life on hold'. All the delays and uncertainties forced her to do some work anyway in preparation for the arrival of her new baby:

> *Because this baby's on the way and stuff like that, I wanted to redecorate the place for a long time, and because they say they're gonna demolish it, I never got round to it. But because the baby's on its way, I literally had to go and do my bedroom again, and the passage and stuff like that, just to make it happy. So if they demolish this house in the next year or so, I'll have wasted a lot of money, 'cos my carpets are coming next week. So d'you know what I'm saying? It's like, you don't know where you stand. If they said to me 'By next year you're gonna be out' or be in a new environment or a new house, then I could budget myself and say, I don't need to do things until then.* (Flowella, East Docks)

Flowella really liked her flat and felt a strong attachment to it, compounding her feeling that neighbourhood conditions rather than housing were the core problems:

> *No, there's not much I'm not happy with in here. There's little things that I'm not happy with, like the windows get damp and there's condensation. Your curtains get ruined and you're forever scrubbing them down. But my house is my domain, I come into my house and I'm in my own little world and I can close my door. There's only little minor things that I see as being minor, there's no major things, like I'm saying 'Oh god this house is falling to pieces and it's terrible', you know. If I could pick up my house, and take it somewhere else with me, and magic another bedroom in there, I would.* (Flowella, East Docks)

The time lag in area regeneration gave neighbourhoods an empty feel, which unnerved some parents:

> *I try and introduce myself 'Hello! Welcome! if you need anything don't hesitate to ask' and whatever. But that's it, it's very formal.... It's still quite isolated around there. Once these new flats are up and running and there's more people living, I s'pose it'll be a bit better but at the moment – it's weird, this area is really weird, you have very built-up areas and then you have very empty areas. So, you know, you can be walking and all of a sudden you're in the middle of nowhere. Like, it's a ghost town and there's no one around and you think 'Hang on, I don't wanna be here'.* (Tamara, East Docks)

Regeneration also had a big impact on other local services like schools:

> *We're losing children fast because they're moving out the area, our numbers are so low. It has affected the school. We don't have a waiting list.* (Barbara, East Docks)

Another parent who worked in a local school commented on the increasing contrast between low-income and new high-income residents, which many parents in regeneration areas commented on. The consequences of major demolition on housing priority were also serious and too often ignored:

> *I notice it more at work — less children coming to school. More children passing through. There's more development going on. At the docks, there's more difference between the better housing and the poorer quality housing. We've been on the council waiting list since 2001–02 but there's loads of people waiting due to the demolition....* (Rachel, East Docks)

One older parent who had lived in the area for a long time and who helped in the local school was deeply perturbed by what was happening, not just to the school but to the whole community. She felt that communities were losing something very valuable in the process of regeneration and on balance she believed that the harm done by regeneration far outweighed the benefits:

> *... the whole area is going through regeneration. Some flats are emptying out. It's a bit worrying, you know, people not moving back in. It's a bit unsettling, because we're part of that regeneration as well, but I think we're going to be one of the last. We're just carrying on as normal.... The school is doing well at the moment, we've had some excellent results but even we're losing our numbers, and they're not being replaced. We've lost the equivalent of a whole class of children over the last year, and that's a bit worrying 'cos we're a good school. We've lost a lot of people where they've moved out the area. When they bought their council houses, they've moved on. And people are not moving back. You know, it's sad. It's all changing. I can't look at it positively really. I have to carry on in my environment as though I'm here to stay. You know, when you're going home in the evenings, you see things run-down. It's just a little unsettling. You know, it's not the same sort of feeling that you got years ago.* (Peggy, East Docks)

Overall physical upgrading that removed the existing homes and communities worked less well than the more incremental, lower-cost programmes, as Andrea explained:

> *There's been a lot of disruption, it's very unsettling for people and a lot of the changes they see happening, a lot of local people don't think they'll benefit from them. The general feeling from the community is that they're not really being considered. Things that are happening are out of their power.... People [rich incomers] don't interact with the local community. It's like being in a different*

*world … and I think local people have feelings about that, about being so separate.* (Andrea, East Docks)

## "It doesn't mean to say they can throw a McDonald's carton"

One mother remembered the time before the original terraced streets of the East End were demolished, when her estate had not yet been built, which was now due for demolition all over again. She had seen a proud community destroyed twice over:

> *Before this estate was built, it was all old houses, terraces. But people were spotless, they'd come out and scrub the whole, you know, a whole bucket of water would go down the front path and down onto the pavement. I know it sounds silly but that's how people lived and their letter boxes shone, you know. It was very, very old houses but they were very clean. They didn't have a lot of money but they were very clean. And they cared, you know. You didn't see rubbish on the street. Perhaps it's because there wasn't McDonald's about at that point, my pet hate! Things were different. I think people need to be a little bit more caring about their environment, wherever it is, you know, whether they're living in the middle of London or not. It doesn't mean to say they can throw a McDonald's carton or leave their rubbish behind, it's horrible.* (Peggy, East Docks)

Many other parents, particularly in London, echoed this sentiment, seeing housing as one of the biggest causes of social dislocation:

> *They've just piled loads of people in and pushed us out. If I didn't know where I was, I'd think I was in a different country.* (Lesley, East Docks)

The lost sense of community echoes the famous East End study *Family and kinship in East London* (1957), which argued that stable working-class inner-city communities had held together by relying on established social networks and a sense of familiarity. That study underlined the damage that slum clearance and re-housing in large council estates would do to communities.[14] Housing policy has never prioritised the long-established social relations that are torn apart by the process of uprooting that accompanies demolition and re-housing in spite of the official recognition of social capital as a community asset.[15] Gillian put it well:

> *This was a working-class area. Everybody knew everybody else, you looked after your own, but it's not like that anymore. It's changed so much.* (Gillian, East Docks)

One mother, living through such upheaval, described the confusion, resulting from misinformation, the loss of neighbours and the mounting social problems. The trust and social bonds that made neighbourhoods secure for families were disrupted and weakened. These intangible assets made areas work and took many years to create but were devalued in regeneration plans which favoured more upmarket private housing and in many different ways excluded many locals:

> *In some ways it's good because it makes the area look better, but in other ways it's housing that's sort of private and expensive, and it's not housing that helps actual local people.* (Joan, West City)

The future seemed very uncertain for low-income families who were not going to benefit directly from the changes and who worried that they might even lose their homes in the process:

> *People see these posh flats going up and say we can never afford anything like that.* (Joan, West City)

## Gentrification: "People who won't mingle"

Gentrification pressures and tensions between existing families and high-income newcomers were much higher in London than in the North. Some families welcomed the improvements in conditions because they attracted people with more money:

> *House prices have gone up so people need more money to live there, so more with money spend on their properties and gardens and take pride.* (Rosemary, The Valley)

Others saw the divisions it could create:

> *Mixed communities just produce high gates.* (Debra, West City)

> *We've got the two extremes – a lot of new yuppie career-oriented people and on the other end of the scale, more drug users.* (Trudy, West City)

The prevailing view seemed to be that private upgrading was good for the area, but not good for low-income families nor the community:

> *That won't help people round here – these buildings are for private sale for professional people who won't mingle. I don't stand a cat's chance in hell of renting or buying one of these new flats.* (Tina, West City)

> *The wealth of the City's coming in. They've closed two parks round here.... An old building that was for pensioners and a youth club, is now apartments. The council are selling off their resources.* (Sinead, West City)

## New Deal for Communities

One of the problems with regeneration schemes was that they relied on private investment and developer interest. There was a direct clash of interest between the desire to make money out of profitable new development in low-value but well-connected urban areas like West City, East Docks and The Valley, and the need to house the large numbers of low-income families who lived in large estates targeted for regeneration:

> *Everywhere you look, derelict areas are turning into luxury flats. For some people it's a good thing, for others it's bad. It's good to have an area looking good but it's too expensive for local people.* (Joan, West City)

A more community-oriented approach to regeneration emerged from the New Deal for Communities programme that was announced in 1998, offering £50 million over 10 years to regenerate 39 of the most deprived urban areas 'with the community at the helm'. The two inner-city areas were part of this programme. The programme had many distinctive and new characteristics that made it different from other programmes:

- its resources would be invested in developing community enterprises and responsive local services and facilities;
- it would support different community groups in different ways, and it would directly fund local activities;
- local initiatives would be 'community-led' with an elected community board.

The funds were too large for a handover to community control and many tensions and conflicts arose over funding, over competition between local groups for resources, over the lack of long-term support, over ethnic divisions and questions of fairness over professional dominance. The haste with which the programme was devised, the lack of trusted partnership structures to carry it forward and the inherent conflicts it unleashed within communities and between communities and local government meant that the programme came in for some strong local criticisms in spite of the funding it brought and the many community benefits it generated:

> *The main thing is people's attitudes have changed. Groups popped up everywhere, trying to get the money, and it's kind of lost that community spirit. People wanted to grab the money for the sake of it.* (Judith, The Valley)

On our first visit, many parents spoke positively and hopefully of the new initiatives being proposed to tackle neighbourhood problems. In The Valley the New Deal for Communities generated a local community forum actively working to improve the image of the neighbourhood and the local environment, producing a local magazine which residents contributed to. Over two thirds of the families in the area knew about its work. In East London, the New Deal for Communities got off to a slower start due to a head-on collision between community activists and government funders over proposals for the transfer of the estates and significant demolition as opposed to community control and local management. Eventually an intensive management and upgrading programme, with many community-owned social enterprises, won support from all sides and improvements began to show.

On our third visit, we asked parents more about conspicuous regeneration initiatives like New Deal for Communities. In the two neighbourhoods with the New Deal for Communities programme, three quarters of the parents knew about the programme. The New Deal for Communities had many positive impacts on their lives, particularly the level of local activity it generated:

*I can see where the money's gone. Lots of courses for community groups, grants for things. A positive feel. Neighbours okay. Kids get on with them too. No negatives really.* (Petra, The Valley)

However, the allocation of New Deal funding to different community groups became divisive, when particular minority groups seemed to be 'favoured' over 'locals'. The grievances of deprived white working-class communities are now increasingly recognised,[16] but some parents felt it took a lot of hammering home for this problem to be heard:

*New Deal is supposed to be working towards community cohesion. But I think a lot of New Deal money is targeted at groups. They do stuff like grills on windows and shutters and satellite dishes and big signs. It's divisive, it creates divisions between ethnic and cultural groups, all segregated by background. Like a local driving school for ethnic minority groups, what's the point of that? Lots of white families suffer more than ethnic minority ones, and there are no groups for them. And no family networks, a complete lack of family support. And most of the kids that are excluded from schools are white. Especially white lone-parent families, kids deprived of emotional, family support, white and also African-Caribbean children.* (Paulo, The Valley)

Other parents referred to the ethnic divisions that were difficult to break down in New Deal for Communities areas:

*There aren't many venues or events that are multi-cultural. There are so many barriers. Can men be there with women? Is the food offensive to anyone? It's difficult to find mutual space.* (Adam, The Valley)

This kind of division over resources also arose in the East London area:

*It had lost 'the old East End feel'.* (Alan, West City)

Paulo was very concerned over the New Deal funding running out. He was particularly critical about the short-term jobs it created:

*I wanted to be involved in the regeneration of the community, et cetera. But I got really disillusioned with New Deal. Because the New Deal money will run out and all who are in New Deal funded jobs will end up with no jobs. I wanted to do my bit for the*

> *community but it's falling apart. New Deal's handout mentality*
> *is dangerous. It will go when New Deal goes, the handouts will*
> *go, but the mentality won't. People won't want to pay for stuff.*
> (Paulo, The Valley)

Many problems arose through the attempt of the New Deal for
Communities programmes in both West City and The Valley to
'put communities at the helm'. The resources over 10 years for this
programme, around £50 million to each area, were far beyond the reach
of even the most advanced community organisation. The conflicting
requirements of public accountability and local 'control' caused many
tensions, delays and sometimes an actual breakdown in communication
and decision making. At our last visit, to families in The Valley, divisions
undermined the sense of community and 'community spirit' that the
programme had initially inspired.[17] Many parents raised this, but Judith
summed it up:

> *The community spirit has gone, due to the funding situation and*
> *the fact you need to jump through hoops to get money. We need to*
> *reverse this problem of 'lack of community' but no, it can't be done*
> *because the funding system has destroyed the community aspect*
> *here. And so the old hard core community people don't do anything*
> *now. I am on the management committee of an after-school club,*
> *that's all I do now.... But it's not reversible.* (Judith, The Valley)

Tension sometimes acquired a racial undertone when disputes over funds
arose. Grants to particular ethnic groups highlighted the community
tensions from particular groups lobbying for particular needs that did
not enjoy wider support, particularly when decisions lacked clarity.
The deep sense of injustice that arose targeting specific ethnic groups
could be overcome by directing such large resources to commonly felt
needs and to inclusive, rather than exclusive, programmes. This active
father was very upset about the impact on community:

> *The New Deal money funded groups for specific ethnic groups,*
> *these are very divisive, dividing the community and ignoring white*
> *people basically, who are often, or can be, very badly off, for example*
> *emotionally, a lack of emotional, family support. It is working*
> *against community action. It is not good for the community at all.*
> (Paulo, The Valley)

Several parents thought that, with more participatory consultation and decision making, a fairer balance could be struck between different priorities.

Other parents had similar worries about the shaky financial future of local groups. One involved a mother in the area who was convinced that money was not being wisely spent, even though she could see some direct benefits and she, like Paulo, worried about the free handouts:

> *The New Deal stuff, I am sure some of the money has been wasted. But we've got all new play equipment in a local park, in May and June, it's done very well.* (Ellen, The Valley)

Another resident had bad experiences, lost his youth work job and didn't have much hope for the programme. He felt bitter that a few professionals had gained good positions while people like himself still felt excluded:

> *Not made that much impact to be honest. Not good that it will end. Like the local recycling initiative shut. Not worked with them or used them. I think New Deal has launched a few careers, basically.*
> *I don't have motivation to get a job through it. I don't want to work in the area.... I don't think New Deal will help me, but I hope young people will benefit.* (Kamal, The Valley)

Another mother saw the huge impact of New Deal but wondered if things were too easy. She recognised that the precarious nature of the projects due to short-term funding:

> *The number of initiatives for local people is the most significant neighbourhood change. I don't know if I am more aware of them because of my work, but there seem to be a lot, everywhere you look, projects for work, leisure, group support, like Halal lunch clubs for old people, and study clubs for young people.... There is so much available and people don't need to try very hard. It is all handed to you, on a plate. If you arrive with nothing, as my brother-in-law did, in a few weeks you can access Job Net, English Language courses, computer groups. I am really conscious of the dodgy foundation of all of this. For example, New Deal nationally had to cut funding by 12 per cent, and SRB [Single Regeneration Budget] cut down too. Learning and Skills Council are withdrawing money for adult learning. We all struggle now to*

> *mainstream it so it doesn't all fall down in five years after New Deal.* (Maya, The Valley)

In fact, Maya's view was rather prophetic as five years later, in 2009, the funding did dry up in The Valley – many local staff lost their jobs and local projects in the area were threatened. However, with the backing of the council local efforts helped to salvage some initiatives:

> *I saw lots of projects getting small grants from New Deal, so it has kept some kind of community momentum going. But it's all ephemeral, nothing permanent. No funding soon, then it all stops. The money should have been invested in lasting things, providing employment in the area, set up small businesses. I thought of a bike repair business and workshop.* (Phoebe, The Valley)

New Deal for Communities needed to provide steady, long-term day-by-day, hands-on problem solving to ensure that improvements, community projects and community involvement itself lasted. It worked out that it was the long-term, low level maintenance and support approach that developed gradually in the two New Deal areas and the large estate that helped make these areas work. Parents recognised the improved management that came with a long-term commitment to their area, making the areas much more liveable and family-friendly:

> *We're getting our money's worth. When we need repairs, they come right away. They gave us an incentive to move but we decided not to. The rubbish is now picked up every day. Before you just couldn't enter the lift…. So I used to struggle up the stairs. The lifts are a bit cleaner now. They're doing a lot of the building…. Generally they're involving tenants and everyone goes about more … they're listening to everyone. We're all in on the community meetings.* (Cynthia, West City)

The West City New Deal for Communities set up its own community trust to invest in the area in order to make sure that improvements lasted, and involved parents were justifiably proud of its achievements:

> *We've the best reading recovery results in the country and a whole series of projects are flagship projects, things we ought to be very proud of.* (Alan, West City)

## Summary and conclusions

Every family has a housing story but there were three main threads to families' housing concerns: first, conditions in the built environment, and their impact on social conditions; second, the impact of major regeneration programmes on communities; and third, the often overlooked challenges of housing management, access to housing, priority need and community stability.

Housing gives families a sense of security and well-being that underpins their ability to cope. It acts as the organising base for social life, fostering social networks and mutual aid. For most low-income families, buying a house, the ultimate security in most people's eyes, is unaffordable, and renting from the council or a housing association is a cheaper, more accessible option. It offers relatively high standards of accommodation for a low price, as it is heavily subsidised by government. However, the social cost of those benefits is high: a lack of control; overriding priority to families in severe housing need; limited choice; low priority to community ties; or other less urgent considerations than actual homelessness. The pressure on councils and government to house those who might otherwise become homeless has led to intense social problems in large social rented estates. Bureaucratic management systems and rules governing fairness made it hard to move. The local environment, social conditions and community instability were not as high a priority for landlords as managing the queues of people and the big reinvestment programmes to upgrade constantly deteriorating conditions. Everywhere there seemed to be a shortage of accessible affordable homes of the right size in the right place, and everywhere rented property occupied by local families quickly became run-down for lack of ongoing investment.

A big problem is that houses are fixed and hard to change, but families are fluid and change constantly. Rented housing for low-income families only works with intensive management and close liaison with communities, to accommodate different priorities and respond quickly to new problems. For parents in disadvantaged areas, the local housing environment is almost as important as basic housing conditions. Parents also saw a clear link between neglected housing environments and young people's misbehaviour – 'the unused is always abused'.[18] This obvious reality was commonly neglected by councils. Local housing managers rarely carried direct responsibility for the wider environment and the spaces that surrounded homes. When the local environment was cared for, it engendered people's respect and fostered better relations; when it was not, it was 'abused'.

In large publicly owned estates, tenants did not have sufficient status, resources or control to take responsibility for the interlocking physical, social and environmental problems that surrounded them. Government recognised the long-term cost of these wider, area management problems, yet ignoring them led to further decay, driving the recurring need for major regeneration. Housing requires constant attention to small detail, because it interacts powerfully with community dynamics. In crowded, urban areas where resources are scarce, it is careful management rather than large capital sums that offers long-term prospects for the survival, rather than demolition, of these areas.[19]

If long-term, continuous, local housing management and maintenance receive priority, then many more serious problems that trigger spending on major regeneration schemes do not arise. Maintenance of parks, secure entrances to blocks, regular cleaning, rapid repair, enforcement of tenancy conditions are all part of this. Yet intensive management to control area conditions, handle difficult social problems, gather accurate information and feedback, to allow carefully tuned responses, requires ongoing, dedicated staff on the ground. Social landlords too often separated their role as housing providers from the neighbourhood conditions in which their housing was located and their tenants lived.

This separation and neglect, caused in part through low rents and in part through the prioritisation of acute need, triggered the regeneration schemes that the families described in this chapter. They worried about the one-off nature of big regeneration programmes and favoured the more low-level, responsive investments that underpinned more gradual improvements and more sustainable management of poor areas. Neighbourhood management cost only a small fraction of the cost of area regeneration and could significantly reduce the cost of large-scale intervention such as the New Deal for Communities.[20] Local neighbourhood and housing management were less conspicuous and less glamorous, but more popular and easier to deliver.

Big regeneration programmes can physically transform low-income communities, mainly through demolition and the re-housing of existing residents. Yet removing existing residents to resolve social problems, which need a more fine-tuned approach, puts families through a nightmare of uncertainty and upheaval that is hard to justify. It often simply undermines family and community stability. In contrast, the less disruptive, more manageable, lower-cost local investments, such as Decent Homes, which preserve and improve conditions within the existing local community, work well. In spite of gaps and problems, parents saw conditions improving, and many more families wanted to stay at our last visit than had at the beginning. They felt more valued as a result of the interventions that supported rather than tore apart their communities. Community stability, family security and a sense of home are the marks of success in housing, and many more families enjoyed a 'sense of home' following the increase in investment and careful management in which they played a part.

**Notes**

[1] Lupton, R. (2003) *Poverty Street: Causes and consequences of neighbourhood decline*, Bristol: The Policy Press; Power, A. and Houghton, J. (2007) *Jigsaw cities: Big places, small spaces*, Bristol: The Policy Press.

[2] Hills, J. (2007) *Ends and means: The future roles of social housing in England*, CASEreport 34, London: LSE.

[3] Mumford, K. and Power, A. (2003) *East Enders: Family and community in East London*, Bristol: The Policy Press; Power, A. (2007) *City survivors: Bringing up children in disadvantaged neighbourhoods*, Bristol: The Policy Press.

[4] Hills, J. (2007) *Ends and means: The future roles of social housing in England*, CASEreport 34, London: LSE.

[5] Power, A. (1987) *Property before people: The management of twentieth-century council housing*, London: Allen & Unwin.

[6] Mumford, K. (2001) *Talking to families in East London: A report on the first stage of the research*, London: CASEreport 09, London: LSE; Power, A., Richardson, L. et al (2004) *A framework for housing in the London Thames Gateway*, CASE Brief 27, London: LSE.

[7] Winkler, A. (2005) 'Analysis of family responses on tenure by family composition, income and work history', Unpublished.

[8] Power, A. (2007) *City survivors: Bringing up children in disadvantaged neighbourhoods*, Bristol: The Policy Press, Cynthia's story.

[9] Power, A. (2006) *One size still doesn't fit all: Final report of the Independent Commission of Inquiry into the Future of Council Housing in Birmingham*, London: LSE Housing.

[10] Department for Communities and Local Government (CLG) (2006) *A decent home: Definition and guidance for implementation*, London: The Stationery Office; National Audit Office (2010) *The Decent Homes Programme*, London: The Stationery Office.

[11] Department for Communities and Local Government (CLG) and Department for Energy and Climate Change (DECC) (2010) *Warm homes, greener homes: A strategy for household energy management*, London: DECC; HM Government (2010) *The Coalition: Our programme for government*, London: The Stationery Office.

[12] Waiting lists are not an accurate measure of housing need but they do indicate a log jam in letting; Hills, J. (2007) *Ends and means: The future roles of social housing in England* CASEreport 34, London: LSE.

[13] Mumford, K. (2001) *Talking to families in East London: A report on the first stage of the research*, CASEreport 09, London: LSE.

[14] Young, M. and Willmott, P. (1957) *Family and kinship in East London*, London: Routledge and Kegan Paul.

[15] Power, A. (1987) *Property before people: The management of twentieth-century council housing*, London: Allen & Unwin; Halpern, D. (2005) *Social capital*, Cambridge: Polity Press.

[16] Denham, J. (2010) Speech launching the Department for Communities and Local Government, *Tackling race inequality: A statement on race*, London: CLG Publications, 14 January.

[17] Power, A. (2007) *City survivors: Bringing up children in disadvantaged neighbourhoods*, Bristol: The Policy Press.

[18] Hill, O. (1970) *Homes of the London poor*, London: Cass.

[19] Power, A. (1987) *Property before people: The management of twentieth-century council housing*, London: Allen & Unwin; Power, A. (1997) *Estates on the edge: Social consequences of mass housing in Northern Europe*, London: Palgrave Macmillan.

[20] Power, A. (2004) *Neighbourhood management and the future of urban areas*, CASEpaper07, London: LSE; Power, A. and Paskell, C. (2005) *The future's changed: Local impacts of housing, environment and regeneration policy since 1997*, CASEreport 2, London: LSE.

# NINE

# How the areas are changing

*I would just say that for me personally, things have improved. It's hard to make a judgement isn't it. But I know lots of people with kids. I know that things have improved for them, and the whole general look of the place, there's not the derelict sites anymore.* (Joan, West City)

*New faces have moved in. There's more foreign people. Before there was a lot of white people in the area, now it's a mixture – it's changed a lot. The children have got somewhere to play football and basketball in the cage. Before they were always hanging around.* (Naomi, East Docks)

*Slowly but surely. More focus on young kids – things need to be put in place for them, instead of them playing on the streets. We still need stuff for kids.* (Patsy, Kirkside East)

*The kids are still hanging about out there, still not good. To be honest, the environment has improved, but anti-social behaviour is a problem.* (Kamal, The Valley)

## Introduction: *"Getting better slowly"*

One basic question we asked on our first visit and on each subsequent visit was how families thought the areas were changing, what was getting better and what was worse. In this final chapter we gather the parents' views on the changes in their neighbourhoods resulting from government efforts, the changes at community level and how changes had affected their families. Parents' views are not always consistent, and the 200 families express a wide range of opinions, varying not just between North and South, inner and outer areas, but also between different types of families with different individual experiences. In spite of these differences, many clear patterns emerge. The 200 families we visited every year over eight years found that the areas had changed in many ways for the better. Yet the families still found it difficult to bring up children in these areas because much more remained to be done and some fundamental social problems seemed to be intractable.

*Family futures* examines seven themes in turn: why community matters; school as community anchors; young people, space and activity; crime, safety and prevention; family ill health and neighbourhood supports; work, training and tax credits; and housing and regeneration. Neighbourhood-level interventions around these themes, supported by government over 10 years from 1998 to 2008, aimed at transforming conditions. We present an overview of how changes have affected families, whether outcomes are positive, negative or mixed, and what remains to be done. We end by summarising our findings on each main theme of the book and highlighting the remaining gaps and discontinuities that threaten to undermine progress.

Change over the decade to 2008 was constant and mainly positive for parents and their children, but inevitably the reality has been more shaded. Education, crime prevention, housing and environmental conditions all seem to have moved in a positive direction but there remain obvious gaps and challenges in unfinished regeneration projects, youth disaffection and closure of some facilities, lack of activities, low skill and limited work experience, job barriers for mothers with children, and too little out-of-school space or activities for children. In almost all aspects, these areas are still highly disadvantaged, in spite of the gap with the average being less extreme.[1]

Many problems remained unresolved: young people's needs as teenagers; enough safe play space for children; low-cost community meeting points; inter-ethnic integration; housing affordability; traffic, pollution and danger to children; the extra needs of children with learning difficulties; and persistent anti-social behaviour and drugs-related crime.

Meanwhile new problems loom:

- What will take the place of the special fixed-funding programmes, given that the task is far from complete?
- How will families overcome the insecurity of rapid population change and increased competition for scarce resources?
- And what will happen to local jobs and incomes as spending cuts and renewed economic problems take their toll?

Many parents at our last visit had ideas and hopes for the future founded on a reassuring sense of progress. A positive sense of direction to the changes they saw had emerged over the decade as a result of efforts to tackle neighbourhood problems directly within neighbourhoods:

- involving families with children in shaping what happened;
- delivering programmes and services at a local scale;
- responding to the minutiae of neighbourhood problems;
- containing the most severe problems; and
- offering better prospects to residents in the most disadvantaged areas.

## How parents' views of their neighbourhoods changed over 10 years

At our first visit, parents identified many local problems impinging on their lives. In all four neighbourhoods, many were dissatisfied with their conditions, recording up to four times the level of neighbourhood problems compared with the average.[2] Gradually, over eight years of visits, the families saw improvements in their children's schools, in their own access to training, in their incomes, in changes to neighbourhood policy, and local council initiatives to supervise the areas, in the condition of their social rented homes and in their children's prospects. However, they also saw increased pressure on community relations because of population change, and they were afraid of letting their children out or allowing them to join in activities because of the 'rough' environment and the bad incidents they often heard about. They did not believe wider social conditions had improved, although they generally wanted to be more involved in tackling problems and felt much more positive when they were.

Schools helped greatly in bringing families together and supporting children's progress, but families with children in difficulty needed far more dedicated help. The most conspicuous and worrying problem for parents was what would happen to young people as they grew up in such tough places. There was simply not enough space, nor organised activities to allow them to 'let off steam' safely. Crime and disorder, closely related to drug abuse, fuelled this worry. Crime prevention initiatives generally won the support of parents in spite of fear, doubts and criticisms; most said they felt safer after visible community policing was introduced.

Health problems in families were more common than average, particularly depression in mothers, and many families struggled with children's health and learning difficulties. Meanwhile job prospects improved rapidly in the course of our visits, and many parents took up training opportunities. Recent economic troubles are hitting these areas hard, however, as low-skilled jobs have disappeared fast, affecting many families. Housing modernisation and regeneration programmes began soon after we first visited and progressed throughout our visits. Parents were particularly pleased when repairs and the immediate environment surrounding their homes improved. New homes being built in the areas were also a sign of progress but parents recognised that these 'high class' new homes were 'not for them' and would not benefit them directly. If anything, they feared being displaced as a result of gentrification.

Parents were frequently struck by the general sense of the areas improving and of leading institutions trying to tackle the bigger problems affecting local areas that were beyond the power of families. They thought that the involvement of families and children in how change was delivered would greatly increase the chances of success. However, they worried about the major regeneration programmes that could simply tear apart fragile communities. Overall, parents' views became more positive over time, but their anxieties for their children's future did not go away; if anything, their anxieties increased as their children grew and faced a more uncertain future.

## The parents' sense of direction

Most parents took the view that changes were both positive and negative, and that some improvements worked while others did not. On our last visit, in all neighbourhoods the share of parents saying that their neighbourhoods were getting better had risen, particularly in the two Northern neighbourhoods, where over half the parents in Kirkside East and nearly three quarters in The Valley felt conditions had improved, a big jump from 2000 when only 10-30 per cent did. In East London there had also been a significant rise in the proportion of parents believing things were getting better, to between 35 and 43 per cent. Figure 9.1 shows the shift in parents' views between 2000–01 and 2006.

While many more parents saw positive changes by the end of the study, fewer believed that their areas were getting worse, except in West City, where the numbers thinking their neighbourhood was getting worse rose slightly alongside a rise in those thinking it had improved. There had been a big fall in all areas in the number of parents believing that there had been no change in their neighbourhoods. Figures 9.2(a) and 9.2(b) show these patterns.

**Figure 9.1:** Parents thinking their neighbourhood was getting better, 2000–01 and 2006

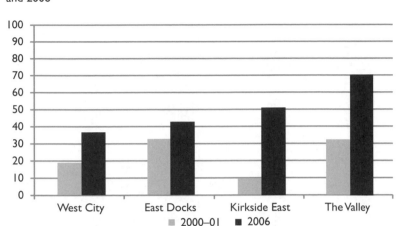

Improved area conditions changed parents' attitudes to staying or leaving the area. Pressures on parents included jobs, homes, family circumstances and children's needs, but particularly the impact of the area on young people's futures. At the outset neighbourhood conditions dominated parents' reasons for wanting to leave. Parents in all neighbourhoods were uncertain about where their future lay, but by the end of our visits many had shifted away from wanting to leave. Continuing investment in the neighbourhoods, a greater sense of involvement, school improvements, less crime, more repair and upgrading all helped stabilise these communities. In the North nearly 80 per cent wanted to stay at the outset and at the end a similar high proportion still wanted to stay. In East Docks, where leaving had been a big priority because of demolition, the numbers wanting to leave had dropped, and half wanted to stay, far more than those wanting to leave (28 per cent). In West City, only a quarter of parents wanted to leave in 2006 compared with 37 per cent in 2000. In Kirkside East, only 14 per cent wanted to leave at the outset, 16 per cent at the end. In The Valley, the proportion wanting to leave dropped from 26 per cent in 2000 to only 9 per cent in 2006, the most dramatic change. Figure 9.3 shows the decline in the overall proportion of parents wanting to leave all the neighbourhoods.

**Figure 9.2(a):** Parents thinking their neighbourhood was getting worse, 2000–01 and 2006

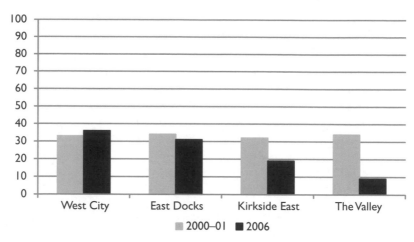

**Figure 9.2(b):** Parents thinking their neighbourhood had stayed the same, 2000–01 and 2006

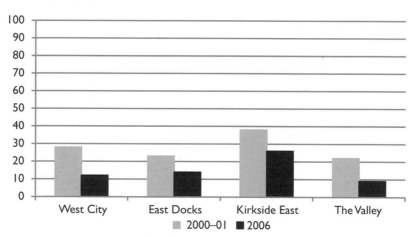

We asked parents for their views on the ongoing problems that made some parents still want to leave. The type of area and the properties families lived in remained dominant problems, compared with more personal factors. In East London, property and area problems ranked higher, whereas in the North, less than a quarter of families were affected by either area or property problems, and fewer wanted to leave, under 18 per cent compared with 25 per cent in East London. In London the repairs and other improvements had reduced the share of families wanting to leave but ironically, continuing dissatisfaction with the area and their housing conditions were partly driven by the ambitious new developments that made gentrification pressures stronger, and the families less secure.

**Figure 9.3:** Parents wanting to leave their neighbourhood, 1999–2000 and 2006

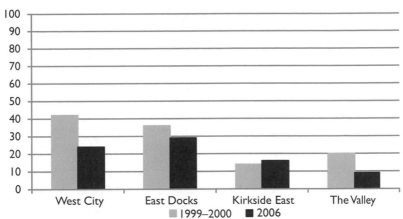

## Biggest marks of progress

Over four fifths of the parents in all four neighbourhoods identified significant positive changes, mentioning many different signs of progress in the different areas, such as better environments and facilities, less poverty and more cash, demolition of selected blocks of socially problematic flats, the addition of new, more attractive housing, and also wider benefits from more subtle changes, such as changes in attitude by outsiders or insiders towards the areas as they improved. Almost a quarter of parents mentioned the upgrading of buildings and the physical environment of the areas as the most significant changes. This was by far the most visible change across all areas. Strikingly, in the two areas undergoing large-scale demolition, fewer parents recognised physical changes as positive, due to the disruption and uncertainty regeneration had caused and the threat to their own future in the areas, whereas small-scale selective demolition of unwanted buildings won greater approval. Physical changes, such as housing conditions, economic changes, such as jobs and skills, hard-to-measure changes, such as attitudes to the area, all figured, but social changes were not so prominent. Improvements in facilities and services were more significant than any changes except the physical. Figure 9.4 shows the most significant positive changes, with a third of parents thinking several things together were changing for the better.

**Figure 9.4:** Parents' views on most significant positive area changes, 2004–05

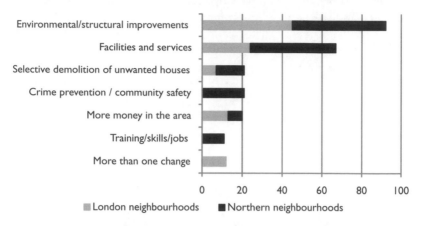

The reaction of parents underlines the fact that 'environmental signals', the look and 'feel' of an area, generate confidence, whereas negative signals from traffic, noise, litter and a general sense of disorder, undermine confidence. The large gap in area conditions between these neighbourhoods and the rest of the city they are located in influenced parents' views on overall progress, even where change was positive, such as physical upgrading or crime reduction.

We asked parents what they most valued about the neighbourhood changes in order to understand better how neighbourhoods affected family lives. Recognition of local problems by wider bodies, leading to local action, represented a turning point. Visible changes such as repair and upgrading, better, more accessible local services, conspicuous inputs into neighbourhood management and visible community policing, made a big difference because they reinforced families' confidence that things could get better. But less tangible changes such as the areas feeling safer, a more positive sense of the changes under way and greater confidence in the future of the areas mattered too, often deriving directly from visible changes.

In all four neighbourhoods, half of all parents rated the visual impact of changes on the areas as the most important aspect of change, and over a third believed that the changes benefited them directly. Only a small minority of parents, mainly in London, did not think the changes would benefit them or would make things worse. Figure 9.5 shows parents' reasons for their more positive attitudes.

**Figure 9.5:** What parents most valued about the changes they saw, 2006

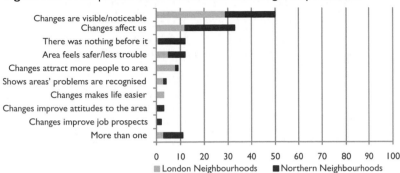

Legend: ■ London Neighbourhoods ■ Northern Neighbourhoods

## Low-income areas are part of the wider city: *"It's not just been forgotten"*

Sometimes the cumulative problems of low-income households concentrated in disadvantaged areas are so acute that the areas feel like 'worlds apart'. This book started with the evidence of acute problems that caused this sense of separation – several parents referred to where they lived as 'islands'. Tony Blair's drive as Prime Minister to 'close the gap' reflected the government's recognition of the dangers this separation, or 'social exclusion' as it was named, could bring.[3] Parents explained, in far more detail than the figures show, how neighbourhood changes affected them and helped them feel more included. A Northern parent was particularly pleased about the visible commitment to the area after it had become so run-down. She firmly believed that intervention was necessary to reverse the problems that had built up:

> *Probably, in a way, the feeling that somebody thinks it is worth putting money into the area, yeah. I suppose because it is recognised there are problems and you can't just let them sort themselves out.*
> (Kerry, The Valley)

Another Northern parent saw the new secondary school in their area as a critical step forward:

> *That'll make a difference. It will bring a lot more to the area. It is a good thing. It is a nice area to live.* (Pete, Kirkside East)

One parent from Kirkside East described how improved conditions restored confidence in the area:

> *They are rejuvenating the estate now, new doors and windows and kitchens and rewiring upgrades and updating what we've got, not leaving it. It makes a difference to you wanting to stay and raise your kids there. If things improve you feel confident to stay.* (Louise, Kirkside East)

In the Northern inner city where some streets were beginning to gentrify somewhat, several parents felt positive about the area attracting more people with jobs, generating additional investment:

> *It is cleaner and the housing market means the house prices have gone up so people need more money to live here, so more with money live here and spend on their properties and gardens, take pride in where they live.* (Rosemary, The Valley)

Another Valley mother saw direct gains for the local community as the area became more attractive, and more resources were dedicated to the local community:

> *The area is generally nicer, the houses on the main bus route are done up.... I can see where the money has gone. Lots of courses for community groups, grants for those. A positive feel.* (Petra, The Valley)

In the large Northern estate, the arrival of a big supermarket had boosted local job opportunities, offering training and local recruitment. One mother directly referred to this change as breaking the cycle of entrenched worklessness in some families:

> *I'd say more people are working. I notice it from people I know and seeing numbers going to work on a morning. Well, you get families who've never worked and now that cycle is stopping.* (Carol, Kirkside East)

Another mother in the same estate talked enthusiastically about training for jobs in the new supermarket. Many of the new courses aimed at job readiness relied on the proactive efforts of parents to take up the new opportunities:

> *The most significant thing is the supermarket and local learning centre. Those are the two major things that improved things for the neighbourhood. They have improved job prospects, provided*

*lots of jobs. People need to use these things though.* (Margaret, Kirkside East)

In East London, better transport links had made a major difference, particularly better and faster buses, which were cheaper than the underground and ran frequently enough to compete with cars. The bus services between central and East London had greatly improved when the congestion charge was introduced in February 2003. The impact of this change was far more significant in low-income communities than in more affluent parts of the city, already better served by the underground:

> *For me, the bus probably is the most significant change to the area, although it sounds crazy to say it, because it just has made places in the east and west directions accessible, far more easily. And so this bus has really transformed things, you know, really.* (Joan, West City)

Some East London parents praised the fact that their areas now attracted better-off people because transport was better and there were more facilities:

> *Think about the children, the people who work. You feel so happy of attracting so many people.* (Sasha, East Docks)

Other parents praised the general upgrading and addition of better quality buildings and shops, even when "they're not for the likes of us".

## *"Better and better"*

A very significant change was the rise in educational performance, closing the gap with more affluent areas, suggesting real progress taking root. One London parent saw rising school standards leading to rising aspirations, and more local children going on to college or university:

> *I think the schools are improving. They get better and better each year, basically. There's much more profile on education than there was before. Nowadays you see, especially in this area, so many kids going to university. Well, years ago it would never have happened in an area like this.* (Barbara, East Docks)

Parents generally believed that 'having a good home', 'feeling confident' in their neighbourhood and 'people taking pride in where they live' were important signs of progress. Tighter control over crime improved family lives directly at a day-to-day level, even though one in seven London parents, compared with only two in a hundred Northern parents, still thought crime had increased in their areas. London families felt more pressured by their environments and more scared for their children. In fact there were declines in crime levels in all areas in spite of the rise in drug crime, which was very small by comparison with the overall downward trend in crime (see Chapter Five).[4] Parents' perceptions and fears were reinforced by worries about loss of youth provision:

> *Years ago there was youth clubs, there's nothing like that anymore. There's nowhere to go. I don't think I could let them out. I'd spy on 'em. Years ago your parents knew where you was. Now it's awful. There's just too many bad people out there.* (Kerry, East Docks)

Yet the positive changes suggested neighbourhood improvements on a scale that inspired London parents too. One parent in West City who was active in the New Deal for Communities listed multiple impacts:

> *The statistics are just phenomenal I think. I ought to be able to reel off a whole stream of them, from street crime level to educational achievement. Across the board actually, if you look at any of the deprivation measures, the area has moved remarkably up on all of them. It doesn't matter what you look at, from the amount of money in people's pockets, employment statistics, education, the whole lot, health – everything.* (Alan, West City)

In assessing overall progress, the two inner areas nearest to the city centres showed more positive progress, even though they were so different from each other – one on the edge of the world's most dominant financial centre, one on the edge of a former industrial city. They were both benefiting from city centre activity and investment, and they were both more diverse, and therefore also experienced more underlying community change:

> *It's a very multi-cultural area with lots going on. Occasionally people moan about stuff for outsiders, something which needs addressing longer term – an undercurrent of racial tension.* (Maya, The Valley)

*It's getting better. There's not so much fighting. There's not so much police presence, so it must be getting good.* (Yetunda, West City)

*Better, definitely. We've had central heating put in. The environment looks cleaner. They've got more after-school clubs for children. The improvements are not on our side of the estate yet, but it's coming towards us. Now we have things down here, that's good. They've improved the local environment a lot. They have wardens now. With graffiti and vandalism, it's got much better. The area looks cleaner, the rubbish has got better.* (Cynthia, West City)

## A long way still to go: *"It just looks like a down-and-out area now"*

It would be a mistake to paint too rosy a picture and suggest neighbourhood problems were solved; far from it. When we asked parents about the problems that still needed to be tackled, they raised multiple issues, although around one in six parents did not have any suggestions to make. The vast majority of parents in all four neighbourhoods, around 85 per cent, felt that some crucial elements were still missing from their neighbourhoods, making them significantly more difficult to live in than standard areas. The neighbourhood improvements that were already working needed much more doing before firm progress was secured. The physical and structural changes already under way needed to continue, particularly on housing, which required repair and upgrading, but they also believed that stronger social and organisational changes were necessary, particularly to reduce ethnic divisions.

Four unresolved issues dominated parents' thinking everywhere:

- more facilities for children and young people were the biggest single need;
- continuing reinvestment in existing homes and expanding the supply of accessible affordable homes ranked second;
- the third big preoccupation was taking more action to prevent crime, tackle drugs and deal with problematic neighbours;
- parents also articulated a sense of urgency about their need for a stronger sense of community.

It was not enough for most parents that crime was falling or that conditions were improving. The distance remaining to close the gap with more normal conditions was still too large. One favoured solution was to move 'problem people' out of the area, rather than feeling forced themselves to move, and it is crucial to understand that such problems are disproportionally concentrated in low-income estates, particularly flatted estates. Figure 9.6 summarises the parents' main ideas on what would improve their neighbourhoods, showing the different priorities of different areas, but reflecting four clear favourites: children and young people; more physical improvements; more community facilities; and more crime reduction measures. Next, but a long way lower down, comes improving community spirit.

**Figure 9.6:** What parents would do to improve their neighbourhoods, 2006

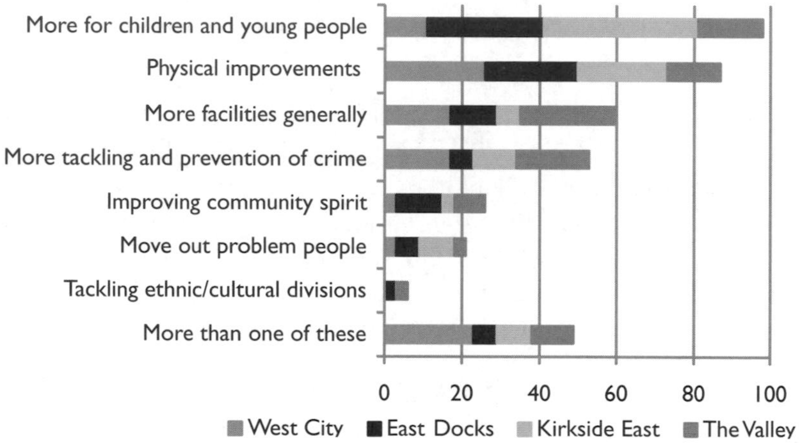

Parents saw where they lived as offering a support system and a resource for their families. They saw neighbourhoods as having many different functions in family life: education, safety, community spirit, cohesiveness, home, play and shared services. They recognised the shared character of neighbourhoods and therefore dreamt of interventions that would help everyone and build stronger communities. Figure 9.7 shows why parents wanted further improvements, most importantly to close the remaining gaps in provision.

Parents also underlined how much remained to be done to equalise conditions, to tackle outstanding problems and complete improvements. They proposed localised remedies that targeted local problems to close the gap. For example, many wanted school modernisation to continue, as this parent explains:

> *Jo's school is in desperate need of re-modernisation and renovation, you know. The government has actually promised some money.*

**Figure 9.7:** Parents' reasons for wanting further improvements, 2006

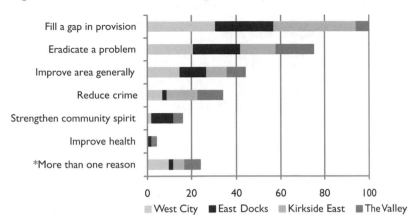

It needs a new roof, new windows, the playground's got terrible subsidence in it. All the cladding all around the school is falling off. I think it's unsafe but I don't know ... the kids play in the playground. The kids've got to play somewhere. One good thing we've had round here is Sure Start. That's been good. (Destiny, West City)

Only a small minority – less than one in five parents – were optimistic that further, deeper problems would actually be tackled:

It made me realise you can clean up the surface, but you need to go below the surface to the people ... I've seen problems over the last year – drugs, I think the council should provide support in the community for such people. It frightens me. (Chandra, The Valley)

## "Two extremes"

Overall progress was clear, but many challenges remained. Nearly half of parents everywhere had mixed views on progress. One third of parents in the North held clearly positive views on progress, compared with one fifth in London. Only 10 per cent of Northern parents compared with 28 per cent of London parents had clearly negative views of progress. Nearly half the parents in both the Northern and London areas had mixed views about the areas, recognising some progress but also remaining gaps, broadly reflecting the reality that much still needed to be done. Figure 9.8 shows this pattern.

**Figure 9.8:** Parents' assessment of progress in the neighbourhoods, 2006

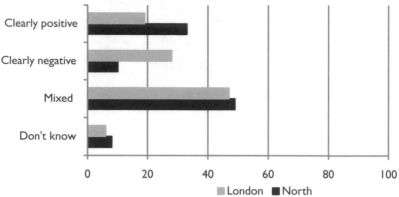

In spite of the parents' overall sense that changes were moving in the right direction, there was a strong awareness of unfinished tasks, of more fundamental inequalities and of local problems recurring, requiring ongoing effort. A Northern mother with mixed views, like many parents, summed up her confused feelings:

> *Got Sure Start up and running, that is something. But they can't get my little one into their nursery because of a lack of funding at the local children's centre, because of New Deal funding. Only the Facelift scheme and park work has happened really, to improve the neighbourhood. Not much done.* (Jessica, The Valley)

Another Northern mother from the large Northern estate could identify substantial improvements, even though she ended by highlighting the remaining gaps, particularly for children:

> *In respect of joy riders, a few years ago you'd see them all, and now I don't see that, not for a while.... And the atmosphere in certain places in the area around here, used to be cliquey, like at the local community centre. It is nowhere near as cliquey as it used to be. Which is a good thing....And more access, linking with nurseries, it is more giving, less blockages. Our Sure Start is the biggest and has branched into three neighbouring areas. It is getting better, slowly but surely. Still need stuff for kids.* (Patsy, Kirkside East)

Another Northern parent saw ups and downs, with improvements in area conditions and appearance, which did not spill over into social conditions:

> *The kids hanging about are still there, still not good. To be honest, the environment has improved but anti-social behaviour is a problem, the police and council not doing anything about it. So, environmentally better but kids on corner so no change in that respect.* (Kamal, The Valley)

London parents often welcomed the improved housing and facilities that were being built while worrying about the possibly negative consequences for them, reinforcing their mixed views. Unequal conditions and unequal opportunities were interwoven themes:

> *I think the place has generally had a lot of tidying up, building work ... yeah, a lot of new flats have been built. In some ways it's a good thing because it makes the area look better. But in other ways it's housing that's sort of private and expensive and it's not housing that helps actual local people. It just brings more people in from outside who can afford it. Which in some ways can benefit the community, it makes the community more mixed. But it does build up resentment, you know. People sort of wander about and see these posh flats going up and say 'We can never afford anything like that'.* (Joan, West City)

Many parents referred to the fact that 'improvements weren't meant for the likes of them', while other parents took a more positive view of this kind of investment, arguing that it was what gave the area a future. Overall parents saw the greater social mix as increasing, rather than narrowing, the gap:

> *We've got two extremes – we've got a lot of new yuppie, career-oriented people, and on the other end of the scale we've got more drug users.* (Trudy, West City)

> *Lots of new building. But stuff like that's not accessible to people who've lived there a long time. Nothing for the community. It's all about money.* (Lola, West City)

This outcome reinforced the sense of powerlessness that many parents felt, because of the harsh inequalities, the lack of housing options and the lack of a sense of control. Joan, from West City, felt defeated by the conditions and her lack of control over them, and by her inability to escape the problems that she couldn't change:

> *So this past year I have got gradually more and more despondent about living here, but it's not just the area, it's other things. Like not having enough money, and thinking 'How can I ever move?'. Because being on benefits, you can't get a mortgage. You know, if you haven't got a paid job, you can't get a mortgage and so you can't move — the thought of moving out is just impossible. And all summer the kids screaming out the front. All the kids from the other blocks come and play outside our flats here, all summer, these kids just driving you crazy out there.* (Joan, West City)

But another parent from West City expressed real excitement at the promise of longer-term progress within a genuinely integrated community:

> *I hear in West London it's segregated, whereas here we have such a lovely community. Some are locals which is brilliant. They're opening an organic supermarket next door, it's turning out like Covent Garden was 20 years ago. The railway extension as well, the station will be one block down. In a few years' time it'll be so busy and bustling.* (Charlotte, West City)

By tuning local projects to local communities, families with children became key beneficiaries:

> *The number of initiatives for local people is the most significant neighbourhood change. I don't know if I am more aware of them because of my work, but there seem to be a lot, everywhere you look, projects for work, leisure, group support, like Halal lunch clubs for old people, and study clubs for young people.* (Maya, The Valley)

### "In a few years time it'll be bustling"

So what does a decade of intervention by government to remedy the worst area conditions add up to? Is it better now for parents bringing up children in poor neighbourhoods than it was? Looking at official measures of progress across the board and weighing these up against what parents told us in the four areas, we find a close correspondence between changes on the ground, measurable reductions in crime, educational progress, housing upgrading and other wider evidence of progress in conditions in poor areas.[5] While serious problems remained, there was nonetheless a narrowing of the gap in the measures of progress that we considered.[6] Progress showed up for parents in the constant flow of initiatives, wave upon wave from 1998, that targeted these areas directly.

Parents hoped that the initiatives underway, for all the huge inputs of time and money, would be continued to maintain the solid foundations that children and parents need:

> *A lot more for youth and children and parents now, like counselling or support or a break for the kids, help, someone to see. Through the holidays they do a lot for children. It has benefited parents, and it hasn't been aimed only at lone parents, which a lot of that stuff is.* (Denise, Kirkside East)

It is the children and young people who count most in family futures and it is progress in making their futures more promising that needs most protection in the era of public spending cuts that we now face. Parents' views on change, their assessment of progress and their views of what worked, what did not, and what still needed to change, are summed up in Table 9.1, which presents an overview of progress.

## Summary and conclusions

Lessons from 10 years of policy activism in favour of poorer communities emerge from the words of 200 parents. Their experiences act as a sensitive barometer of change. Since neighbourhood conditions affect families deeply, and families are a mainstay of local communities, their views offer a highly shaded measure of what works for families and communities at the bottom. If parents can bring up children successfully in particular places, reliant as they are on many local services, then those places serve their function and we should invest to protect and enhance their value to society. If families struggle, it is worth responding to problems because problems at a local scale that seem intractable from afar are often easier to solve directly on the ground. *Family futures* shows why bringing up children in disadvantaged areas poses special challenges for parents, no matter how committed and concerned the parents are to their families' futures. It considers the major changes unleashed by government commitments to tackle child poverty and to equalise conditions and opportunities between poor areas and the average. It shows what interventions can achieve, what fails to make a positive difference and what remains to be done. It also shows that more fundamental inequalities require more than local initiatives.[7]

**Table 9.1: Balance sheet of progress and impacts of neighbourhood interventions**

| | Outcomes – based on parents' views |
|---|---|
| Sure Start | ✓ with very few criticisms |
| New Deal for Communities | ✓ with some mixed views |
| Decent Homes | ✓ with a lot more to do |
| Neighbourhood management | ✓ but requires long-term commitment to stay in place |
| Wardens | ✓ but need more of them and more frequent patrols |
| Community policing | ✓ but back-up needs to be clear |
| Crime prevention | ✓ but fear of crime still high and actual crime still above average |
| Safety | ✓ but more preventive policing; still needs tighter control on drugs |
| Mixed housing development | Some gentrification and some expensive flats but areas remain predominantly low income |
| Open space | ✓ but not enough of it and needs more supervision |
| Sport | ✓ but needs a lot more organisation and lower charges |
| Schools | ✓ but secondary not as positive as primary |
| Training | ✓ but more work experience would help |
| Youth provision | ✓ many big gaps, definitely a high priority |
| Public transport | ✓ generally big improvements |
| Community activity | ✓ when it happened, but a lot more needed |
| Consultation | ✓ but most parents don't join in formal consultations – need more 'fun' approaches |
| Demolition | ✓ some hope that it might help, if on limited scale, but very negative impacts from large-scale demolition |
| Large-scale regeneration | ✓ very slow, creates a lot of uncertainty, very expensive – lower-level investments help more |
| Job access | ✓ local services and programmes often offer openings to parents with low skills, with accompanying training |

The parents' views over 10 years are summarised chapter by chapter to show just how much changed and how much remains to be done. Chapter Two, about community involvement, showed why community matters to families and underlines the importance of familiarity, informal links and local activities. Parents wanted more say and influence. When they got it, they felt much more in control. They wanted to help and nearly half of the parents played some local, helping role. A sense of community is all-important to parents with young children, but is clearly undermined by over-rapid change, a shortage of meeting points or common ground between very different layers of the community. Sure Start offered a positive community focus and support to parents as well as helping children.

Chapter Three, about the role of schools in local communities, shows how much schools help low-income families, and their children, as well as teaching, providing a focus for community activity, supporting parents and responding to social problems. Secondary schools are more difficult to manage and harder for parents to access than primary schools, however. Children who struggle with academic learning need more consistent, more long-term help than schools alone can provide, and boys in particular, especially those with learning difficulties, often struggle with too little individual help. But overall parents were satisfied with schools and felt they had improved over time.[8]

Chapter Four, about young people's need for space and activities to 'let off steam', shows just how disadvantaged children in low-income communities are through a combination of high charges for facilities, particularly sport, inadequately supervised play areas and loss of community space to other uses. Commercial pressure on land, the growing problem of traffic, fear of crime and drugs and a shortage of revenue funding for youth provision have exacerbated this problem. Parents' top priority for their areas was to engage young people more fully through more and cheaper facilities and activities to keep them away from trouble. Schools now play a bigger role in play and sport, through out-of-school clubs, but could do more – as could local councils, churches and other local groups.

Chapter Five, about crime, illustrates how powerful the fear of crime and drugs is in undermining a sense of community, influencing parents' choice of poorer schools that they know about and are nearby, restricting their children's freedom to 'play out', to explore and to join in local activities. Crime levels fell in all areas, following spates of serious gun crime, as a result of a dramatic increase in levels of street policing, particularly using PCSOs. But a major rise in drug offences, particularly in London, kept fear alive among most parents. Community-level crime fighting initiatives generally won support, built parents' confidence and curbed street disorder. But parents still felt that more needed to be done to reduce crime as a high priority.

Chapter Six, about family health, showed that ill health, disability and depression were all more common among the low-income families in these poor areas than the national average. GPs were a major source of help but in East London health services were under pressure and sometimes seen as inadequate. Where children or parents had serious disabilities, they generally received a lot of help. The biggest problem for mothers was depression and anxiety, made worse by personal circumstances. The local environment, traffic, pollution and lack of space often have damaging effects on family health, but so do unhealthy drinking, smoking, diet and lack of exercise. More could be done to reduce the pressure on mothers to help and counter mental health problems, and more could be done to raise awareness through public health campaigns promoting preventative measures such as a more balanced diet, less junk food and so on.

Chapter Seven, about work, showed that most low-income parents come from low-skill work backgrounds, have on the whole done only low-paid jobs, are reliant on modest skills, and at least a quarter have only flimsy work backgrounds. Lone parents and parents with the least work experience (often connected) have by far the greatest difficulty securing work after a break to have children. Many mothers work only part time, although in London full-time working is more common. Many fear losing the security of benefits. Many take up training opportunities and progress over time. On balance tax credits helped mothers into work in spite of a shaky start, but the main issues were availability of jobs, low-cost childcare, the need for more training and 'hand-holding' support for mothers wanting to work.

Chapter Eight, about housing and regeneration, highlights the cumulative problems of low-cost housing areas dominated by social renting. It shows that basic investment in essential repair and modernisation such as the Decent Homes programme, along with local environmental improvements, helped to upgrade poorer areas and that costly, large-scale regeneration involving major demolition could damage community stability as well as proving extremely slow, expensive and divisive. Social management problems in large estates, such as those that dominate three of the areas, were more easily tackled alongside lower-level investment, more local involvement and locally based staff, than through higher profile special initiatives, separate from day-to-day repair.

This final chapter has two central themes: how much the areas changed in a positive direction over 10 years, leading to better schools, housing, environments, street supervision and community involvement; but how much remains to be done to build on the positive momentum of the last decade, as well as to tackle the complex new challenges of population pressures, housing affordability, community instability, loss of public resources, job losses, skill shortages and mismatches, and continuing environmental pressures. Many of these problems will show up most clearly in the experiences of the youthful generation now growing up in these areas. Already they are beginning to form future families, and their progress largely depends on holding in place things that work, such as Sure Start, while plugging the most pressing gaps such as youth provision and play spaces.

Lots of relatively modest and manageable interventions to improve poor areas make a vast difference to families' outlooks and ambitions – building greater family stability, stronger children's development and more positive community relations. Many promising activities are now under threat, in spite of evidence that different strands of activity, tried over decades of cross-party efforts to integrate poorer areas, need to be continually woven together on the ground. Fast evolving, low-skilled communities contribute to the wider society and should at the same time be able to achieve their overriding ambition to build their families' futures. Many of the families we spoke to underline this. Our society has a major stake in helping low-income families as the most cost-effective way to tackle deep-set and troubling community problems.

Given that children are only children for a quarter of their lives, their futures will not wait for large-scale, long-term changes, so action has to happen now if it is to help today's children cope with today's problems. Relatively modest but steady ground-level investments, based on our evidence, would provide the quickest and surest return to society in developing productive and cohesive communities.

## Family futures

Parents worry about their children's future from the day they are born. This book has explored what families do to help themselves, their communities and neighbourhoods, as well as what governments need to do to help them. But there is no such thing in modern cities as a fully autonomous community, and dependence on public infrastructure is high in rich as well as in poor neighbourhoods.[9]

The 200 families, through repeated visits over eight years, told us much more about their lives and experiences than we dared hope for.

Their confidence in sharing ideas with us has allowed us to draw some broader conclusions beyond their views of area change and government programmes. There are five factors that make bringing up children more challenging in these areas.

First, low-income families living in low-income areas rely more heavily on a sense of community than people without children and more affluent areas. The severe limits on household and area resources make pooling more necessary and more valuable. Being able to call on someone nearby, a neighbour, a relative, a local service, is often vital. Sharing is a stronger imperative and local ties are more directly important than weak, distant ties to these families.[10]

Second, there are more direct threats to families in disadvantaged areas than in more advantaged areas: more crime, less play space, weaker informal controls and less opportunity for young people, leading to a stronger need for security, enforcement and local management of conditions.[11]

Third, there is more rapid population change. Different ethnic groups do not readily understand or accept cultural divisions and often challenge the distribution of scarce resources as seemingly unfair.[12] Without proactive efforts to increase understanding and create common ground, these tensions can spill over, and parents, particularly minority parents, often articulated the need for more bridge building.[13]

Fourth, they are often isolated from more affluent families. The idea of building more mixed communities by simply encouraging luxury developments within poor communities did not work to bring about the greater mix, better social control or more affordable, accessible housing that low-income families need. Nor did it seem to integrate ethnically diverse communities in highly unequal cities.[14] A much more sensitive effort to encourage younger working households to stay or move into these areas would create a lower profile, more proximate and harmonious mix of incomes.

Fifth, many parents have limited skills and some parents are more proactive, and therefore more successful at winning resources, than others. It is the majority of low-income families with multiple disadvantages who are not able to 'fight their corner' that lose out most heavily. This shows up most clearly in access to school support for children with learning difficulties, in parents' uneven access to jobs and training and in some parents taking on wider community roles, while the majority felt overcome by a sense of their own powerlessness.

One message is clear – without a wider social, physical and governance infrastructure to support families, disadvantaged neighbourhoods would over time fall apart.[15] This is because local resources are too limited to repair worn-out or damaged or obsolete infrastructure, because the constant inflow of newcomers makes it impossible for the existing community to carry the full social costs of integrating strangers, and because disadvantaged areas are used by society as a catch-all for societal problems caused by chronic low wages, deep inequality, subsidised social housing for vulnerable groups, providing a receptacle for rejects from the wider society, and so on. Such 'residual' neighbourhoods are always at risk of falling off the edge, or falling back to where they were.

There remains a pressing, but unanswered question: to what extent are these areas, and society as a whole, battling to overcome an endless flow of problems, pushed to the bottom rungs of society? If this is inevitable in a competitive and individualistic society, then how much more urgently does this underline the evidence provided by the families that more needs to be done and successful approaches need to be kept in place? *Family futures* shows that the constant efforts to pull neighbourhoods 'back from the cliff edge' work to prevent extreme ghetto formation, such as occurs in the US, with its far weaker public and social investment in poorer areas.[16] The new Coalition government has talked much about promoting the 'Big Society', the idea that we should take more responsibility for each other, that we should share and act on local problems, that we, as citizens, should do more alongside the state, and that the state itself should devolve more of its power and resources to local communities.[17]

Only by keeping in place a wider framework of support, exactly the ingredient that is too often missing in US cities, will local communities where the 200 families live be able to contribute as fully as they want. For local communities in today's complex urban settings are only rarely self-organising. By investing in our shared future, society as a whole encourages a sense of cooperation, of neighbourliness, of better futures for the children of today growing up in poor urban areas.

### Notes

[1] Hills, J., Sefton, T. and Stewart, K. (eds) (2009) *Towards a more equal society? Poverty, inequality and policy since 1997*, Bristol: The Policy Press.

[2] Mumford, K. and Power, A. (2003) *East Enders: Family and community in East London*, Bristol: The Policy Press.

[3] Hills, J., Le Grand, J. and Piachaud, D. (2002) *Understanding social exclusion*, Oxford: Oxford University Press.

[4] See Chapter Five, this book, and Annex 9 (available online at www. policypress.co.uk).

[5] Sure Start National Evaluation Reports: www.ness.bbk.ac.uk/; New Deal for Communities National Evaluation Reports: http://extra.shu.ac.uk/ndc/; Social Exclusion Unit (1999) *National Strategy for Neighbourhood Renewal, Report of Policy Action Team 4 – Neighbourhood renewal,* London: Cabinet Office; Power, A. (2004) *Neighbourhood management and the future of urban areas,* CASEpaper 07, London: LSE.

[6] Power, A. (2009) 'New Labour and unequal neighbourhoods', in J. Hills, T. Sefton and K. Stewart (eds) *Towards a more equal society? Poverty, inequality and policy since 1997,* Bristol: The Policy Press, pp 115-33.

[7] Hills, J. et al (2010) *An anatomy of economic inequality in the UK – Report of the National Equality Panel,* CASEreport 60, London: LSE.

[8] Hills, J., Sefton, T. and Stewart, K. (eds) (2009) *Towards a more equal society? Poverty, inequality and policy since 1997,* Bristol: The Policy Press.

[9] Hills, J. (2004) *Inequality and the state,* Oxford: Oxford University Press.

[10] Halpern, D. (2005) *Social capital,* Cambridge: Polity Press.

[11] Power, A. (1997) *Estates on the edge: The social consequences of mass housing in Northern Europe,* New York: St Martin's Press.

[12] Cantle Report (2001) *Community cohesion: A report of the Independent Review Team,* London: Home Office.

[13] Trust for London (2010) *Building our futures: The employment and human resources needs of deaf and disabled people's organisations in London* (www. trustforlondon.org.uk/media-centre/news/building-our-futures.html).

[14] Lupton, R. and Tunstall, R. (2008) 'Neighbourhood regeneration through mixed communities: a social justice dilemma?', *Journal of Education Policy,* vol 23, no 2, pp 105-17.

[15] Power, A. (1997) *Estates on the edge: The social consequences of mass housing in Northern Europe,* New York: St Martin's Press; Mumford, K. and Power, A. (2002) *Boom or abandonment: Resolving housing conflicts in cities,* Coventry: Chartered Institute of Housing; Power, A., Plöger, J. and Winkler, A. (2010) *Phoenix cities: The fall and rise of great industrial cities,* Bristol: The Policy Press.

[16] Power, A., Plöger, J. and Winkler, A. (2010) *Phoenix cities: The fall and rise of great industrial cities,* Bristol: The Policy Press; Jargowsky, P. (1997) *Poverty and place: Ghettos, barrios, and the American city,* New York: Russell Sage Foundation.

[17] Cabinet Office (2010) *Building the Big Society* (www.cabinetoffice.gov.uk/ media/407789/building-big-society.pdf).

# Index

Note: The following abbreviations have been used – *t* = table; *f* = figure